NO ONE ROUND HERE READS TOLSTOY

NO ONE ROUND HERE READS TOLSTOY

MEMOIRS OF A WORKING-CLASS READER

MARK HODKINSON

CANONGATE

First published in Great Britain, the USA and Canada in 2022 by
Canongate Books Ltd, 14 High Street, Edinburgh EH1 1TE

Distributed in the USA by Publishers Group West
and in Canada by Publishers Group Canada

canongate.co.uk

1

British Library Cataloguing-in-Publication Data
A catalogue record for this book is available on request
from the British Library

ISBN 978 1 78689 997 2

Typeset in Van Dijck by Palimpsest Book Production Ltd,
Falkirk, Stirlingshire

Printed and bound in Great Britain by Clays Ltd, Elcograf S.p.A.

For Jean and Roy

'I recall a bigger brighter world,
A world of books and silent times in thought.'

The Go-Betweens, 'Cattle and Cane'
(McLennan/Forster)

CONTENTS

Part Two: Where Am I Going?

PREFACE

The walls are closing in. They used to be over there, a few metres away. Now, if I lean over I can touch them. This is what happens when you collect books and store them on big shelves in a small house. The process occurs imperceptibly, similar to the passing of time, where you think little has changed but then see a picture of yourself from a decade ago and sigh, 'Bloody hell!'

I had no idea that 3,500 books (and ever rising) was an especially large number. The same as I thought having *one* book in my childhood home wasn't particularly unusual either. I'm much the same with music. I have thousands of CDs and filled three iPods with more than 60,000 tracks before subscribing to a streaming service. We are what we are, we do what we do, and it takes others to point out deviations from 'normal'.

I first saw books in a house, lots of them, when I was seventeen and had visited the family home of a college pal. I'm not one to use the word awestruck or act in a way revealing such a state.

But, that day, in my Italian combat jacket and with my hair at its flick-fringe best, I was struck by awe, hard. I want all this, I thought. Books upon books. All around me.

Even back then, I knew this wouldn't be a mission undertaken for the sake of it or to show off, a sly appropriation of look-at-me cleverness. I was already aware of the true appeal of books, their brilliance and their beauty. As I saw it (and still do), each book was a portal to a new world or a new version of the world, where, afterwards, you should feel slightly or, better still, radically changed. Was there anything more irresistible? Also, if you are brought up in a home almost entirely devoid of culture or any acknowledgement of the arts, you are free to build your own personality, and I did this through music and books.

Initially, the main theme of this particular book, my book, was to be deferred gratification – a term beloved by sociologists and psychologists – and how it related to the accrual of a personal library. In short, what did it say about someone? What did it mean? And when, exactly, would all these books ever be read? We even had a provisional title, *How Soon Is Now?*

The best books, the same as the best days, skitter on the breeze. They go their own way. While there remains a robust appraisal of the original topic, the beating heart of this book lies elsewhere. Only in the writing of it did I come to appreciate the relative singularity of a kid from a working-class home where books were objects of disdain, and who struggled in a CSE* group in a comprehensive school ('I pity you with this lot.'), later becoming a bibliophile. Not to mention a journalist, author and publisher.

Class is often used as camouflage for self-pity. Or, in a 'we had it worse' race to the bottom, it can take on a comedic aspect

* Certificate of Secondary Education. More on this later.

– see the 'Four Yorkshiremen' sketch featuring members of Monty Python. For my part, I've written about my background, my family and my town as I found it and remembered it and with no other agenda, at least on a conscious level.

As my *working-classness* came out naturally, so did the interwoven story of my poor, tormented grandad. It was he, in his vitality, wisdom and mutiny, who did most to shape the boy who became the man who collected the books. I wanted to tell this tale of an ordinary bloke because I sense there were many John William Duffys. One on every street perhaps, where families did their best, day after day, to cope, get by, with little support or even acknowledgement.

This is a book about books by a book lover, a hotchpotch of metaphorical byways, lay-bys and even the odd thoroughfare. To complete it I locked myself away for the best part of a year with my collection. I have included a stand-alone section at the end to faithfully reflect this period. There are notes on items found within the pages of my books; a run-through of titles I hadn't read but finally did and a résumé of my various To Be Read piles. Please view this section as similar to extra features on a DVD or, if you're of a certain age, the bonus track on a 12-inch single (gatefold sleeve, with satin patch).

I have seen books all ways up, inside and out, author to publisher, reviewer to collector. I have shared all I've learned, including concise histories of favourite authors and publishers; the importance of blurbs and author photos; the aesthetic of design; the role of agents; a self-help guide to publishing and, of course, there's Dirty Raymond and a box marked 'Brainy' (in felt tip). Books upon books.

Mark Hodkinson
2022

PART ONE

How Did I Get Here?

CHAPTER ONE

A couple of years ago we were moving to a new house on the same estate, round the corner. People often say 'round the corner' when it's really about a mile or so away, past the petrol station, a church, row of shops and a car park of a shut-down pub turned into a hand car wash. But we were literally moving *round the corner*; Google Maps lists the journey as three minutes on foot and one minute by bike. Too near, then, to make it worthwhile hiring a removal firm. The plan was failsafe: load up the cars a few times with boxes and bin bags while family members and friends lugged the beds, settee, chairs, bookcases, coffee table, drawers and wardrobes through the streets. And we'd start early in the day to minimise the number of witnesses to this meticulously organised if irregular flit.

I had piled hundreds of books onto the bed and was putting them into appropriate boxes, marked in pen: 'history', 'media', 'politics', 'novels A–C' and so forth. I looked out of the window.

A railway embankment runs parallel to the estate and the line is level with the first floor of the houses, forming a pleasant ribbon of nature. Buddleia, gorse and bramble fight for growing space with the rhododendron, lilac bushes, cow parsley and birch saplings. It was early August. Everything was still, not a leaf shuddered or a stem swayed. When we conjure thoughts of late summer it is light and bright but that day, the day we moved house, the weather was bellyaching between absent and overcast. At least it wasn't raining.

The house we were buying was being sold by Steve and Steph. Their near-matching names should have been a forewarning. He had extremely smooth and shiny skin for a man in his fifties, as if polished on an hourly basis. She wore a constant grimace that suggested either a recent catastrophic health diagnosis or the loss of a winning lottery ticket. On this designated 'completion day' we were in a chain with four other sets of people buying and selling houses. The assorted solicitors had advised that, as contracts had been exchanged on the various properties a few days earlier, completion (i.e. moving out and in) was a formality.

Steve met us at his – soon to be my – front door with a furtive nod. We could put the boxes and bags in the garage, he said. I recognised the implication; it was evident in the set of his shiny unhappy face and perfunctory tone of voice. Behind him, down the hall, was that grimace, cheese-wire tightened to prissi- ness: tell him, Steve, the garage and no further. She didn't actually say this but it was easily discerned as she sat perched tight on a wicker chair, arms crossed. I didn't want confrontation so early in the morning and with so much ahead of us. I did what most people do when faced with a looming predicament: skirted it, hoped it would go away.

Friends turned up and began filling cars with boxes. Soon, they were joined by my parents and two sons, both in their early twenties. Everyone began asking whether they should start carrying round 'the bigger stuff'. Judith – the woman buying my house – arrived, followed by more piled-high vehicles and a huge removals van. Within minutes, there were about twenty people in the cul-de-sac. Van and car doors were opened. Items of furniture began appearing on the pavement and in the road. Neighbours joined the throng and little groups were holding discussions, each looking occasionally towards the house, expecting me to appear and make an announcement. This stand-off lasted a couple of long, tense hours. I rang Steve.

'I'm not at liberty to let you deposit anything in the house until all monies have cleared into our account,' he said, as if reading from a script.

I told him that everyone else in the chain was moving out and I had a swarm of people outside, restless because they had nothing to do. Steve said I was lucky they had granted access to the garage. I then heard shrieking and wailing and realised it was Steph. I guessed Steve was holding the phone to his chest so I'd not be able to hear, but it didn't work. He told her to calm down, love, take it easy, darling, he'd deal with the matter. Finally, he informed me that they were about to leave the house and deposit the keys at their solicitor's office; I'd have to deal with them from here on.

While I'd been on the phone, Judith's removal team had set about my garden shed, moving my lawnmower, spades and saws onto the street. My heart was thumping, mouth dry, head aching. I had an idea. My sister lived about 200 metres from the house I was buying. She was on holiday but at least we could use her drive and front garden for temporary storage space. I briefed everyone and within minutes a procession formed through the streets carrying my belongings. The experience was unsettling, seeing personal items tucked under arms or held between two people, on show to anyone passing or staring from their houses. Amid the hurry-hurry panic I hadn't noticed time moving on: it was now mid-afternoon and the estate was beginning to hum with life, people returning from work, kids on their way back from school. One or two did comedy double takes, staring beyond this haphazard train of mattresses and wardrobes as if expecting a film crew to come into view at any minute.

At regular intervals I phoned the solicitor to see if the money had cleared and the keys released. I was told at 4.30 p.m. that it had been received but they were closing at 5 p.m. The office was only five miles away but I had to negotiate rush hour traffic. I got there with minutes to spare. The grumpy lady on reception asked for identification. I didn't have any; no one had said it was needed. I reasoned with her, asking how plausible it would be that I had randomly walked in twenty-five minutes after someone had phoned and said they'd be there in about twenty-five minutes to collect these specific keys and could also name and describe the vendor (smooth-skinned, shiny, irritating) so accurately.

'Well, we have to be careful,' she said, passing them to me, pleased to have the final word.

At last. I was near-euphoric as I drove back, slamming the heel of my hand on the steering wheel in time to the music. As I entered the estate I looked over to the railway embankment. The rows of shrubs were arched, forming shimmering waves. Leaves on the birch trees quivered as if electrified. I knew what this meant. I leaned forward to better see the sky through the windscreen. The blue of earlier had been replaced by a grey slab of cloud. The first few drops of rain fell lonely on the bonnet but quickly built up momentum. I switched on the wipers. I could see the removal party hurrying from my sister's to the new house, using my belongings to shield themselves from the rain or huddling over electrical equipment to avoid it getting wet.

I parked and entered the house, still fearful of finding Steve and Steph *in situ*. They had gone, of course. As people funnelled through out of the rain, into the hall and on to the various rooms,

10

it felt like a spiritual transference. I was glad it had become instantly noisy and told everyone they could keep their shoes on; Steve had insisted I remove mine when I'd called round to discuss the purchase. (I've always found this bothersome; a house is a home, not a temple.) I stood at the doorway directing the human traffic. I looked across to my sister's. Standing tall in the drive was a wall of cardboard boxes. The rain suddenly intensified and began bouncing from the ground and past my ankles; August shunted to a raincoat afternoon in November.

'What's in those boxes?' I asked.

'Your books.'

My books. *My books? In this rain?* Within two or three seconds I had a pile-up of thoughts: how water resistant was your average cardboard box? Some had been sealed with parcel tape – this would keep out the rain for at least a little longer, wouldn't it? Why hadn't I put them in those plastic containers with clasp-shut lids? Hardbacks, at least those with laminated covers, would withstand more rain than paperbacks, probably. Maybe I could save a few of them or even most of them – a curled up cover here and there, a bit of staining or pages smelling musty, possibly, but still readable, still recognisably books. What if they were turning to pulp? I dashed with the others to retrieve the boxes.

At that instant, as I straddled the low chain-link fence, I realised what my book collection meant to me. My head was busy, all full up with the moving, the stressing, and so the feeling hit me elsewhere. I'm not sure where exactly but in the middle and all around – whack. I had been forced, for those few seconds, to imagine life without *all those books*. I had collected them from first learning to read and they had travelled with me through my growing-up years, several relationships and numerous house moves. On any photograph of me taken at home – family groupings; larking about as a teenager; arm around my first girlfriend; amid the beer bottles and vinyl records of a house shared with a pal;

beaming smile in my first bought house and then cradling my baby children – the books are behind me or at the side, always there. They are crammed in the MFI unit of my childhood bedroom and then on the mantelpiece of that clothes-strewn house where we played the latest Smiths single before running hard at Friday night. At first, the collection fits on a shelf beneath the mirror and Debbie Harry poster in my bedroom. Later it is in a specially made bookcase with sagging shelves which my dad had to reinforce with blocks of wood. Thereafter, it grows until it takes up alcoves on either side of the fireplace and covers whole walls. Then it flows into more bookcases, some glass-fronted with a key (invariably missing) to fasten shut the doors, others faux Gothic and chunky with acorns and oak leaves chiselled into the wood.

A sudden stabbing contemplation of all these books possibly lost to me does not let loose an eddy of nostalgia or make me rue the money or time spent on the collection. I'm struggling to understand the feeling until, eventually and limpid clear, it comes: it feels close to the ache of bereavement.

It was a false alarm. The cardboard boxes held firm. My library was intact. I'd probably magnified the danger they were in but isn't this inevitable when you love something dearly and think it might be lost?

During the move my mother had commented a few times, 'You're not going to read all these books.' She has said this regularly over the years but I have good reason to mistrust her when it comes to books, for she be (crack of thunder, clouds parting) a biblio-phobe – 'a person who hates, fears, or distrusts books'. On this occasion, however, I properly heard her for the first time: the statement hit home. Perhaps it was my age or the realisation that this might be my last house move. Either way, a reckoning of sorts.

I counted the boxes. There were more than eighty. If they each contained, say, forty books, that would make a total of 3,200, and already dotted around the new house (by the bed, on the coffee table, in my bedroom-office) were piles of newly acquired books, ranging from three or four to nearly twenty. Of the grand total, I had probably read between a quarter and a third but, in some cases, this was more than thirty years ago; a reread was probably in order. I carried on doing the maths. The shortest work of fiction in my collection was *The Vigilante* by John Steinbeck at about 1,500 words and the longest, *Women and Men* by Joseph McElroy, at an estimated 775,000. The average novel length was generally accepted to be 90,000 words and non-fiction, 65,000. All told, if my collection was three-quarters fiction and one-quarter non-fiction, and it took two or three days of continuous reading to finish a book of average length, I'd need more than twenty years to read them all, and that's if I didn't take time off to sleep, eat and have the occasional sup in the Red Lion.

'You're not going to read all these books.' There it was again. I couldn't dislodge my mother's truth. I had succumbed to what Americans call BABLE: Book Accumulation Beyond Life Expectancy. How did I get here? Asked this on a Friday night after a few pints and I'm looking for a chair to stand on. Appealing for quiet, please. Amid the chest thuds, quiver in my voice, I'm telling everyone (two pals and the barmaid) that it's because I'm ambitious and hopeful and ever seeking and each new book bears witness to a restless desire, of wanting, *needing* more, always more. And, and, if I were to divest myself of these books would I not be conceding that my time on earth is finite and that I'm going to die without reading everything I own? Who of us can defer so meekly to mortality?

Walking home afterwards, too many pints downed, it's me and the streets and creeping, seeping self-doubt. *Listen up, kiddo* (you're always a child to the voice in your head)*: you've only got all* *these books because you want people to think you're clever. But you're not, are you? You're a CSE-er; always will be. And, admit it, you're still moping about stuff that happened to you as a kid, which you're trying to blot out with all these walls of books. You're not fooling anyone, especially yourself.*

The day after, I call on a writer friend (this was an urgent matter, make no mistake). He tells me 3,500 — the latest count — is 'a lot of books'. The statement is made assertively, as if everyone knows it is an unimpeachable fact.

'Really?' I said.

'Really,' he echoes, which further implies, I feel, that there is something awry, pitiful even, about a man owning so many books.

As the hangover began to fade, I defended stoutly my right to have so many books and said, now we're here, that I found it peculiar that other people, writers especially, did *not* have huge collections of books. What was wrong with them? How did they avoid them these days when second-hand books were as good as free, left on the windowsills of supermarkets or on trestle tables outside people's houses, next to a biscuit tin in which you were invited, on a handwritten note, to place 'a few pence'.

Maybe my writer friend and the rest of the sane wide world read books and then dispensed with them, whether by passing them on to friends, or strangers at train stations. Or perhaps, God forbid, they *threw them away*. Imagine a book so reduced, so besmirched, as to be put in a wheelie bin to be recycled with other paper and cardboard waste, the spine broken, pages concertinaed, all those words and ideas jammed down hard with card that had once sheathed microwave meals or Amazon packages. Books in a bin or skip? The tragedy, special circumstances aside.*

*

* See later.

14

How many, then? Marie Kondo, the world's most famous tidy-upper (she'd probably prefer interior consultant or organisational guru) believes thirty books is enough for any home. Her philosophy, which came to her after a two-hour fainting episode, decrees that every item in a home must 'spark joy', otherwise it has to go. Understandably, her view had book lovers at the barricades. Leading the way was the peachy keen Irish-Canadian author Anakana Schofield. She warned the book populace on Twitter: 'Do NOT listen to Marie Kondo in relation to books. Fill your apartment & world with them. Every human needs a v extensive library not clean, boring shelves.'

The literary website Shelfari* volunteered a more rational maximum number of a 'few hundred' for a personal library but decreed that more than 1,000 books was 'too many'. So here I am, significantly beyond too many. But how did I get from there to here – boy to man, a dearth to a surfeit? What and who is a person with nearly three times more than too many?

* Merged with Goodreads in 2016.

CHAPTER TWO

The following aggregate of arbitrary, quickly recalled facts lead to a middle-aged man choosing to live in a book cave. I was born in Manchester in the mid-1960s. My dad (never 'father'), now retired, was an electrician. My mum (rarely 'mother'), also retired, a sewing machinist. They met at Bernard Manning's 'World Famous' (*sic*) Embassy Club in Harpurhey, Manchester; it was the wrestling night. Mum said she liked that my dad smelled of cigarettes. She considered it 'manly'. Dad was twenty-one when I was born, Mum, twenty-three. Although they were easily young enough to embrace the 'Swinging Sixties', there is not a whiff of patchouli or tie-dyed clothing or free love about them – I don't think the 1960s made it to north Manchester.

We owned a car (inexpensive) and had our own house (modest, boxy, three bedrooms, on a small estate). I had a sister, four years younger. We didn't go on foreign holidays – Devon was regarded as exotic; it had palm trees. I don't remember drinking water, unless I was ill, when I imagine it was thought to have vaguely medicinal qualities. I drank a lot of pop instead. Usually blue pop. In fact, we had a man (the 'Alpine Man') who traversed the streets in a truck leaving huge bottles of 'Alpine'-branded mineral on doorsteps each week.

I went to a comprehensive school. A lad in my class said I was posh because my parents were still together. I had a chippy dinner every day for three years from the age of thirteen to sixteen ('Steak and kidney pie and chips on a tray with gravy and vinegar, please, Mr Wan.'). None of my friends had parents who were teachers. No men in my family or anyone I knew worked in an office. Dad smoked heavily; Mum, five or six a day. They seldom showed tactile affection but their love and loyalty to me and my sister was constant, absolute. No one I knew owned or played a musical instrument. The soundtrack of our house was provided by Elvis Presley (his schmaltzy period, especially 'The Wonder of You', etc), Del Shannon and the Platters, played on scratched 45s kept in a device that resembled a toast rack.

Outside of visiting cafés while on holiday, we never ate out as a family. At home, we had the same meals depending on the day of the week. Fish was always on a Friday and potato hash on Wednesdays. Our midday meal was 'dinner' and our evening, 'tea'. We didn't really have family days out. Both Mum and Dad assumed the 'countryside' was private land with a farmer at every stile, gun in hand. Mum was usually cold, too. We'd walk a few yards and she'd announce: 'It's bloody freezing. What are we doing out here?' We'd run back to the car and pick at sandwiches wrapped in tin foil, usually corned beef with piccalilli. We went to the cinema only once as a family, to see *Planet of the Apes*, and the theatre, once also – *Jack and the Beanstalk* starring Jimmy Clitheroe and Anita Harris.

Everyone's house – family and friends – was full of ten-bob

ornaments and religious trinkets. Most had a budgie and a dog which was let out at regular intervals during the day to roam free. The television was always on. No original artwork was on the walls. My parents drank tea; coffee was considered 'hoity-toity' – their words. They had a bottle of Camp liquid coffee that remained in the cupboard for at least a decade, unopened. I was in my late teens and had left home before I first drank wine and tried olives, lasagne, hummus, guacamole, moussaka, garlic, asparagus, mozzarella, couscous, chick peas, cashew nuts and avocadoes. The only pasta we had was tinned spaghetti or spaghetti hoops.

Tesco was the first supermarket that came to town. On those early shopping trips Dad went with Mum; it was as if they were going somewhere special. When they came back they said how warm and well lit it had been. Girls dressed in funny costumes had offered them samples of cheese and foreign food from trestle tables. I asked if they'd had any.

'Not likely. That stuff gives me indigestion,' said Dad.

Supermarkets meant we had (frozen) pizzas and cheesecake. Mum served up our first cheesecake with chips because she was unaware it was a dessert. As a treat, when she got back from shopping (Dad, after those first few trips, never went again, the same as he never did the cooking or housework), she occasionally gave me and my sister a raw sausage to eat or tore off a couple of chunks of Chivers jelly. Yummy. Dad went to the pub every night. At closing time he and his small circle of friends would order a last round of two or three pints of beer each. He sometimes brought animals back with him – cats, dogs and, one time, a brood of chickens. Mum accompanied him to the pub at least once a week.

Every weekend, on an alternate basis, my nana (Dad's mum) or my gran and grandad stayed with us. All the grown-ups I knew were pleasant and kindly enough, but their world was parallel to mine. Only one person, my grandad, followed the Sigmund Freud maxim (not that any of us had heard of it): 'There is little that gives children greater pleasure than when a grown-up lets himself down to their level, renounces his oppressive superiority and plays with them as an equal.' Grandad spoke and listened to me this way; being schizophrenic – one of several diagnoses of his condition – might have made this easier for him.

Parenting wasn't a complex issue in the 1970s. They didn't fret or read self-help books. The definition of being a good parent was feeding and clothing your children, keeping them warm, loving them – what more was there to worry about? Noel Gallagher knows. He took the country there during a television interview with Michael Parkinson in 2006. Against his wishes perhaps, Gallagher had been steered back to his growing up years in Manchester, specifically the role played by his father, who was often errant or violent. For a gilded second Gallagher let go the swagger, the control and cool. It was in his eyes. He was back there, reluctantly sharing a bedroom with his fidgety younger brother Liam, developing a stammer because he was anxious about his bellicose father who routinely sought confrontation. Parkinson pushed, maybe expecting Gallagher to retreat to self-pity or at least acknowledge the magnitude of the issue.

'You used to lie in your bed at night wondering if your dad was going to come in and whack you, didn't you?' said Parkinson.

Gallagher scratched his head, picking out time to think. He responded:

'It was the Seventies. This is before the New Age Man was this trendy thing to be. It was a violent time, know what I mean?'

Parkinson persisted, asking what it was like to be 'without hope and no future'. The camera closed in on Gallagher's face, framed by meticulously tatty hair. Unusually for a rock star, he was listening.

'I don't consider my upbringing to be any different from anyone else who lived on my street or any of the guys that I used to knock around with,' he said.

I recall a similar tension, although my dad didn't hit me. The snarl was enough. He worked hard and came home at night knackered, his skin coated in muck, made irritable by the slog. Building sites were tough places, where there was often someone ready to turn a trick. Dad had learned to wrap up tight and show the white of his teeth if necessary. He'd been in a few scrapes. As a kid, when I went on jobs with him I could sense this aura he carried. It would remain with him always: was anyone trying to pull a fast one, backing him into a corner? He had a temper which served him well and made sure he was heard, made sure he was paid. He had kids to feed, a mortgage. You wouldn't want to cross him but if it came to it, you'd want him on your side.

We were, then, in all respects, an Every-family, perfectly normal until it all started with me and the books. Firstly, I developed the habit of collecting – just about anything that was collectable. I have a clear memory of when it began and it's nothing fanciful or possibly imagined, such as when they plonk Laurie Lee, aged three, down in the grass in Slad and he's recalling chirping grasshoppers and tiger-skins of sunlight. I was about seven years old. It was playtime at school. All these kids were running about, jumping here and there, shouting. I passed through; I have always enjoyed *passing through*. Along the perimeter wall of the playground, boys were wuzzing (so much more precise than 'throwing') football cards. Technique was everything. Liam Brady or whoever (footballer in kit on bended knee, ball pressed to the ground under palm of hand) would be positioned carefully between index finger and middle finger. A flick of the wrist and the card was away, almost too fast for the eye. If the hand was driven down with a sudden upturn at the point of flick, it was possible to send the card into a narrow arc and cover a greater distance. The boy who threw his card nearest to the wall or further than the other received his competitor's card as prize.

My hands weren't clasped behind my back and I wasn't wearing a cravat but, much the same as the posh, twittish kid in literature – Little Lord Fauntleroy, Dick Bultitude, Harry Potter et al. – in my mind's eye, as I stride across that playground, I am aloof, slightly superior. I have a plan, see. All this wuzzing. Why the effort? I had decided, coolly and magnificently, on a strategy. I would wait until this phase had passed, when all my fellow schoolmates had become bored with football cards, and I would either buy or swap them at ridiculous discount – they might even give them to me for free, such was the fickleness of children. I am both discomfited and proud that seven-year-old me could be so shrewd, though shrewd is a first cousin to sly, of course.

So, I didn't decide it, I wasn't persuaded to be it, I didn't become it: I was it from the start – a collector. Already, my reach was preposterous. Before the age of ten I had assembled collections of postcards, PG Tips cards, stamps, football programmes, beer mats, badges, coins, football cards, comics and conkers. And it was a total sensory experience. I liked the parched texture of paper rubbed between my fingers and the grooves in the coins, soft on the face but gritty ridged on the sides. I sniffed football cards for traces of the sweet smell of bubblegum with which they had once been wrapped. If a PG Tips card came loose from its book, I'd seek out the slightly salty smell of Pritt Stick or the more acrid UHU. I bought the tiny gummy hinges with which you could affix stamps to a book; they were always coming loose as if alive and shimmying to the fold on the inside edge of the page. I loved the evidence of ageing – discolouration caused by sunlight or damp on paper; pockmarks of rust on the back of badges; the ring stain of a glass on a beer mat or runny, blurry words on the back of a postcard that suggested it had been posted on a rainy day in Keswick, Oberammergau or Vladivostok.

Of all my sets, duly logged, mounted, framed or filed, I accepted reluctantly that there was one I could not complete: I would never own all the conkers in the world. All the same, to this day, I cannot pass a conker without picking it up and putting it in my pocket. Sunlight reflected in the deep reddish brown of a fresh-from-shell conker is a handful of heaven.

Everything I collected as a child was easily accumulated. My parents, my gran and my uncle Ronnie furnished my tea card collection. They drank the tea, I got the cards. A plastic bag full of stamps 'from all over the world' was available for about 37p by writing off to an address in Bungay, Suffolk; I was always 'writing off' to places. Relatives usually had a few postcards on their mantelpiece which later came my way. I'd find beer mats and badges on market stalls. I was too young really to barter but if I wanted something badly enough I did the deal, even if it took several laps of the market to summon courage.

As per my plan, I 'inherited' hundreds of football cards from kids at school keen to move on to the next fad. Sometimes I was so embarrassed by the quantity I had at any given time, I concealed them evenly about my person (coat pocket, inside coat pocket, sleeve pocket, front trouser pocket, back trouser pocket). I knew that there was something odd, weird even, about one kid having 647 football cards when the usual, the normal number, was a pocketful. Who wanted 17 Bob Latchfords, 11 Ray Kennedys and 5 or 6 Graham Paddons, anyway? I did.

Various psychoanalytical explanations are tendered for why people collect. The most common is that unloved children seek comfort by accumulating belongings. I was loved but I was, and remain, unlike the rest of my family. Maybe, as a very young child, I'd sensed this intuitively and the stamps and cards became my 'friends', a family within a family. Another theory is that it is motivated by existential anxieties – the collection, an augmentation of identity, lives on after we die. In my case, I can't imagine mine lasting much longer than I do. None of the next generation of family members (sons and nephews) have shown much interest ('What are these, like, actually, you know, *for*?'). The skip awaits or, if they want to convert artefacts into holidays or training shoes – and why not? – eBay. A third hypothesis is that a male seeks to attract potential mates by signalling his ability to accrue resources. If the collection boasts cars and yachts (full sized, the real thing, not pictured on beer mats or postcards) this is plausible but it's doubtful that a man overly proud of owning – full set, no creases, no stains – 'Transport Through the Ages' or 'Flags and Emblems' from the Brooke Bond PG Tips collectors' cards series will be considered irresistible. In fact, it may significantly reduce his appeal.

I knew it as a child, as I do an adult – why I collect. I wanted to store up sufficient stuff, *my* stuff, so that tomorrow, next week or at some point in the future, near or distant, I could surround myself with it, submerge myself, become it. I am suspicious of anyone who doesn't feel the same way. How can they live so much in the now with no regard to a better, quieter, reflective, rainy day tomorrow – which is what a collection guarantees. To them, tomorrow will be like today, so life becomes merely a run of routine, samey, in-the-moment days. Surely what makes it all worthwhile is the promise of all this material to wade through and cherish, *any day now*.

As a young teenager I moved seamlessly from beer mats and the rest, to books. They were mere foothills compared to the mountain range of amassing a personal library. Books are substantially more collectable, more of everything. A book is not a passive, peripheral object. Consider books as people, as a family. Who wouldn't want a house full of challenge and chatter and, should the racket get too much, the covers can be closed, the silence sweetened by the earlier hubbub.

Everyone has a different feel or need for books, a different relationship with them. To some they are functional carriers of information. To others they span the phantasmagorical to the ordinary, through which they can recognise, validate and bolster their own lives. And some turn to books to daydream or escape. They want smart plotting, twists and turns, characters so sordid or saintly they could only live within the pages of a book, couldn't they? Some readers want to return to the past, a definitive point or somewhere, anywhere, that is safely a long time ago. Or they want to read a story that tells them of the present, the now. Or to be sent out to the future, away from here, outer-places sculpted sheer from the imagination.

We lived in a district of Manchester called Blackley, three miles from the city centre. Around us were streets, redbrick houses and occasional tracts of wasteland where buildings had been flattened during the war. Luckily, we lived near a park rich in trees and valleys, streams and marshes, so we could build dens, hang swings from branches, collect conkers and birds' eggs, dam brooks or wander to the boating lake on the far side.

I was locked into a close relationship with Grandad from my earliest memories; I had no idea that he was so different from other adults. Later, I saw him a little in the character of Joe Margery, the kindly brother-in-law and guardian of Pip in *Great Expectations* by Charles Dickens. 'I always treated him as a larger species of child, and as no more than my equal,' said Pip. Grandad was missing a filter, what was appropriate to discuss or say to a child and how and when to say it. Gran or Mum often scolded him for starting out on a tale about someone falling into a mincing machine at the butcher's or rats as big as dogs running loose in the side streets of Manchester. He had all the best brilliant horrible stories.

'Give over,' they'd chide. 'The lad'll be having nightmares.'
He talked a lot about death.

'Everyone's scared of dying,' he'd say. 'But it's coming to us all, we're all going to the soil. You've got to imagine it as one big long sleep, with no one bothering you or out to get you. What could be better than that?'

I didn't know how to answer; I was seven years old.

He had a few sayings which he'd repeat often. A favourite was, 'There are eight million stories in the naked city. This has been one of them.' He'd say this usually after telling Gran something mundane such as the council had replaced the manhole cover at the entrance to the flats where they lived. I learned years later that he'd stolen the line from a police drama called *Naked City*. He was both a storyteller and a man lit by a halo of stories. He was interested in people and could sum them up in a few words, see them for what they were. Spend a few hours with him and something would happen or, in his gentle sing-song voice, he'd tell you tales from last week or the week or year before, sometime back then.

I seemed to spend more time with Grandad than I did Dad, at least until my teenage years; this was a pattern among a lot of my friends. Dad was still fizzy with youth when I was born, a good part of him drawn to the pub and pals. He often worked at the weekend or away from home for several weeks at a time. Despite the manic episodes and various 'breakdowns', in between, Grandad's presence was usually more settled. I think of him often, how large he was in my life, our lives, and yet minuscule in the history of the world, the same as most men, especially of his class. His is a story made special by what occurred at the very end, a *happening* – that's probably the best word for it – that involved me and him, which was as true as the sun and the rain but felt drawn from a book: magic realism or supernatural even. I have, ever since, felt to be an envoy, trusted with this tale of misfortune and heartbreak, and where it led. If, as they say, we each have a book in us, or a story at least, this was mine. And his. He is the book within the books, the first among 3,500.

During the two or three decades before and after the Second World War, there was a strand of the traditional working class that embraced a certain trilby-wearing, worsted clad, pipe-smoking, medium-brow culture. They had hobbies. They listened to folk and classical music. They frequented pubs with flagstone floors and drank real ale or brewed their own in sheds kept in good order, creosoted once a year, new felt for the roof every other. They had allotments. They attended classes held by the Workers' Educational Association (WEA). They visited mechanics' institutes to read or listen to lectures given by scientists; the UK had more than 700 of these institutes, some of which evolved into colleges, universities or public libraries. They learned foreign languages. Women were as eager for knowledge as men while also embracing 'domestic science': sewing, baking, flower arranging et al. The men were gentle and soft spoken. They built radios. The more radical, men *and* women, trespassed defiantly across Kinder Scout in 1932, knapsacks bulging with butties, a fold-away Bartholomew map in the side pocket. They painted. They even read books, usually drawn from the Everyman's Library, a series set up in 1905 whereby world literature was made available to 'every kind of person'. I imagine these sturdy, earnest folks reading the likes of John Ruskin, George Bernard Shaw, H.G. Wells and, most of all, J.B. Priestley, specifically his gem, *Delight*, a series of essays celebrating the simple pleasures in life – the thrill of waiting for a play or film to begin after the house lights have dimmed, for example.

My lot was not of this subdivision of the working class. Our house was noisy, busy, messy, neighbours and family passing through (my uncle and aunty lived next door), doors banging, the dog barking, budgie whistling, Mum and Dad bickering, the telly blaring and Elvis crooning everlasting love for his mother on 'Mama Liked the Roses'. I don't remember us having a Bible, which was unusual. They were in a lot of friends' houses, side-on among the shelves in the chipboard display cabinet. I'm not sure they were ever read; it was more a talisman to ward off evil spirits.

Pot shire horses significantly outnumbered books at our house. In fact, we had only one book. Dad sent away for it after seeing an advert in a newspaper. I can only ever remember him doing this once; it must have been a palaver because we never had stamps or envelopes. *Folklore, Myths and Legends of Britain* was leather bound with gold writing on the front and spine. Dad treated it with reverence, keeping it on top of a wardrobe with other items of great worth such as their wedding album and my National Cycling Proficiency certificate. If you asked to read *the* book, he kept a watchful eye, making sure you didn't crease the pages or slam shut the covers. By about the age of ten this book had given me a profound but narrow field of expertise. I knew everything about grisly murders at vicarages; one-eyed giants; the wretched life of the alleged witch, Alice Nutter, and whether it was true that anyone spending a night alone in Madame Tussauds' Chamber of Horrors would emerge as a 'gibbering idiot'. It was. I've seen the drawings.

(*Folklore, Myths and Legends of Britain* is now out of print but available on several websites. When I see the front cover again, an illustration of Cernunnos, the Celtic horned god, looking startled and irked, his leafy beard bedraggled, I fall through time. I am a child once more and this is the only book in the world, a book as dark, dense and forbidding as a night-time forest.)

If I should call upon my parents today there is about the same likelihood of my finding them trampolining in the back garden as reading a book. They're both in their late seventies. I have never seen them read a book, not even on holiday or over Christmas, those times when there is often a fleeting union of page and person. I don't remember seeing books at the houses of my childhood friends either, aside from those belonging to visiting grandmas, usually a Mills & Boon or Catherine Cookson. Any bookcases that found their way into homes were used as shoe racks or receptacles for snow shakers and ornaments brought back from seaside holidays in Llandudno or Rhyl.

Books and my parents didn't stand a chance. There has to be peace and quiet, inside and out, to properly read, to indulge. No one can read in a chilly place. Virginia Woolf recognised this in *A Room of One's Own*, an entreaty on behalf of womankind but also resonant to the poor. Woolf lived in a five-storey house containing a library in Hyde Park Gate, Kensington, and spent summers at Talland House, a villa overlooking St Ives Bay in Cornwall – she wrote in *The Waves* of seeing the reflection of the shimmering sea on her bedroom ceiling. While her brothers received a university education, the sisters were taught at home, hence her plea for personal space.

My parents, by contrast, came from backgrounds where everyone was busy getting by, staying warm, covering the rent, caring for children, putting food on the table. There was no time or space or encouragement or inclination to ponder on authors, artists or anything other than life's essentials. They are still proud of the districts in Manchester where they were raised and are affronted if anyone refers to them as slums, even if they fit the definition in the *Oxford English Dictionary*: 'an area of a city that is very poor and where the houses are dirty and in bad condition'. Many of their neighbours might have robbed and fought and boozed but underneath, deep down, they were good sorts, *really*.

My dad grew up in a rented terraced house with his parents and older brother and sister in Harpurhey. It had two bedrooms and a toilet in the back yard; my nan remained there until she

28

died in 1980 – my paternal grandad died a few months before I was born. The house was close to Carisbrook Street where Anthony Burgess (then known as John Anthony Burgess Wilson) was born in 1917. Mum lived in a terraced house a mile or so away, in Collyhurst, near the River Irk. Almost a hundred years before, Friedrich Engels had written about the area when he worked nearby for his father's textile company, Ermen & Engels. He wrote in *The Condition of the Working Class in England*:

> Right and left a multitude of covered passages lead from the main street into numerous courts, and he who turns in thither gets into a filth and disgusting grime, the equal of which is not to be found – especially in the courts which lead down to the Irk, and which contain unqualifiedly the most horrible dwellings which I have yet beheld . . . Below it on the river there are several tanneries which fill the whole neighbourhood with the stench of animal putrefaction.

Although the neighbourhood had improved considerably by the time Mum lived there, the Irk regularly burst its banks, driving sludge into nearby homes. Mum has memories of kids being lifted above flood waters by policemen so they could get to school on the other side.

Grandad had seven sisters and was the only son. He had the same name as his father. He'd occasionally fish out photos of his dad from the sideboard and sing:

'Roll up, roll up, here's the original John Willie Duffy and a right old bugger he was too.'

As he sang, he'd lift his knees and pretend to play the spoons. On the photo, the original John Willie was standing with his shoulders back and chest pushed out. His eyes were hidden in folds of puffy skin, one of them almost shut. He'd suffered an industrial injury. A shard of brick had caught it while he was working on a building site. Mum said he soothed it with a damp handkerchief but the continual soreness made him cantankerous.

A family called the McGurrans lived next door to my mum's. When their parents went to the pub, which was often, the three kids were locked in the house on their own. They were all under eight and the eldest, Patricia, had to look after the little two, Michael and Bernadette. Gran used to jam comics through the letterbox for them to read. They didn't have an inside toilet so they'd go on the stone tiles in the kitchen; their mum cleaned up the mess when she got back.

Dad isn't as talkative as Mum. I know much less about his childhood. He's pragmatic to the point of bluntness and, should you ask what he felt about this or that, the response most likely will be: what do you *think* I felt? Or he'll shrug. He's good with body language, much better than he is talking. I know only a few details: his school didn't have a playground, so they played in the cellar. He spent a lot of time combing the local tip on the lookout for anything to sell on. He has always been proud of 'having a trade' and did well for a boy from his background – discovering and nurturing his talent, serving an apprenticeship, attending night school and eventually qualifying as an electrician. He loved his job.

Instead of reading, everyone watched the telly, lots of telly. The saturation was remarkable considering we had only three channels and one of those was BBC2, with its documentaries and Proms, which hardly anyone watched. In the late 1970s almost one in three people in Britain would view a particularly gripping episode of *Coronation Street*.

Lives were played out to this steady, easy beat of game show, soap opera, sports, sitcom, news and the occasional film. Adverts were especially loved and became fixed in minds as much as programmes, more so when combined with catchphrases or ditties: 'For mash get Smash' (Cadbury's instant mash potato); 'Every bubble's passed it's fizzical' (Corona pop); and 'Tea, best drink of the day'. When the clock struck midnight or thereabouts, the national anthem was played before a homely voice reminded everyone to turn off their television set. Should they forget, they'd be hissed to bed with a shrill monotone.

CHAPTER THREE

I was often sick as a child. I missed a whole term of infant school and when I returned everyone had learned to read and write. I had asthma. I'd develop a wheeze and would soon be cough-coughing through the night. When the breaths became brittle, Mum or Dad took me downstairs and I'd stand on the doorstep, hungrily drawing in fresh air. A heavy cold would set in and I'd be in bed for days, usually with a fever. I made regular visits to the doctor's and hospital, where I had to blow in tubes, give blood, have X-rays. They tested for allergic reactions, injecting my arm with traces of dust mite, bird feathers, cat and dog hair. I was given an inhaler and had it with me at all times, jangling in my pocket. Mum put a plastic under-sheet across my bed and vacu-umed the room every day to keep down the dust.

Maybe this poorly time was when I discovered my love of reading. I was sealed off from the noise of the house and the rest of my family, shut into the quiet, where I was happiest. Unlike the author Francis Spufford I can't remember a particular book that took me to this other place but I had a variety of reading material – comics, football programmes, magazines and perhaps an Enid Blyton Famous Five adventure. Words and images rose from the page and became intertwined with the fever; I'd drift off sickly-happy. Spufford, meanwhile, had been six years old when, stricken by mumps, he realised he could read as he turned the pages of *The Hobbit* by J.R.R. Tolkien: He later recalled this in florid prose:

> The first page of *The Hobbit* was a thicket of symbols, to be decoded one at a time and joined hesitantly together . . . By the time I reached *The Hobbit*'s last page, though, writing had softened, and lost the outlines of the printed alphabet, and become a transparent liquid, first viscous and sluggish, like a jelly of meaning, then ever thinner and more mobile, flowing faster and faster, until it reached me at the speed of thinking and I could not entirely distinguish the suggestions it was making from my own thoughts.'*

Although we are of hugely different backgrounds – Spufford is the son of extremely high-achieving academics (his late mother had an OBE) – our reading began on our sickbeds, as it did for many others. Bram Stoker had an unspecified condition that meant, 'Certainly till I was about seven years old I never knew what it was to stand upright.'† At the same age, H.G. Wells, known to pals as Bertie, broke his leg when he fell down hard on a tent peg while camping. He referred to it later as the 'luckiest day of my

* From *The Child That Books Built*.
† *Personal Reminiscences of Henry Irving* by Bram Stoker (1906).

life' because it allowed him to retreat to a favourite settee and read scores of books. Hilary Mantel, twice winner of the Booker Prize, had mysterious fevers and severe headaches in childhood and was nicknamed 'Little Miss Never Well' by her GP. She wrote evocatively in *Giving up the Ghost* of her self-diagnosis of endometriosis. Robert Louis Stevenson had numerous bronchial problems, as did Katherine Mansfield and D.H. Lawrence, two close friends who both died of tuberculosis at the ages of thirty-four and forty-four respectively.

Ill-health has, in many cases, added to a writer's standing and lustre, a presumption that they were too delicate for the demands of the world, that suffering brought depth and insight to their work beyond the reach of the everyday healthy. A close look at the lives of most writers (who were all readers before they became writers, of course) reveals the sickbed reading epiphany as a staple. Almost all of us, writers and avid readers alike, it seems, spent our childhood wan and unwell among the bed sheets, sipping tomato soup, either reading a book or propped up with pillows so we could look out over the garden.

Grandad told me that his dad would sit for hours in a chair by the fireside bossing everyone around. He chewed tobacco and spat it into the flames. When the kettle whistled he refused to budge; it was his wife's job to leave whatever she was doing, lift it from the hob and make the tea.

He was a prodigious boozer and was twice run over while drunk, by a horse and cart and the other time by a car. Grandad told us this with pride.

'Not once but twice he got fast under a set of wheels while he was roaring drunk. What a fella!'

The patch of lawn I looked down upon from my bedroom in Blackley was about the size of an opened-out tablecloth. In the corner was the leg of an electricity pylon; we shared a leg each with three neighbours. Dad's shed was perched on a small island of concrete that had become brittle and broken away under the onslaught of rain; woodlice and spiders busied themselves in the debris. I was still coughing. The prognosis issued by doctors in Manchester in the 1970s appeared to belong to the medical profession of a century earlier. Mum was told I needed plenty of fresh air and would 'grow out of it'. All the same, I was given tiny, bitter-tasting pills which she concealed within a teaspoon of jam.

On a drive out, my parents strayed onto a road that crossed moorland. They noted that this grassy sea bordered Rochdale on three sides. A few days before my tenth birthday, largely in a bid to improve my health, we moved to this Lancashire mill town. Although only twelve miles away, it might have been a different country, such was the difference. Many streets had mills on them, standing tall and wide like battleships, completely out of scale with the rest of the surroundings. We sometimes caught the bus to and from the city, visiting relatives and friends. I recall waiting for the 461 and my apprehension as it set off along Queensway, one of Rochdale's main roads. Almost two miles long, it was hemmed in by mills and factories. When you finally reached houses and pubs and streets again, it felt as if you'd emerged from a brick tunnel. If you did the same journey by train, you passed Dunlop Mill, believed to be the largest mill in the world; it employed 3,200 people in its heyday of 1929, making fabric used to reinforce tyres. Most of the mills had peculiar short names to fit snugly on the chimney when read horizontally: Elk, Era, Ena, Orb, Rex and Roy.

Dad took me with him on jobs in these mills and also in offices, schools and warehouses – places that had to be closed to carry out electrical repair work. The mills had a distinctive starchy smell. I liked exploring these empty buildings, but Dad was uneasy about my leaving the site where he was working. I'd read notices pinned to the walls and check on the postcards and pin-ups near the frames or lathes. There was often a drinks machine in the corridor.

'Fancy a cup of tea, Dad?'

I usually had hot chocolate, feeding in the coin and hearing its insides shunt into life. I imagined the noise on a weekday, the machines thundering and people shouting above the din; my gran had learned to lip-read from working in sewing factories. I wasn't much use at practical work so took along books to read. Dad didn't mind; he liked the company. I read George Orwell's *Animal Farm* in one of the largest factories in Lancashire.

The first glimpse I had of a different way of living was through David Johnson, one of the first friends I made in Rochdale. Most evenings, before he was allowed to play out, I had to sit in his front room until he finished violin practice. The house had a rich, pleasing odour comprised of furniture wax, coffee and pipe smoke. While I waited, his mum would give me a biscuit and a glass of orange and ask questions about school or talk about an item in the news. I don't recall other parents doing this; in fact, some barely knew my name even though I'd been calling at their houses for months. I'd look through his dad's record collection. The albums were classical and in pristine condition, the covers depicting autumn woodland scenes or indigo seas lapping against a harbour wall. A folded newspaper was usually on the coffee table revealing an almost finished crossword. They had an antique wooden clock on the mantelpiece with a loud tick; it was so peaceful in there, the rhythm almost counted me down to sleep.

When we moved up together to secondary school, it was soon discovered that we had two David Johnsons in our year. On the first day, the list of the various classes was read out by the headmaster in assembly. One David Johnson was assigned to A, the other, E. The classes A and B consisted of pupils deemed the most intelligent, who would study for O levels. The rest, C to M, a huge group spanning average to remedial, were to undertake the much inferior CSE courses. I had been placed with these, in E. My friend Johnson, in a rare moment of humility, had wandered down a corridor and joined the E class. The other Johnson did the same, sitting on the back row. The difference between them could not have been more apparent. My Johnson was clean, smart and clear eyed. The other was a rained-on rat of a boy, folded in on himself, messy hair, with a fringe covering most of his face. He was already engraving his nickname on the desk with a compass: 'Spud'.

'Now then,' said our form teacher, Mr Cooke, taking obvious delight in the conundrum. 'Which one of you two is in the correct class and who should be up there with our brains trust, the "A" form?'

'I think it's probably me who should be in "A", sir,' said my Johnson.

Mr Cooke took this as audacity and snapped:

'And what makes you so sure about that?'

'I was told I'd probably be doing Latin and they only do that in the O level group.'

Mr Cooke was angry with this easy victory and waved Johnson out of the room contemptuously. Spud Johnson confirmed it was the correct outcome by flicking a dried corn flake from his jumper and shouting:

'It's got to be him, sir – I'm thick!'

As David passed my desk, he whispered:

'I pity you with this lot for the next few years.'

Mum often told us about a time when she was about seven and had called at her grandparents'. The front door was open. She went inside looking for her gran. The 'original' John Willie was snoozing in his chair, sleeping off a drinking session. Her footsteps must have woken him. He sat upright and snarled:

'What are you doing, walking in here like this? Get out. Get out now.'

He hadn't recognised her. He had more than fifteen grandchildren and they all looked the same when you'd just woken up and had only one good eye to see through.

The school was formed from a mismatch of low-cost buildings plonked on a scruffy council estate. The streets were full of potholes. Door numbers were painted three feet high on brickwork outside houses. Blokes worked under cars jacked up on bricks across pavements. Garden fences were kicked down and dogs barked all day long. The school uniform policy wasn't enforced because teachers knew the homes from which most of the kids came. They made their own breakfasts and probably their siblings', too. If you went home with them at dinner time, perhaps to collect a PE kit, their mum might still be in bed, the breakfast plates on the settee, a milk bottle on the table. The gas fire they'd forgotten to turn off would be blazing out heat on three bars:

'Shit, better switch that off. Mum'll kill me if she finds out.'

There was usually a small mongrel dog curled up on the settee or yapping at your ankles.

'This is Rusty,' they'd say as it set about you with its tongue, happy to see a sign of life.

The kid would wrestle playfully with it and pour a few biscuits from a box onto the floor. The kitchen was bare, dirty plates piled high in a bowl. The place smelled of dogs and chip fat.

'Shall we see if there's anything to eat?'

He'd open the cupboards to reveal packets of custard, small bottles of blue and green food colouring, cream crackers and bottles of sauce: nothing you'd really want for dinner.

The other Johnson, 'Spud', was typical of my classmates. He had his hands perpetually dipped in the front pocket of his cagoule, where he kept his Space Dust. Most of us had grown bored with it after a packet or two but Spud was addicted. He'd hold his mouth open while it popped and cracked in his teeth and along his tongue.

'Fucking hell, Space Canaveral or what?' he'd yell.

Teachers tried to include him in lessons but soon accepted that his life was as combustible as freshly dampened Space Dust.

At least Spud was likeable. Many of the others were unpredictable and violent. Teachers spent a good portion of lessons settling everyone down and dealing with constant interruptions. Kids shouted out, answered back and provoked facile arguments. If anyone showed an interest in the lesson or did homework, they were mocked, told they were creeps and arse lickers. The teachers soon gave up, stressed out and worn down.

It was going on everywhere, this disaster. The British educational system of the 1960s and 1970s suited the few and failed the many. Comprehensive schools had been introduced purportedly to address the inequitable nature of the previous system, where pupils passing the eleven-plus exam (25 per cent) went to grammar school and those failing it, secondary modern. At a secondary modern, pupils received, according to the Department of Education guidelines, 'training in a wide range of simple, practical skills'. In straightforward terms, children were prepped to work in manual labour. Meanwhile, grammar schools offered an academic education suitable for a white-collar and management career. More fundamentally, falling on either side of this division formed a mindset that remained with people for life, literally marking their cards. Grammar school kids felt chosen, important, validated. The secondary modern, irrelevant, discarded.

The victims were many, among them the art historian and novelist Michael Paraskos, still seething more than thirty years later. 'You knew you were a failure from Day 1. Because they told you! So they [secondary modern schools] weren't pleasant places to be if you were into art, or books, or anything like that.* He wrote more on the subject in the *Guardian*:†

> I do not think people who gained grammar school places
> . . . can understand the crippling effect of failing the
> 11-plus exam.
>
> Apart from hobbling your opportunities, it embeds
> deep in your mind a feeling of absolute failure no matter
> what you do in later life. Although I hold a doctorate,
> am widely published, and have taught at some of the
> top universities in Britain, thanks to grammar school
> selection there remains to this day a voice in the back
> of my head telling me I am a failure. It undermines
> everything I do.

The comprehensive system had been rendered as a panacea, equal opportunities for all. Unfortunately at my school (dubbed a 'community' school, such was the specious pursuit of the ideal) and many others, it was purely a cosmetic modification. They replicated the previous regime by streaming pupils on admission.

The Certificate of Secondary Education had been introduced in 1965, primarily as a 'leaving certificate' – effectively proof to an employee that you had actually gone to school. CSE subjects were aimed purposely at those earmarked for blue-collar work, so we did woodwork, metalwork and technical drawing, and made regular visits to workshops and factories, as if primed specifically for local firms.

* *Cyprus Mail*, April 2016.
† September 2016.

I often recall David Johnson's sneer and remark as he passed my desk that time:

'I pity you with this lot.'

I'm not sure how and why I ended up with the CSE-ers. No one explained how this worked. No one asked. Back then, parents trusted teachers, schools and systems. I have often pondered: who made the decision? Had I performed badly at junior school? (It didn't feel that way.) Were they filling a quota? Did they, for a few seconds, imagine how this might shape a personality and affect a life? At least with the eleven-plus exam there was an element of self-determination: you actually sat a test, even if it came at a young age.

Two or three years later, the school (or more likely the council's education department) changed its policy and pupils were streamed into CSE or O level groups on a subject-by-subject basis, rather than en bloc. Too late for me, of course.

The CSE stream was broad and included several who, these days, would be considered as having *special educational needs*. They were on the outer edges of the behavioural scale and labelled by kids, with typical insensitivity, 'spackers' or 'mongs'. They rocked in their chairs or held their hands awkwardly by their sides. They had speech impediments and formed habits such as rubbing the desk repeatedly or nodding their head vigorously. Ian Miller licked his lips constantly until the skin around his mouth turned red and sore as if he'd dipped his face in Vimto, which became his nickname. They were made to join in PE, which seemed especially cruel. I remember watching Mark Peake in the changing rooms. His hands were shaking and he grimaced as he slowly took off his clothes, almost as if he were removing a layer of skin. He put on his rugby socks with absolute precision, tongue protruding from his lips as he concentrated. During the games, they were lost children at a busy railway station, fearful of being struck by the ball, turning their backs and screwing up their faces if they

41

thought it was coming their way. These kids would eventually leave the class to be housed in the 'remedial block', a prefabricated building set back from the main school.

Occasionally kids turned up part-way through a term and it was clear they were 'special' in a more ominous way. It would be obvious in their manner (agitated), their eyes (a manic 1,000-yard stare) and what they said ('Let's find a cat and kill it.'). One lad lasted a single day. During a chemistry lesson he rubbed a rag soaked in ammonia in a girl's face and, at afternoon break, set about someone with a bicycle chain. Another lad, Carl Bebbington (Bebz) was obsessed with violence. He regularly said a gang from a nearby school was on its way.

'They're bringing loads with them. You watch, it'll kick off. Bound to.'

He had made plans:

'If I'm cornered, I'm going to get a cup of boiling-hot water and make sure the first one who comes near me gets the fucking lot in his face. I'll blind the bastard.'

Often, he claimed to have witnessed a gang fight 'in town' or 'in that ginnel behind the Lord Howard pub'.

'You should have seen it. They gave one lad a right hammering. His face was a fucking mess.'

On my own with him, on the bus or walking home from school, there seemed a splash of truth in his stories, especially on dark wintry afternoons. The recurring theme was of being trapped and outnumbered. His face flushed red when he became excited, as if licked by flames. When you left him it felt as if he was on your skin.

Grandad's first job after leaving school was on the railway. He shovelled coal, carried sleepers, swept platforms and painted the station. At the age of nineteen he was struck by a wagon that had careered down the track after breaking free from its coupling. He was knocked unconscious. His sisters said he 'wasn't the same lad' afterwards. He'd not been dating my gran long when Lizzy, one of the eldest, warned her:

'You'll have nothing but trouble. He's not right.'

I read my first grown-up (252 pages) book in May 1976: *Vet in Harness* by James Herriot. I have the evidence. In celebration, the twelve-year-old me (flares, centre parting, star-patterned jumper) scrawled my name and the date on the first page. I don't remember ever doing this again; this claim of ownership goes against the communality of books.

I'm not sure what attracted me particularly to this fourth instalment of the memoirs of a vet working in the fictional village of Darrowby in the Yorkshire Dales. I hadn't seen the film based on the books, *All Creatures Great and Small*, released in 1975, and the television series wasn't broadcast until three years later. The draw may have been the sheer popularity, the sovereignty of James Herriot (real name: James Alfred Wight). His books were everywhere. They were borrowed in huge numbers from libraries and available on revolving stands at gift shops and newsagents. Herriot was an author with rare cross-gender appeal; others such as Mario Puzo, Jack Higgins, Frederick Forsyth and John le Carré were bought almost wholly by men, while Jackie Collins, Colleen McCullough, Jilly Cooper and Barbara Taylor Bradford were their female counterparts.

Reviewers in the UK (many of whom were authors themselves, usually of lofty pretensions) viewed Herriot's work as provincial and lowbrow. Not that it mattered; he sold more than sixty million books throughout the world. The branding was distinctive. Each cover featured a literal, funny ha-ha cartoon of a hapless vet drawn by Norman Thelwell. My edition cost 60p. The press notices on the back cover are drifting clouds of text without the now familiar anchoring of a barcode; they were introduced in the autumn of

1979. On rereading the book, the genial characters and bucolic wheezes are the main charm but it is not without reflective moments: 'And, walking face on to the scented breeze I felt the odd tingle of wonder at being alone on the wide moorland where nothing stirred and the spreading miles of purple blossom and green turf reached away till it met the hazy blue of the sky.'

Later that same summer, the habitual spitting rain to torrential rain and every version of rain in between was chased away by shafts of sunlight. And the sun stayed, over Rochdale and the rest of England, day after day, week after week. Roads melted to sticky black glue. Police were allowed to remove their ties for the first time in the history of the local division. Firemen were called out 300 times in one week, mostly to moorland fires. Scores of people were taken to hospital with sunstroke. A reservoir evaporated to nearly twenty-five feet below its normal level and the outline of the village on which it had been built was visible again. Water rationing was introduced and houses had supplies cut off for long spells.

Our little gang played out all that summer. On some days it was so hot we flopped down on the grass, closed our eyes and watched the shapes and colours shifting across the underside of our eyelids. The area by the canal came alive with insects, chirruping and scratching. They jumped around your feet as you walked and each step detonated a small explosion. Grass grew longer than ever before, past belly buttons, and it was difficult to see paths snaking between the trees. Colours were brighter and deeper and heat set water sparkling. Footpaths dried and split into tiny fractures. Kids stripped off and jumped into streams and rivers. They formed parties and tripped through streets with towels under their arms, dogs at their heels.

In the evenings, with my bedroom window open to let in precious cooling air, I read the three earlier books in the James Herriot series – *If Only They Could Talk, It Shouldn't Happen to a*

Vet and *Let Sleeping Vets Lie*. I had no mentor or guide to the landscape of books but already had the tenacity and resolution of the completist.

On his death in 1995 Herriot left an estate of nearly £5.5 million. The obituary in the *New York Times* said of his books: 'Each was filled with heart-warming stories, told in simple prose, of ailing animals and their owners and the veterinarians who tramp across muddy fields at all hours of day and night.' A museum remains open at the original base of his veterinary practice, 23 Kirkgate, Thirsk. World of James Herriot (oddly, without a definite article), thrives, though dog lovers are upset that pets are prohibited. 'Herriot would turn in his grave,' complains 'Paul' on Tripadvisor. The response from the museum is phlegmatic: 'Dogs can be unpredictable.'

I made my way through an assortment of books borrowed from the school library. The desire to read was wholly innate, neither shaped nor encouraged by anyone. Only in childhood is this possible, where there is a purity of thought and deed: it feels good, so we do it. This meant there was no discernible selection process at play. One of the first books I read, cover to cover, was a western, *First Blood* by Jack Schaefer. The dust-coated tale is of Jess Harker, a young stagecoach driver in awe of the company's top messenger, Race Crimm. I wrote a review in a notebook that I'd bought specially: 'Fast paced and full of action.' I determined to write one for every book I'd read from there on but failed at this mission within a few weeks. I next borrowed two books whose titles and authors I have forgotten but when I try to recall them I think of books similar in themes and tone which I read much later in life. The first was slow and dark and claustrophobic, much the same as *One Day in the Life of Ivan Denisovich* by Aleksandr Solzhenitsyn, and the other was a journey-of-the-mind exercise similar to *The Star Rover* by Jack London.

I was heartened – even at my hopeless school, you could be spirited away from everydayness by merely slipping two curious, esoteric books into your bag, then reading them later.

A cultural and social revolution had ignited during the time I was reading the James Herriot series and books from the school library. Nine miles north of Thirsk, running parallel to the North York Moors National Park and passing three Thorntons (Thornton-le-Street, Thornton-le-Moor and, finally, Thornton-le-Beans, where Bill Bryson has expressed a wish to be buried), was the market town of Northallerton. On Wednesday, 19 May 1976, six months before the release of their debut single, the Sex Pistols performed at Sayers nightclub on a backstreet in Northallerton town centre; it was the first time they had played outside the conurbation of London. That summer, as they passed through unlikely venues in far-flung towns, they collected disciples anxious for change. I was too young, at twelve, to understand and embrace this celebration but this would come over the next few months and years. And when it did, sure and steadfast, music (punk specifically) and books, and all the ideas and energy and intrigue contained within, would merge and remain for a lifetime.

Punk arrived at our little bit of Rochdale on an overcast autumn morning when we'd almost forgotten the hot summer just gone. Paul Kennedy, known to everyone as Kenny (even teachers), marched into the school yard in leopard-skin trousers and a capped T-shirt covered in zips. His hair was spiked high and a small white feather dangled from a stud in his ear. He was a couple of years older than me and my pals. Until this point, most self-aware kids had been big on a kind of sullen pseudo-spirituality forged largely in the image of David Carradine from the television series *Kung Fu*: eyes down, hands in pockets, lank hair and slouched body. A mob gathered around Kenny asking questions; it was almost as if it were a press conference.

'Why are you dressed like that?'

'I'm a punk.'

'What's a punk?'

'A punk is a punk is a punk, that's what a punk is!'

After a few minutes he parted the throng by putting the backs of his hands together and moving his arms in a large arc as if doing the breaststroke. Over the next few weeks, under pressure from teachers, he moderated the look, adopting a sort of militaristic chic with an Italian combat jacket, sharply pressed trousers and black-framed glasses without lenses. I was hugely impressed.

Punk blow-torched the school. Anyone still smelling of patchouli oil and padding around in Trax desert boots was turned into a relic. I saw Kenny a couple of times at Bradleys Records in town. On the second occasion he called me 'matey' and rubbed my hair. He had a small box of 7-inch singles that he took everywhere with him. He passed them around, telling everyone how rare they were, that the see-through vinyl with hand-printed sleeve was limited to the first 1,000 copies. Most of the artwork was cut-outs, the kind you could do in a few minutes at home with scissors and glue.

'That's the whole point,' he said.

Gran and Grandad made plans to marry. My gran told me, many years later, that she loved him so much because he was 'great fun when he was well'. His sisters urged her to call off the wedding. She was suspicious that it might be a ruse; she felt she had never had their approval. How could she possibly conciliate eight women – seven sisters and a mother? Already she had a fierce devotion and wasn't going to desert him at the start of their life together. The wedding went ahead.

I had a morning paper round. If I walk-ran the landings in the old people's home, I could sneak a few minutes of reading on the

bench by the canal, book in hand. Before sitting down I'd sometimes stare out across the water. The canal was viewed in those
days as a semi-legal repository of refuse. In the gloomy half-light
of an early morning it was swamp-still with strips of wood, tyres,
plastic bottles and traffic cones floating on top, the odd shopping
trolley breaking the surface. A few sparrows or starlings were the
only signs of life. They picked at crumbs that had broken off from
discarded polystyrene tiles, mistaking them for bread. One time,
vandals had thrown in a whole section of road works.

My round finished at Ashfield Valley, a council estate made
up of multistorey flats running alongside the canal. The flats,
exactly 1,014 of them, had been built in the late 1960s following
the utopian ideal of 'Streets in the Sky', influenced by French
architect Le Corbusier. The blocks were like giant futuristic creatures turned inside out with their guts put on show – pebble-
dash, corrugated edges, metal cages set in concrete. Within a few
years, tenants complained that the dark utilitarian structure made
it feel as if they were living in a prison. Vandalism and drug
dealing were rife. Drunks slept in corridors. Walls were covered
in graffiti. A mummified body of a man was discovered in a bin
room; he had been dead for about six months. Tenants were black-
listed by local traders and businesses. Television rental shops, gas
showrooms and furniture stores refused to supply goods, or when
they did, insisted on sizeable deposits. Such was its notoriety,
anyone from the estate seeking a job was advised to use another
address when applying. Dad joked that the canal served as a moat
between our estate and the flats, though anyone wishing to cross
could easily hop from thrown-in shopping trolley to pram to pallet
to reach the other side.

Even in the early mornings, there felt to be danger. The lifts
stank of urine. Some of the graffiti was about teachers at my
school. On the stairwells between floors were cartoon penises and
messages: 'Julie is a slag', 'Paul is a tosser'. One morning, new

graffiti appeared. The names of what I presumed were bands – Crass* and the Fall – had been stencilled underneath the Norweb† sticker of the matchstick man having his belly zapped, warning of danger by electrocution. I made a mental note to ask Kenny whether he knew of these groups.

A few weeks later I saw Kenny sitting on a wall near the Dicken Green pub. Out of school, he had reverted to full-on punk again. He was wearing tight red trousers, a blue artist's smock and Doc Martens boots up to his knees. His hair was dyed red and fixed into thin spikes with flaky dried soap. He nodded. I'd almost walked past when I decided to speak to him.

'Kenny – have you heard of a band called Crass?'

'I have indeed,' he said. 'Total anarchists. I was reading about them in a fanzine the other day. They look scary fuckers, all dressed in black.'

'What about the Fall?'

'I *fucking* love the Fall,' he said. 'I was at their first ever gig earlier in the summer. They played in this basement in Manchester. Mad, it was. I met the singer, Mark, afterwards in the Sawyer's Arms on Deansgate. He bought me a pint!'

I asked him why he was hanging about.

'I'm waiting for a lift. A few of us are going to the Leccy.'

'What's that?'

'The Electric Circus. It's this club in Manchester.'

'Who's on?'

'The main band are the Rezillos but we're going down really to see the support, Warsaw. They're fucking great. The singer gets completely into it, spazzing out.'

* More of Crass later.
† North Western Electricity Board.

CHAPTER FOUR

Raleigh Chopper bikes were perfect for transporting books. The seat was padded, long and thin, with a piece of curved metal as part of the backrest, ideal for hooking over a carrier bag containing four books – the maximum number permissible on a single loan from Castleton Library, Rochdale. The library was a 'Carnegie' – one of more than 2,500 in the English-speaking world part-funded by the Scottish-American industrialist Andrew Carnegie, who donated $350 million to libraries in his lifetime (1835–1919); today's equivalent would be $4.8 billion.

I cycled to the library most Saturday mornings. While it was a joy to be among so many books, it wasn't the sacred experience which many recall and romanticise ('I had found my religion: nothing seemed more important to me than a book. I saw the library as a temple' – Jean-Paul Sartre). To me, the library was a city without a map. The etiquette was intimidating, the staff unhelpful. Was I allowed to take out three from the fiction section and one from the non-fiction, or had they changed the rules again so that you could take out any you wanted so long as it wasn't from the local history section or a big picture book from the shelves under the stairs? The library ladies (always ladies) weren't as portrayed in films: all soft smiles, half-rimmed glasses and encouragement. They tutted as they went about their duties, looking at their watches, ready for home. They clearly didn't think children should be there; streets and parks were for kids, not libraries. I'd sometimes lose my cards or bring the books back a day or two late. I'd present myself as cheerfully contrite as possible:

'Sorry, but one of these books is a bit overdue.'

'Well, there'll be a fine.'

David Johnson was my only friend who also read books but our tastes, nascent as they were, were already diverging. He lent me *Foundation* by Isaac Asimov. I would have been happy enough if he had merely passed it over but before it left his hand, he started:

'It's the last days of the Galactic Empire and this mathematician called Hari Seldon – spelled H.A.R.I. – spends his life developing a theory known as psycho-history. Using statistical laws, it means he can predict the future of large populations. He sees the imminent fall of the Empire, which encompasses the entire Milky Way and a dark age that lasts 30,000 years.'

I nodded, hoping to reveal that I was being courteous rather than enthusiastic. He began telling me Asimov's life story.

'He was born in Petrovichi, about 250 miles south-west of Moscow in Russia,' he said. 'Along with sixteen other children in his village he caught double pneumonia in 1921 and was the only one to survive. When he was three years old his family sailed on the RMI *Baltic*, the world's largest ship at the time, to America. I bet you're thinking the family spoke Russian, aren't you?'

(I was actually thinking that I preferred listening to his screechy violin rather than being talked at in such a manner.)

'Well, you'd be wrong. His parents spoke English and Yiddish.

Have you heard of Yiddish before? It's a secret language that Jews speak. Anyway, he became professor of biochemistry at Boston University . . .'

'Great,' I said, almost snatching it from him.

Over the next week or so I read about twenty pages of the book. I couldn't understand it and didn't like it. I told him so.

'It might be a little bit beyond you for a first try at science fiction,' he averred. 'That's what it's called, that type of book. Maybe you should try Michael Moorcock to get you started. He's like an English Asimov. Well, sort of. If I were you, I'd begin with *The Cornelius Quartet*.'

'Sounds like a jazz band,' I said.

'It is *not* a band,' he said, oblivious to my facetiousness.

The sisters were right. Soon after they were married Grandad began acting strange. He drew on the wedding photographs. On the wide-angle shot of the assembly outside the church he daubed a pair of horns on his head and an arrow pointing downwards at his feet.

David's final petition, with him acting all sigh-sigh, exasperated, was on behalf of J.R.R. Tolkien. This time, he passed me the book straight away as if it were a tablet of pure gold: *The Hobbit*. I had managed to make my way through a reasonable number of his other recommendations but every page of this felt weighed down. Wizards, dwarves, trolls, goblins, dragons, secret doors, magic rings, speaking spiders? What was this claptrap when outside (in pubs, venues, on the streets) and inside (on television and the radio) there was a cultural revolution under way called punk, where keeping it real was the new manifesto. It felt an abrogation of duty, a waste of time and energy, to be indulging in the baloney of Tolkien when there were bands to form or see, fanzines to publish, records to buy and songs to celebrate: Hey! Ho! Let's go!

A week later I handed back *The Hobbit* and declared that I'd 'struggled with it'. We stayed friends and I realised you could share a great deal with people but enjoy completely different books. More importantly – for David told me *The Hobbit* had sold *millions* – I had embraced the role of an iconoclast for the first time. I didn't care how lonely my island and noisy or sure of themselves my adversaries, any book beginning 'In a hole in the ground there lived a hobbit' could play no part in my life.

Castleton Library contained many books which, a few years later, would form the bedrock of my collection. Without any literary counsel, David Johnson aside, they remained invisible at the time, friends-to-be walking along the other side of the street. Instead, I still had my magpie eyes out for books that correlated to my various collections, such as the Ladybird series (with their fabulous illustrations) and the chunky, authoritative Observer's Books, which ran to a hundred subjects, from 1937 (*British Birds*) to 2003 (*Wayside and Woodland*). Another wonderful series was the Bancroft Tiddlers. These were forty-eight books on an eclectic range of subjects, from *Life Under the Sea* to *Heroes of the Wild West*, *Famous Churches* to *Beautiful Butterflies*. They were first published in the mid-1960s by Bancroft & Co. and were, as the series title suggests, small – about as big as a young teenage boy's hand – and each had a number in a red circle on the front. Was there anything more enticing to a collector?

At his worst, Grandad lit candles around the house and wrote on the walls. He brought pieces of wood from the railway and boarded up windows; he said people were spying on him. He could hear voices. He shouted at the neighbours, told them to stop whispering through the walls. He kept saying to Gran that he was leaving; he had to go somewhere, soon.

I see-sawed between being a kid and a trainee grown-up, trying them both out. I'd spend quiet evenings with a book, maybe pondering on punk, and then I'd be out with friends, ripping up bits of cardboard to skid down a grassy ramp or floating down the canal on a railway sleeper. I was further conflicted because I was simultaneously 'old-headed' (probably imagining myself to be somewhere in my mid-thirties) but I looked years younger than my real age; at thirteen I could have passed for nine.

Most of us from school went to the youth club at St Luke's church hall on Wednesday nights. Kids were in and out of side rooms, bumping into one another, mock-preaching from the stage or whizzing each other across the dusty floor. Fights broke out. A kid would be hurried to the toilets with a bleeding nose, a trail of red splashes behind him. Others found sweeping brushes in stock-rooms and galloped around as if they were taking part in jousting tournaments. Fluorescent tubes were waved triumphantly until a leader intervened:

'Put that away, will you? This minute. Those things can explode.'

A karate club used the large room above the hall and, under no circumstances *whatsoever*, were we allowed up there. Steve Fitton and me gave the leaders the slip. Steve pressed his face to the glass in the door panel and I sneaked a look over his shoulder. They were dressed in white baggy suits and, as they ran through their routines, pulled bizarre, strained expressions. Steve said they looked as if they were trying to have a shit. He started imitating them, for my benefit at first but then so they could see him. The sniggering stopped. The door crashed open. I'd already turned to run and was racing down the stairs when Steve passed me three feet from the ground. He hit the wall and fell in a heap. The karate bloke was at the top, shaking in rage.

'You've been told time and time again not to come up here.'

'Fuck off,' cried Steve, rubbing his backside.

'If you come up here again it'll be more than a boot up the arse. Do you hear me?'

'I'll get my dad on you,' shouted Steve. 'He won't bother with all that kung fu shit. He'll just beat you up.'

Mr Day was our science teacher and overseer of *the* school video player.* Every few weeks he wheeled out this huge contraption and asked for hushed reverence as he positioned it at the front of the class. He said (repeatedly) that we had no right to share room space with this mechanical deity; it was usually exclusive to posh schools. He had a video tape dedicated to anatomical oddities, many filmed in an eerie, fuzzy monochrome.

'Shall we watch the freaks?' he'd sing.

'Yeah.'

Flattened cardboard boxes were placed against windows to blot out the light as Mr Day cheerfully clunked down the huge buttons at the front of the recorder. The film began, the sound trembly, the picture scratchy. We saw babies covered in hair, people joined together, men with tails at the end of their spine, bearded ladies. There was a pianist with eleven fingers. He played joylessly as if at his own funeral. Mr Day asked us to remain seated at the end of the lesson so he could whisk the machine away without us knowing where it was stored. He was worried we might pass on information to older brothers or friends keen to acquire it.

PE offered no respite. Most of us wanted to play football but rugby league was the official 'school sport'. In the gym, Mr Benson, the PE teacher, made it seem an elegant, courtly pastime. We ran through play-the-balls and passing drills and there was

* It must have been among the first VCRs (video cassette recorders) imported into the UK. They became available in 1975 at a cost of about £1,000 – a family car was about twice as much at the time. By 2001 the price had fallen by 96 per cent. They are no longer manufactured and second-hand ones are considered worthless.

gracefulness in the shapes and formations. On the pitch, it was a glorified gang fight. The big lads, at last, had consent to manhandle their underdeveloped classmates. They came charging through. We were birds clinging to the backs of wildebeests.

'Get down to his ankles,' screamed Benson.

He wanted us to launch ourselves, head first, at the feet of a rampaging man-boy wearing rugby spikes. Some kids went through the pain barrier to win his approval. Munir was one of the wildebeests. Once, he was six yards from the try line when ambushed by about six waifs. He was slowing down but drove on through the mud. Spud Johnson had slipped beneath him and was on his back looking upwards. He reached out and took hold of the underside of Munir's shorts; it was obvious immediately that he had also grabbed his balls or dick, possibly both. Munir yelped. Benson was imploring him to drive for the line. Spud wasn't letting go. Munir's face set like a death mask and he made noises none of us had heard a kid make before – high-pitched wails to deep, gurgling groans. Spud slid across the turf on his back, clinging on. Munir made the line to score a try. Benson slapped him on the back. Munir said he felt sick.

'You'll soon feel better, lad. Keep moving.'

Underpants and vests were banned in PE lessons. Benson believed that boys should put on clean, dry underwear after they had showered. If he saw the faint outline of a 'Y' beneath a pair of shorts or spied the shoulder straps of a vest, the transgressor was beckoned and told to remove them 'at once'. This meant he sent us out on frozen February mornings in flimsy nylon shorts and shirts, shivering, skin turning red, turning blue. The icy, chuckling wind wrapped itself around your legs and there was an immediate sensation of tightening around the genitals.

Back in the changing room afterwards, a shower was compulsory. Some ran through the jets of water, a towel wrapped around their waist. If Benson detected the ruse, he made them go through again while everyone looked on, sniggering. Later that day, perhaps towards the end of double maths in the afternoon, you'd feel an unusual sinking sensation in your lower stomach. You'd clutch at your ball bag and find that they had finally returned: one, two.

When Grandad was uneasy his movements became frantic, edgy. Gran would become afraid. She fled the house once and walked the few streets to Lizzy's, where she knew she'd also find another of his sisters, Irene (the pair was inseparable). Gran wanted their help; he was their brother as well as her husband. This was the start of a family feud. The sisters refused to believe what they were being told: their brother, swearing and shouting and carrying on? She must be dreaming. Sure, he'd gone a bit doolally after the bang on the head but he was a peaceable, easy-going lad: she was making this up. When Gran told them she might move out for her own safety, they admonished:

'How can you think of leaving your husband at a time like this, when he needs you the most?'

She went back home and dealt with it as best she could, as she did for the next fifty years.

Music lessons could have been scarce moments of accord between teacher and pupils; most of the kids actually liked music, after all. Unfortunately, the music teacher, Mr Crompton, was a snob and completely unable to relate to children, the same as most of the other teachers. He had short-cropped fuzzy hair and long, wiry limbs, much like an Action Man figure come to life. During one lesson he wanted to show us how to sing properly and was looking for someone to stand in front of the class to illustrate breathing techniques. He kept asking and asking. In fact, he had asked so much that it had become quite amusing and he seemed aware of this, half smiling and sitting further back in his chair, scanning the class.

'Come on, I need a volunteer.'

No one moved.

'Just one, don't be shy.'

He asked again. He was making us anxious now. We were in the last year at school, a bit old for this. He pushed up his glasses with the back of his hand, loosened his collar. It wasn't funny any more.

'What is it with you lot? Why won't you have a go?'

I didn't hear or see Jenny Henstock volunteer because the commotion that ensued was so loud and violent. She must have held up her arm or muttered 'I'll do it, sir' and, almost immediately, David Roach had made his impudent remark. Crompton was on him, knocking over a table in his haste. Under his breath, Roach had mumbled that Jenny was a 'mug'. Crompton dragged him from his chair and almost lifted him from his feet as he moved him to the front of the class. He pushed him with the heel of his hand on the shoulder.

'Mug, did you say? Mug? Who's a mug now, Roach, hey? Who's the mug now?'

The Action Man was melting in the heat. Roach rocked back on his feet but kept righting himself to stand in front of Crompton. Roach was a skinny kid; every jab will have left a blue-black print on his chest. Crompton took hold of him and began shaking him.

'Do I have to shake it out of you? Do I?'

He gave up and shoved Roach away. He looked down at his hands and frowned as if he had suddenly noticed they were covered in shit. He wiped them on his corduroy trousers.

'Get out of my sight, Roach, just get out.'

Even now, Mum gets defensive when I talk about my schooldays.

'We didn't know you were so unhappy. You seemed okay,' she says.

As a kid, you know no different. I thought everyone regarded

58

their schooldays as a warty toad on the palm of their hand. It's only through meeting and getting to know people in adulthood that your schooldays and childhood are placed in perspective. I had no idea that kids, other kids, went to schools where the teachers were interested in them and they applied themselves and actually enjoyed being there, *learning*. Similarly, I hadn't noticed that my school was shabby with barely any facilities or that we were constantly treated with suspicion in case the video recorder or a box of pens was stolen. I am envious of the happy, enriching schooldays of others and the even-tempered nature it usually bestows.

My compensation was that I learned how to survive amid hostility, to conceal my intelligence and ingratiate myself with mad or degenerate kids who might have otherwise picked on me. I wonder, too, if it forged independence. Nothing was handed down, from either pupils or teachers; I had to find it myself. Maybe, in a world where books, for example, were shared, recommended, deconstructed, they might have become an easy currency and soon felt ordinary, nothing special. Instead, books became crucial in reinforcing my outsider stance, getting me through and forming my personality.

Mum was born into a war, outside and inside the house. A few weeks before her birth, the Luftwaffe had begun bombing missions on Manchester. In one weekend alone 684 people were killed and 2,000 injured in the city. The other war was being waged by her dad, with himself. At bedtime she prayed for two things: 'Please make my dad better and let us one day have a garden.'

Years after leaving school I was contacted by a former teacher who had read one of my books. We met in a Rochdale pub. He asked me what I'd thought of the school. We'd both had a few pints. I blew away the froth of diplomacy and told him straight: I had endured it as I might a prison sentence.

'Think about it from our perspective,' he said. 'Most of us were straight out of teacher training, finding ourselves in a dump like Rochdale, herding all these juvenile delinquents. Most of the older teachers were misfits who wouldn't have got a job anywhere else. It's no wonder we were disillusioned after a few weeks.'

He had made a reasoned petition and I could see that both pupils and teachers had been institutional victims. But this wasn't to excuse the peevishness, apathy and bullying of most teachers.

'What was *I* like?' he asked.

'Not as bad as some,' I replied, which was the best I could offer without letting down either myself or former classmates, wherever they might have been on that dark night with the rain lashing against the windows of the Flying Horse.

He left and I carried on drinking, staying for one or two more pints. It felt, there and then, memories fading to grey, as if those way-back days might not have even existed. The school had been knocked down, pupils and teachers dispersed, the kids now had kids of their own, possibly even grandkids; some of my schoolmates had died. Where did the days go anyway? Were they piled up in a magical other-place, waiting to be rerun, reshown? Or were we supposed to agree, by mutual consent, that they had existed once but we now had to move on, forget them and live in the here and now? I ordered a taxi.

After the night with the teacher I realised that he'd probably been one of thousands caught in the prevailing idealism of the 1960s – duffel coats and CND marches – that led many young teachers to view education as a means to foster egalitarianism, to make a difference. But these teachers had struggled to relate to the impetuous, agitated working-class kids sitting before them.

As an adult myself, I could see that he was only a few years older than me, maybe nine or ten, whereas back in school he'd felt at least a generation away. He said he'd moved from Southampton specifically to work at the school, leaving behind family and friends. Imagine moving, on your own, to live in Rochdale and for such a demanding, thankless job. I shuddered.

'It's what we did back then. I'd done teacher training in Hull, so I'd already made that break from home,' he'd said.

History has not recorded how *A Kestrel for a Knave* by Barry Hines was added to the school syllabus in the early 1970s, but it had a remarkable and lasting impact and was the bridge by which these young teachers and teenagers could cross and meet. It changed my life. Billy Casper, the book's protagonist, was the definitive emblem of a ragged generation. Everyone knew a Casper — half-boy, half-pigeon, disowned by his family and school, left to hobble through life in a ten-bob anorak and half-mast trousers. Viewed from a modern perspective and an improved standard of living, Casper can appear an exaggerated literary creation, but he was real and he was everywhere.

Some nights Mum was woken by Gran standing over her bed, shaking the bedclothes. As soon as her eyes opened, Gran was holding a finger to her lips, beseeching her to be quiet.

'Come on, get your slippers. We've got to go.'

They tiptoed across the room, down the stairs and out of the front door. Grandad had fallen asleep after another outburst and they had to move quickly.

We had about four Caspers in my school class alone, lads from 'broken' homes dressed in hand-me-downs, not sure from where their next meal would come, dodging bullies, irate neighbours or members of their own family. These were shadow boys, a few yards behind the rest of us, unwilling to join in. They often played alone on the margins, down by the river near the chemical factory or on a piece of oily scrubland between the road and railway. Gerald Swanson was typical. We'd often ask him to join us but it was like trying to tame a feral cat; he didn't trust us enough to draw close. He was always yawning and sometimes fell asleep in class, his forearm a pillow for his head. During the summer holidays we found him sleeping on a pallet near the canal, curled up tight. His face was mucky and looked to be tear-smeared.

'Swanny.'

Gerald opened his eyes, blinked and scanned our faces. In an instant, he was off. He charged through the shrubs and bushes and was on the towpath within seconds.

'What's up with you? We're not going to beat you up or owt.'

'Fuck off,' he yelled and jogged away.

The image of Billy Casper flicking an insolent V-sign has endured and is available on posters, mugs and even fridge magnets. The defiance was important but far more significant was the passion. Billy had no family to speak of, no education, no friends, but, through Kes – in finding, nurturing, training, even loving this bird of prey – he had discovered a passion, the kind that evades most people all their lives. The pivotal scene is where Casper is encouraged by his teacher, Mr Farthing, to tell classmates a 'factual story' about himself. 'Tell him about your hawk,' a kid pipes up. At first Casper responds in a monotone but soon builds up confidence, relating how he has trained (but not tamed) the kestrel. He recalls the bird's first flight: 'She came like a bomb. About a yard off the floor, like lightning, head still, and you couldn't hear the wings. There weren't a sound from the wings – and straight onto the glove – Wham! And she grabbed me for the meat.' The kids are rapt. They suddenly see a kid who is made strong and valid, a knave becoming a prince. Here lies the hope, for Billy has found himself and, with it, a poise and sureness to carry through life.

On a wider level, the novel, published in 1968, authenticated the north and its people. This had been Hines's intention: 'English literature was reading books about people who had been dead for hundreds of years. I wanted to read about a world I could identify, where people had to work for a living,' he said.

Northern provincial Britain was as bleak as he had portrayed it. I was there. Industries that had forged communities were on their last wheeze – coal, iron, steel and textiles – and this decay had seeped into people, left them without faith. Worse, a sense of having a 'rightful place' had set among the poorest, so they were taught to accept their lot. This lack of self-worth dogged my generation of working-class kids and led to wasted and thwarted lives or, worse, early deaths. Gerald Swanson killed himself in his early twenties by stepping in front of a train. He left a note for his mother – it was read out at the inquest and reported in the *Rochdale Observer*. He wrote that he was 'fed up of not having a job and feeling like I can't get on with life properly like everyone else'. There were other victims. Paul McMahon, high on glue, was stamped to death by his best friend, Francis Harper – while hallucinating, Francis believed Paul was on fire and thought he was putting out flames. Simon Humphries jumped from a veranda of a town-centre flat. Most of the rest got make-do, better-than-nothing jobs that were supposed to last a few weeks but had stretched out for most of their lives or until redundancy.

After we had read *A Kestrel for a Knave* we were set an essay by Mr Selwood, our English teacher. We had to compare Mr Gryce, the head teacher in the book, with the brutal Wackford Squeers from *Nicholas Nickleby* by Charles Dickens. Squeers, one of literature's most abhorrent figures, ran Dotheboys Hall, a boarding school in Yorkshire where 'there were little faces which should have been handsome, darkened with the scowl of sullen, dogged suffering; there was childhood with the light of its eye quenched, its beauty gone'. Our school wasn't quite that bad.

Hines had been brought up in Hoyland Common in South Yorkshire, where the novel was set. He was confounded when he passed his eleven-plus for Ecclesfield Grammar School in Sheffield because it took him away from pals. 'Just because I sat down one morning when I was ten years old and got a few more sums right than my mates seemed no reason for trying to make me into a snob,' he wrote in *This Artistic Life**. He said he would probably have become a 'plumber or electrician', had he gone to a secondary modern. Instead, he studied to be a PE teacher at Loughborough College where, on a languid Sunday afternoon, he borrowed a friend's copy of *Animal Farm* by George Orwell, chiefly because it was a thin book and wouldn't take up too much of his time. Hines, then aged twenty-one, found himself reading for pleasure for the first time in his life. He moved on to Ernest Hemingway and, as he had done with Orwell, admired the economy of style, realising that literature did not have to be ornate or melodramatic.

He drafted *A Kestrel for a Knave* while working as a PE and English teacher at Kirk Balk Secondary Modern School for Boys in Hoyland Common. The novel was completed on the island of Elba in Italy; he used a bursary from the BBC to fund the sabbatical. While working as a teacher, Hines often read aloud – expressively, according to former pupils – the stories of H.E. Todd, from the Bobby Brewster series of books. Throughout the 1950s and 1960s Todd had visited schools and libraries where he accentuated his plummy voice to lend greater absurdity to his tales of talking household objects, predominantly spoons. Hines

---

* I commissioned and edited *This Artistic Life*.

knew that the silly motifs (Brewster's love of sardine sandwiches, for example) and the inevitable arrival of the sentence, 'And then a funny thing happened . . .' had a warmth and rhythm that ensnared the class. Hines was asked in a radio interview what he remembered most of being a teacher: 'It was good fun. The lads were so funny, so humorous. It was a treat to be among them. I think in South Yorkshire it was like a mining humour.'

Sadly, the humour tripped out in Rochdale schools was of a meagre standard. Most of us had tapes or records of *Monty Python* and were familiar with the sketches about dead parrots and cross-dressing lumberjacks. These were learned verbatim by a handful of kids. While impressive on first recital, by the ninth or tenth, it was a wasp in your ear.

A pornographic magazine appeared in one lesson. It wasn't the usual pouty, quick flash of *Men Only* or *Fiesta* but a near-gynaecological exposition, the pictures barely comprehensible no matter which way round the magazine was held. The 'joke' was that every time the teacher turned to write on the board, a page featuring a pinky outspread of flesh was held aloft. Again, the pantomime element inspired a chuckle on the first or second occasion of this being played out – porn held aloft, kids giggle, teacher looks round bewildered, magazine shoved under desk. By the last lesson of the afternoon, only the same two or three lads were still laughing.

I joined in occasionally with the frivolity; it helped maintain credibility within the pack. Once, I was invited to play with about four or five lads where we bashed a path through bushes on a roundabout of a dual carriageway and slid down a muddy incline on our backs. As we were doing it, amid their shrieks of joy, I was aware of being bored and also that it was ruining our clothes, ripping them to shreds. Similarly, I joined a fountain pen free-for-all where we repeatedly flicked ink over each other. During one lesson – where the teacher carried on as if nothing untoward was happening – we ganged up on one giggling kid, wrestled him to the floor, lifted up his shirt and sent ink criss-crossing all over his belly. I was about fifteen, exams looming and far too old for this. As I flicked the pen one more time, I remember thinking: what am I doing?

Sometimes the 'humour' had a sinister edge. A teacher's chair was replaced with a broken one from the stockroom and we all had to anticipate the collapse onto her back and then our shame because we'd dared not say anything and risk the wrath of the class bullies. Another 'joke' was to secretly manoeuvre (usually with crafty footwork) the pole used to open the top windows, so it would topple and hit a kid or, even better, a teacher. By far the most sadistic episode saw a lad cornered and stripped while getting ready for a PE lesson. As a final ignominy, he was hurled into the girls' changing room. He ran home naked.

Grandad was routinely sectioned to Springfield, a former workhouse that had been transformed into a psychiatric hospital. Mum's school friends asked about her dad's whereabouts and she told them he had gone away because he was poorly. They said they had never heard of anyone being so ill that they had to stay in hospital for months.

Kes, as the book became better known (reflecting the popularity of the film adaptation), had been thrown down as a blunt truth from the frontline of working-class life. As such, it was meant for the poor and the let-down and never-stood-a-chance, and holding it on high was a statement of partisanship, similar to the passionate support of a football club. Mr Benson, for example, the PE teacher at my school, could well have been Mr Sugden, the bully in a tracksuit in *A Kestrel for a Knave* ('We'll play with the wind, down-hill . . .'), and my futile end-of-school careers appointment was similar to Casper's with a youth employment officer. I was once caned by the head teacher for picking up a piece of paper from the classroom floor (he was passing in the corridor, stared in and judged that I 'wasn't paying attention'). My caning mirrored those dished out arbitrarily by Mr Gryce in the book ('Yours is the generation that never listens. No guts, no backbone. Nothing to commend you whatsoever. Mere fodder for the mass media.').

The novel wasn't for the posh and the privileged, as acknowledged by Robert Butler, writing in *1843*, the culture and lifestyle magazine of *The Economist*:

> When I first read *Kes* I was at a prep school in the south of England. The backdrop there was a great Gothic cathedral, and daily life was punctuated by the peal of its fourteen bells. A chalk stream flowed through the school grounds and the walls round the playing fields were the ruins of a bishop's palace. Except for the familiar references to nibs and ink pots and the football legends Bobby Charlton and Denis Law, Billy's harsh life in the industrial North seemed impossibly remote.

Butler's standpoint and world-view contrasted hugely with that of Hines, as revealed in *This Artistic Life*: 'The view from my window is very inspiring. What? they say. Those horrible blocks of flats, all those mucky factories and all that smoke pouring out? Those ramshackle houses down there, that faceless council estate? Well, yes, I say. Most people live and work in places like that. And I can't think of anything more important to write about. Can you?'

CHAPTER FIVE

I had heard *Rule of the Night* talked about reverentially at school but I'd never actually seen a copy. The book was perceived as an item that might belong to an older brother, much the same as a Yes double album with gatefold sleeve or a heavily embroidered Wrangler jacket. I detected from overheard conversations that it was a dark, tough book with an aura of the *verboten*, and it was about Rochdale, specifically the area where I had grown up – its streets, alleyways, lock-up garages, pubs, working men's clubs and waste ground.

Before the internet, out-of-print titles were extremely difficult to track down. The only real way was to comb second-hand bookshops and, should they not have it, register your interest with the owner and effectively augment the search party. Charity shops were not as prevalent as today, so this also reduced the number of possible sources. In such circumstances it was relatively easy for books such as *Rule of the Night* to attain cult status.

Dawn visited our house every few weeks to cut Mum's hair.

They'd make space in the living room, pushing aside the coffee table and settee, bringing in a chair from the kitchen. The telly would be switched off for a couple of hours and the procedure – hair washing, cutting, blow-drying – was carried out with them talking non-stop. One day, nonchalantly, Mum told me:

'Dawn's dad is a writer.'

'A writer? What kind of writer?'

'He writes books, I think.'

It was as if she viewed having a writer as a family member about as commonplace as a bus driver or school caretaker. Rochdale, to my knowledge, had only one bona fide published author at that time: the man who had written *Rule of the Night*.

'What kind of books?' I asked.

'I don't bloody know.'

'What's he called?'

'She did tell me but I've forgotten now.'

'Well, what's *she* called?'

'Dawn.'

'No, her surname.'

'How would I know that?'

True, Mum and Dad barely knew anyone's surname, wouldn't think to ask. Dad had known people for years and referred to them only by their nicknames. He got antsy if you pushed him on the subject: 'I don't care what he's bloody called as long as he does a decent job or pays me on time,' he'd say. He knew at least four Johns: John the Pole (he was Polish); John the Ghost (he disappeared when any serious graft was required); John the Bog (he was Irish) and Chicken John (a daily consumer of home-made – wife-made – chicken sandwiches, picked out of a Tupperware box).

During the war Grandad was posted down south. He absconded frequently, saying his family needed him more than the army. He'd arrive home with his ration of chocolate saved for Gran and Mum. He'd spend a day or two with them until the military police knocked at the door. They knew him well:

'Come on, John. Let's have you back.'

He'd give Mum one last kiss on the cheek and tell Gran not to worry because he'd be home again soon. On the way out, he'd appeal to his captors:

'You shouldn't be taking a bloke from his wife and kid like this. What use am I down there, marching up and down all bloody day?'

I came home from school and saw a book upright against the telephone: *Rule of Night* by Trevor Hoyle. So it wasn't *Rule of THE Night*. On the cover was a glinting razor held between grubby fingers, all set to cause distress and damage. Above, the copy read: 'Kenny is savage, sensitive, menacing and unpredictable. This is his story – a haunting novel of teenage violence, crime and kicks.'

I read the book in two days, frustrated because I had to fit a night's sleep in between. While marketed similarly to the teen pulp novels popular at the time and featuring a typical protagonist – football hooligan and skinhead, Kenny Seddon – *Rule of Night* was of far greater literary worth. Hoyle said in an interview that he had the idea for the book after seeing a football fan arrested during a match.

'He was frogmarched around the pitch by a policeman with his arms up his back,' he said. 'He was growling at the crowd and they were spitting at him. It was an ugly sight and I remember thinking, "Christ, this is a violent reaction." I wanted to know more about people like him and started hanging around with a group of skinheads.'

As I'd heard at school, the book was set in Rochdale but this did not matter particularly. The rainy fluorescent-lit streets where Kenny and his mates prowled, smoking Players No. 6 and hunting down greasers to fight or girls to chat up, could have been anywhere in northern England. Hoyle wrote it 'as found' with no sentimentality or condescension.

The book, published by Futura in 1975, fell into the genre forged by the prolific Richard Allen, whose real name was James Moffatt (his editor chose the pseudonym). Moffatt wrote 290 novels under forty-five pseudonyms, averaging 10,000 words per day. *Skinhead*, his first novel as Richard Allen, was published in June 1970 and sold more than a million copies.

I recall seeing these pulp novels in second-hand bookshops and they were usually well worn, with scuffed covers or bendy spines; they'd clearly passed through many hands. Before *Skinhead*, its publisher, New English Library (NEL), had made a loss for the previous fifteen years. 'We wanted to publish books about what was happening on the streets,' said Peter Haining, an editor at NEL. 'We would literally read the papers for ideas and very quickly turn them [news stories] into books.' Moffatt, in his late forties, a jobbing writer, pipe smoker and cardigan wearer, had volunteered himself to his agent, Victor Briggs, as a prospective teen-pulp author. 'It was ridiculous. He was no more a skinhead than Greta Garbo,' said Briggs. Moffatt's 'research' was said to have been chatting to a group of drunken east London skinheads in a pub before dreaming up the close-cropped psychopath Joe Hawkins who kicked and punched his way into eighteen books. *Skinhead* was written in six days and, the same as all Moffatt's work, his first draft was the final draft; he refused to rewrite or edit copy.

Moffatt gorged on episodes of racism in his books, along with violence, gang warfare and rape. 'It's a business – it's the way I make my money. I write to live,' he said at the time. The thrill for his young readers was voyeuristic and vicarious, a visit to the dark side. Skinhead culture was originally multiracial, co-opting much of the fashion and music of Jamaica, but Moffatt's protagonist, Hawkins, mandated the neo-fascist version of the skinhead which took hold in the 1970s and beyond: 'He leant against the bar between

71

two coloured men. The stink of the blacks made him sick . . . "Spades" or "Wogs" didn't count. They were impositions on the face of a London that would always be white, Cockney, true-British.'*

When Moffatt wrote the books he was living in a seafront cottage in Sidmouth, Devon. He earned a good amount from royalties but when sales declined in the 1980s he drank a bottle of whisky a day. He was also a heavy smoker. He died of cancer in 1993, aged seventy-one, declining treatment. Another popular 'youthsploitation' author, Peter Cave, lived a few miles from Moffatt, in Torquay. His theme was books about bikers, predominantly Hell's Angels, beginning with *Chopper* in 1971. Cave had previously written for the soft porn magazine *Flirt 'n Skirt*.

Although I was young (and possibly a little bit pious) I resisted these books, sensing there was an elemental *wrongness* about literature used in such a grubby way. I'd sometimes find discarded porn magazines by the canal and, paradoxically, these seemed more wholesome; at least they existed in their own right and not within a framing shared by great and earnest authors trying to fathom the meaning of life. Later, I'd feel similarly about the burgeoning subgenre of football hooligan and 'hard men' books. They were a source of cheap, sordid thrills, lighting up names and deeds that should have remained unknown or forgotten.

Dawn the hairdresser must have told her dad how much I had enjoyed *Rule of Night* because a couple of weeks later two more of his books were waiting by the telephone. *The Adulterer* (1972) and *The Hard Game* (1973) predated *Rule of Night* and had been published by NEL. Both had cover shots featuring near-naked women with, respectively, the straplines: 'The sex games ad-men play' and 'He was a king-pin in the pornography racket'.

* *Skinhead*.

72

The protagonist in *The Adulterer* was Jon Jones, an aspirational rascal working at an advertising agency in Manchester, scooting around in a Triumph Stag, invariably with the top down. The of-its-time misogyny was probably considered true to life, knock-about banter but would inflict a considerable jolt to the post-Me Too generation: 'I looked at her face for the first time. She was indeed an ugly cow,' is Jones's assessment of Thelma, a barmaid with whom he has frequent sexual relations. After a liaison in a parked car on a moorland road, he states: 'Thelma sat there like a sullen lump of dough, the dashboard glow reflected in her glasses. Her body was anybody's; it didn't belong to her; it belonged to men.' The theme was revisited in *The Hard Game*, where Kyle Rossiter, a hard-core pornographer and the book's narrator, says: 'Women are cold, heartless creatures . . . you can't trust them, they are deceitful and full of trickery.'

Reading them again nearly fifty years on, *The Adulterer* in particular has an insolent energy. Hoyle sculpts a world all his own where wheezing taxi drivers and other dead-end heroes pursue mucky sex, shuffling across worn linoleum to the tap room where they can talk of their lay-by conquests until closing time. Hoyle can also do descriptive prose, writing of the moors that swaddle Rochdale: 'The clumps of dry, hardy grass lay close to the earth, permanently bent and disfigured by the wind; high in the cloudless sky flickering black dots of birds hung on that same wind, singing with hunger, and scanning the ground with eyes like telephoto lenses.'

Trevor Hoyle had drawn inspiration and material from this dirty old town and had become a published author. Maybe, I thought, one day I could do the same.

Mum had a sister, Linda, born a year after the war ended. Gran let Mum, who was six at the time, help wash and dress the new baby. Mum liked to nuzzle up close and smell the baby's skin after

73

she'd been bathed in front of the fire. Grandad was the worst he'd ever been, a train tipped from the tracks, engine revving, metal grinding sparks. Gran watched over the baby and she also watched out for Grandad.

Mum caught whooping cough. Linda had a runny nose and also started to cough. Gran said there was a draught. They shut all the doors and windows. Linda still coughed. They put another blanket over her. A few days later, they heard the distinctive 'whoop' as she struggled for breath. Grandad heard it too. He fell quiet in his chair, staring at the fire. Gran had mastitis and was unable to feed Linda properly. Linda lost weight and was coughing continually. She died at two weeks of age. The journey back from the hospital, the same hospital where she'd been born, was only about a mile but was the longest of Gran and Mum's life. Grandad circled, furious, blaming them for Linda's death.

I don't think Mum and Dad or me had noticed that the school's annual holiday was to a *Christian* centre. Great play was made in the brochure about it being an *adventure* holiday; the godly aspect was included as a footnote. The school otherwise had no religious dimension whatsoever; maybe teachers thought a week in Wales would form a spiritual power surge to see us through. All these years on, the centre remains open and its website says, 'a simple epilogue is held each evening in the lounge and this usually comprises of a song, one of our famous sketches, Bible reading and a short talk'.

I've still got the photographs from the holiday, halfway up Cader Idris and then by the deep blue of Llyn Cau, everyone gurning and snarling to the camera, wearing or waving aloft clunky chains and outsized padlocks – such brattish behaviour was considered 'punk'. Kicking out at sheep and telling them to fuck off was another popular gesture, repeated ad nauseam ('It's 1977 and we are going mad' – 'Plastic Bag' by X-Ray Spex). I didn't join in. I'd had some insight from Kenny. He'd told me devoutly that punk was a 'state of being', an uprising beyond the grasp of what he called cartoon or plastic punks. And it didn't matter what you wore or how you looked; the revolution was of the mind.

'It's about originality, doing your own thing, thinking your own thoughts, not booting old ladies or sticking out your tongue at policemen,' he'd told me. 'Let it suffuse your consciousness, kid, and set your path for life. It's a movement of acceptance and tolerance, and always remember your C's – the war on complacency, compliance and conformity.'

This all meant I was working at a more intellectual level than most of the others. I kept this quiet, of course.

After a few days at the centre based on the Mawddach estuary, near Barmouth, a few of us made friends with two leaders, Andy and Clive. They were about ten years older than us but the age gap didn't seem to make any difference. They were gentle and trusting and cheerful; we didn't know many men like this back home. They told us they were Christians and we started going round to their chalet, asking them about God and the Bible. On the last night Andy read us a poem called 'Footprints', about a man who dreamed he was walking along a beach with God while scenes from his life flashed across the sky. During the saddest times the man noticed there was only one set of footprints.

'He asked whether God had forsaken him,' said Andy. 'God replied that he would never leave him and during times of trial and suffering, when he could see only one set of footprints, it was because he had carried him.'

He closed the book and as its covers came together we heard snuffling. Stephen Killroy was crying. Andy and Clive went to comfort him. We scrambled to watch.

'Is he okay?'

'He'll be all right in a minute,' said Clive.

'What's upset you, Killy?' asked Jackie.

'It's what Andy's read out, that poem.'

He was looking around the room as if surprised to find himself there. Darkness was fanning through the doors and windows, the sun blood-red and tired over the estuary. Something strange and brilliant had happened and we all sensed it.

'That poem, it's beautiful, isn't it?' said Killroy.

I'd never heard a kid say anything like that before. He started sobbing again and Clive held him. None of us giggled or mocked him, not even when we were back at school again and it had all felt like a dream.

I turned up one Friday night at a Christian youth group that met in the basement of a church in town; I had seen a notice for it in the *Rochdale Observer*. Candles were on the tables and flickering light lit up pastel drawings on the wall depicting Bible stories. I sat among these kids and grown-ups I'd never met before. For the first time in my life, I wasn't shy or self-aware; it *did* feel as if I was 'born again' and that Jesus Christ walked with me, phrases I'd heard Andy and Clive say on the holiday. I had an extraordinary sense of well-being formed from conflicting elements: energy and serenity, confidence and humility, and it came without side effects or at a price.

Ralph was the most popular lay preacher at the youth group. He wore jeans and check shirts and rode a motorcycle. A large leather crucifix dangled from his neck. As we were leaving one Friday night he asked if I'd like to go to his house the next day and help wallpaper his front room.

'It would be a lot easier with two.'

I don't remember telling my parents or feeling there was anything untoward in being invited to the house of a single, middle-aged man. I took two buses to reach his bungalow. He opened the door, smiling broadly. A few buttons on his shirt were undone and he had a white T-shirt underneath. The house was extremely tidy. A large tapestry of a dove flying past a cross was on the wall above the gas fire. Beneath, it said: 'Jesus is Life.'

We worked well together. I cut the paper to length, pasted it, and he put it on the wall. He had small, supple fingers and stuck out his tongue as he brought the edges together. He told me about himself. He'd been a biker for 'years and years' and had once been a heavy drinker. He kept saying, 'I liked a drink,' and staring at me solemnly. He was wearing tartan carpet slippers.

'Do you know what changed? Do you know who made me see where I was going wrong?' he asked.

I shook my head.

'The Lord. He spoke to me. He tapped me on the shoulder and said, "What are you doing with your life?"'

He glared at me:

'Do you know why I've asked you here today?'

He still had the pasting brush in his hand and was waving it as he spoke. The bucket of paste was behind him and I thought if he took a step back he might stand in it, Laurel and Hardy style. He asked me again:

'Do you want to know why?'

I shrugged.

'I asked you here because I have the feeling that you want to talk about Christ. I mean – *really* talk. You told me that you read a lot of books and I sense that you are a seeker. Am I right?'

He was making me uncomfortable. When I didn't answer immediately, a look of despondency fell across his face.

'Well, that's up to you, but I'm here when you do want to talk. And I'll always be here.'

He said this as if he was rallying himself. We didn't speak for a while and I had the impression I'd disappointed him.

Gran wanted to bury Linda in the same plot as her father, who had died a few years earlier. Grandad insisted his baby daughter wouldn't

77

be buried with members of his wife's family. He refused to sign the forms and Gran had to arrange the funeral on her own. Linda was laid in a pauper's grave, placed into the earth among strangers whose coffins were laid on all sides of hers.

I was happy going to the meetings, the youth groups and the get-togethers at different houses, but they kept pressing the point, perplexed that I still hadn't found myself a church to attend. At one meeting I was sitting cross-legged on the floor (we'd formed a circle), feeling pretty good about myself because I'd caught the bus in the pouring rain and found this house on an estate miles from anywhere. A bloke in a denim shirt with a neatly trimmed beard called me by my name and asked if I'd found a church *yet*.

'Nope,' I said breezily, hoping he'd sense that I didn't want to talk about it.

'You should do, really.'

I smiled and said I felt okay.

'I'm not sure you can consider yourself a Christian if you don't go to church.'

I suddenly felt homesick. I could hear my dad in my head: this wasn't normal, it wasn't what lads my age should be doing. The beardy bloke softened his approach and forced a twitchy smile.

'Honestly, it's fantastic in church. It's where we all feel at one with God. It's like, instead of visiting your friends' houses, which is cool and everything, you're visiting God's house. It's where his love exists, where you can feel it strongest.'

At the point when he'd said 'cool and everything' I looked around to see if anyone else had noticed how disingenuous it sounded on his lips. No one responded. I was also wondering why Christian blokes wore either check or denim shirts, as if it was a uniform.

Finally, I went to a service at the church nearest our house.

A few pensioners were sitting in the front pews. The building was cold because the sun wasn't high enough yet to send light through the windows. I had a pew to myself halfway down the nave. One or two old ladies turned round and smiled. The vicar's voice reverberated and I could barely hear what he was saying. He spoke in a monotone and kept his body perfectly still. The hymn numbers were set in a wooden frame at the side of the pulpit. When the singing began it was a cheerless drone without any recognisable tune.

Afterwards, the vicar was fast on his feet, cassock flowing as he zipped down the aisle to greet me.

'Hello,' he said. 'I don't think I've seen you here before.'

'No, it's my first time.'

'Has your family just moved into the area?'

I noticed some of the old ladies had stopped and were craning their necks to hear. I was embarrassed by the attention.

'No, we've lived around here for a bit.'

He wanted to ask more but I'd already partially turned away. As I shuffled between the pews, he raised his hand to wave:

'I hope we'll see you again soon.'

That afternoon I caught a bus to a youth group on the other side of town. I told them about the church, how chilly and forlorn it had been. They said I should go to *their* church, which had a 'modern outlook'. They played guitars and sang, and the vicar was a 'real character'. I didn't like the sound of that either.

Within a year, and like a suntan fading over winter months, I lost my faith. I stopped going to the church groups and reading my New Testament. I was tired of seeing acoustic guitars released from unzipped cloth cases and the sound of tambourines. I'd had enough of chinking coffee cups and the rigmarole of communal washing-up and checking diaries to organise the next meeting. I wanted to leave behind the people I'd met as a Christian. Their jolly, open lives and bright-lit eyes began to feel fake; I didn't believe in them.

Mum and Dad had probably noticed my waning commitment but didn't mention it. Maybe they thought it might prompt a return to my old ways, back to God. They still teased me with 'Go and look in a bloody Bible' if I asked them an awkward question or they'd yell, 'You're supposed to be religious' whenever I did something they considered nefarious, such as not tidying my bedroom.

(A peculiar legacy of my time as a Christian is that I can't bear to see papers inserted into a book. I'm fine with a bookmark but when I see multiple papers, presumably acting as page markers, I'm back among the Christians, irritated by their prissiness, over-polished joy and, perhaps most of all, their habit of using leaflets to signpost their way through a Bible.)

I had Barry Hines. I had punk rock. And then I had J.D. Salinger. It was a Saturday morning, approaching noon. I was drifting through Rochdale town centre, my usual haunts: frothy coffee in the San Remo; check out the mark-downs in the crates at Bradleys Records; peruse the music papers in WH Smith and stare at the electric guitars in Tractor Music. I usually passed through Boots, the perfume and the corn plasters, on my way to the record stall on the market. I hadn't noticed before that Boots stocked books.*

The bookstand looked lonely in the middle of an aisle. There were just a few titles, no more than twenty-five, and each turned so the cover faced out. This rectangular frieze of colour, words,

---

* Boots ran a 'book-lovers' library' out of its 460 pharmacies from 1899 until 1966, with more than a million subscribers. The company also republished classic books under the imprint Pelham Library, named after the flagship Boots shop in Pelham Street, Nottingham.

photographs, typefaces, shapes and cartoons was overwhelming. After a few seconds, a particular cover set itself to my eyeline. And to my heartbeat. The author's name and the title were placed relatively small against a block of gunmetal grey. While the others were shouting 'buy me, buy me' in lots of different ways, this one was passive, indifferent, sure of itself. *The Catcher in the Rye* by J.D. Salinger made the journey from rack into the palms of my hands.

It seems incredible now – considering its great fame and repute and my association with Salinger* – but, on that day, I knew nothing of him or the book. I opened it and read the first page. No book has had the same impact since. I was breathless; within the first few paragraphs it felt like reading a letter sent exclusively to me. I flicked through more pages, unable to believe that a novel could be so consistently truthful and personal. I was unsure at first whether I had enough money to buy it. I decided there and then: if I have to, I will steal this book. I disgorged £1.25 from my pockets at the till. By mid-morning the following day I had read the book, viewed Holden Caulfield as a best friend and, to paraphrase Salinger, knew of all the madman stuff that happened to him around last Christmas just before he got pretty run-down.

There was no internet where I could carry out research and I certainly wouldn't have sought illumination from a teacher or snooty librarian. This meant I was unaware of the book's notoriety (more than thirty incidences of censorship or prohibition from schools in the US for being, take your pick: communist, immoral, vulgar, blasphemous, satanic and for featuring prostitution,

---

* I commissioned and edited the biography *J.D. Salinger: A Life Raised High* (2010) and presented and co-produced *J.D. Salinger: Made in England* broadcast on BBC Radio 4, February 2016.

transvestism, premarital sex, alcohol abuse and 'negative activity'), or its popularity (selling 250,000 copies per year throughout the world, equating to 685 per day). I also didn't know that Salinger was thirty-one when it was published in 1951 and had spent a decade working on it before retreating to Cornish, New Hampshire (population: 989) in 1953 to live out the rest of his days, eating alone at the Windsor Diner or calling for shopping at the Plainfield General Store.

Grandad used to scrawl on newspapers, envelopes and scraps of paper left around the house. He had spidery close-together writing and never tired of scribbling his name. It was like a barometer; the letters became more condensed and jagged when trouble was imminent. He'd mumble to himself and become fastidious: counting his money, checking through bills and insurance policies. He moved around the furniture, agitated, twigs crackling in an internal bonfire. He was turned in on himself, as if he'd swallowed a thunderstorm and it was pressing against his skin.

Calm briefly fell over him and the house when, six years after Linda had died, Gran gave birth to a healthy son, Peter.

I thought I was the only one, or near enough. I had no idea that I had forged a union with millions of others across the globe by simply reading a book. The experience of reading is isolated and fragmented, each to his own, and mostly undertaken by those who fancy themselves as originators, outsiders, freethinkers. But by falling deeply for Holden Caulfield and imagining him as a blood brother, I had succumbed to a prevailing cultural trope of young adulthood and beyond, although wasn't this unavoidable with such a novel? As Holden himself says: 'What really knocks me out is a book that, when you're all done reading it, you wish the author that wrote it was a terrific friend of yours and you could call him up on the phone whenever you felt like it.'

The modern reappraisal of Holden often has him as a whiney, uptown kid fastened to egocentric angst. Under an agenda of cultural revisionism, he is deemed too male, too white, too privileged, too American, too heterosexual and, for good measure, flagrantly misogynistic, referencing women solely by their hair colour, for example, or subdividing them as 'pretty' or 'whory'. Salinger owes no apology for placing Holden – a sixteen-year-old *boy* – in a circle he knew intimately (male, white, heterosexual, affluent), and social mores drawn predominantly from the 1940s are bound to jar in a modern context; it's one of the reasons why we read: to understand and interpret the present through the past, how we got here.

Many readers, especially critics who revisit Holden in their middle age, renounce him as they would a religion. His was a world-view, a people view, they held in youth, before they had wised up to his conceit, self-absorption and, sin of sins, phoniness – the vilification he holds as a sabre to much of the rest of humankind. They feel, by disowning Holden, that they have *moved on* and become advanced and urbane, no longer gripped or intrigued by the crisscrossing neuroses of a kid wandering through bars and Central Park, pondering on everything but nothing of real consequence.

Once a year, every year, I read the book and the feeling remains the same: it still smarts with a lust for life. There is no schism between our childhood and adulthood; this is largely a construct to account for and excuse mistakes and mishaps ('I was only a kid') made along the way, from minor to catastrophic. Life is a continuum and we are what we always were, always will be. What we see in Holden, we see for life but are perhaps afraid to admit. Life *is* angsty and we mewl and fret and embrace both self-love and self-doubt. We merely become more adept at the cover-up, further falsifying our adult version of self. Salinger created this forever-character almost as an act of philanthropy, a gift. While we age, Holden stays a teenager, caught within those pages, reminding us that the world is skew-whiff and unfathomable and that the best way to deal with this is to stay as Holden, young and sharp, cocksure and vulnerable, perfectly imperfect.

Most of all, *The Catcher in the Rye* is a supreme work of literature. Salinger writes absolutely in the voice of his protagonist, almost as if spoken in one take into a recorder. Many believe this to be an easy assignment – writing as speaking – but it is extremely difficult to sustain rhythm, energy, consistency and authenticity. Only the very best writers can master it and, even then, it takes a great deal of honing and paring down; it is no surprise that the book took years to complete.

That day in Boots, and the one after, and all those after that, *The Catcher in the Rye* made me believe I could become an author. I was fooled by the talk-writing, how simple it appeared, and thought I could do the same and also bring in the vernacular of my life to close-dance with his 'goddams' ('we went to a *goddam* movie'), 'as hells' ('it was always rusty *as hell*') and 'and alls' ('I didn't feel like getting in a long conversation with her *and all*'). On reading Salinger, with its limited vocabulary and paucity of description, it didn't seem to matter that I'd grown up in a house without books. All those words and insights and literary devices were rendered superfluous when you could write down your life and thoughts as he had done, so simply. Over many years and many attempts to emulate it, I (along with thousands of others) have learned that *The Catcher in the Rye* is proof of the Einstein maxim that 'the definition of genius is taking the complex and making it simple'.

Within a few weeks I had read Salinger's other books – *Raise High the Roof Beam, Carpenters / Seymour, An Introduction*; *Franny and Zooey* and *For Esmé – with Love and Squalor*.

I bought *Franny and Zooey* from Paperchase in Manchester, an independent shop selling posters, badges, pamphlets, novels and political books. There seemed a lot of these types of places in the 1970s, usually under-heated and staffed by shouty people who brought their dogs with them to work and let them sniff about your legs. I went there with Craig Radcliffe, a kid from school who barely spoke but, when he did, whispered single lonely fragments rather than sentences, usually extolling Genesis or Judas Priest ('*Rocka Rolla*. Great album. Priest. Class.'). It was midwinter, dark and icy, and when we got off the bus in the city centre the streets were almost empty, as if we were in a sci-fi movie.

'Bit eerie,' said Craig.

Snow started falling. We called at a few record shops and bookshops and both had a baked potato with cheese and beans at Spud U Like across from Piccadilly Gardens. When we got back to the bus station we were told they had stopped running because of 'inclement weather'. Craig asked what this meant. The woman in the kiosk said she wasn't sure exactly but there were no buses to Rochdale 'until further notice'. We set off walking. Snow turned to slush at our feet. We fell into the same pattern, side by side in our ox-blood Doc Martens shoes. I had *Franny and Zooey* in a plastic bag and he had two button badges (Rush and Rainbow) in a brown paper bag in the pocket of his duffel coat.

'All this to buy a book and a couple of badges,' I said.

'It's our life,' he responded cryptically. I soon gave up trying to engage him in conversation; it was hopeless.

The thunderstorm inside Grandad broke once while Mum and me were at their flat. Dinner plates were first, held aloft and hurled to the floor, pieces skittering towards the skirting board. Gran shouted for him to stop but he couldn't hear. He moved on to the drawers containing knives and forks and these made a different sound, metal cling-clanging in a harsh deluge. He set about the kitchen efficiently, destroying it with fierce purpose. The aura of energy from his strong, tense body was both majestic and terrifying. I thought that if he chose to, he could lift off the roof and hurl it aside. I had no fear for my own safety during this; I knew he would never hurt me, at least not intentionally.

The police were called. He didn't have time to barricade himself in as he had done on previous occasions, nailing planks across the door or bits of wood he'd salvaged from the frame and headboard of their bed. Neighbours gathered at the entrance to the flats. Two police cars arrived and a group of officers ran upstairs. I was with Mum on the landing. They tried to force the door with their shoulders but couldn't make it budge.

'It's probably open,' shouted a neighbour, Mrs McAvoy.

They pressed down the handle and entered.

Surprisingly, I found *Raise High the Roof Beam*, *Carpenters/Seymour*, *An Introduction* and *For Esmé — with Love and Squalor* next to one another on a second-hand book stall at Rochdale market; the trader had probably bought them together. Most of the stall was given over to romances, westerns and thrillers, which people purchased and then sold back at a reduced price; there was a lot of passing around of paper bags containing books. Jammed among them was a small cardboard box with a flap up, on which was written 'Brainy'. I was with another mate, Steve Kershaw.

'Have you seen that?' I asked.

'Brainy? I don't get it.'

'Brainy!' I said.

He shook his head. I thought it was the best classification ever — still do — for a certain type of book. I kept giggling.

'It's not that funny,' said Kersh.

I was desperate to read the Salinger books but we'd arranged to go to Kersh's afterwards. He'd bought the first Black Sabbath album from an older kid at school and wanted to play it. After the revolution of punk, Black Sabbath were among two or three rock bands it was still permissible to like (Hawkwind, Motörhead and AC/DC were the others). At his house, Kersh asked if I'd ever *headbanged*. It was brilliant – similar to being drunk, he said. We nodded our heads, picking up the rhythm but had to break off for a few minutes when his mum knocked on the bedroom door and passed us plates of roast beef sandwiches. We resumed with gentle head rocking, the sound of church bells and thunder providing respite while we nibbled the butties. As the beat progressed Kersh slipped off his glasses. When the guitars and drums came in, we began shaking our heads furiously. The music stopped abruptly. We heard a loud scraping sound. Kersh sat upright, eyes spinning.

'What the fuck?'

We stared about us, all at sea. The grating sound was traced to the record player. The lid was up and the top half of a roast beef sandwich had jammed against the arm, causing it to lift and fall intermittently. The other half was in Kersh's hand. He cracked up laughing:

'Christ, I thought we'd summoned the devil.'

I wanted *all* of Salinger's work. Who would not want more of something so exceptional? I am astonished that everyone doesn't do likewise and investigate a writer's back catalogue – many furnish their shelves with only an author's most famous or acclaimed books. The communion of great book and reader is so potent, surely there is a call to find it again, even if, in the other work, the pleasure is less intense or intermittent.

This pursuit of *everything* has played a significant part in my having so many books. Largely, in truth, it has gone unrewarded and the excellence I found in a particular book has been sporadic across the author's career. Sometimes it can feel as if brilliance is a visitation that is then spirited away. Afterwards, the author is left to stab at a keyboard, day after day, smashed to the graft, wielding a metaphorical butterfly net, should it pass this way again.

While accepting that very few writers reach a level of outstanding consistency and breadth of material – not even Salinger, for he had his own literary tics, themes and indulgences (a writer can only ever be what he or she is, which is a personality fed through a thought process into words) – by owning the full canon of work, the overall character emerges clearer from the mist. Fascinatingly, it also allows the reader to plot the development of a writer through the years, to see whether maturity burnishes the prose or slows it down, burdening it with self-consciousness perhaps or, worse, cynicism. A writer's relationship with the ever-shifting perspective of ageing is a parallel story, which readers delineate only by sticking with it, following the clock of life through each new book.

Salinger was one of very few authors with the dominion and desire to impose strict conditions on how his books were presented. While this reflected a heartfelt belief that the words and story did not require adornment, his standpoint led to subtle typographical designs which, whether inadvertently or not, became an authorial branding. It wasn't always this way. The cover of the first edition of *The Catcher in the Rye* featured a vivid orange-red horse (not particularly well drawn), evoking a critical scene in the penultimate chapter where Holden's sister, Phoebe, rides on a carousel in Central Park – though the 'beat-up-looking old horse' is actually brown in the book. The first and second printing carried a photograph of Salinger on the dust jacket but, by the third, he insisted it was removed.

The novel was picked up in paperback by NAL (New American Library), which specialised in popularising pre-existing titles, operating similarly to Penguin in the UK, with whom it had a brief union. Under pressure from Victor Weybright, NAL's co-founder, Salinger agreed at first that Holden could be pictured on the cover, so long as it was a specific illustration – from behind, sitting on a park bench in the rain. James Avati, whose rich, expressive paintings had adorned hundreds of covers, was duly commissioned. Avati had several fraught meetings until, finally, he confronted Salinger and told him: 'Look, what do you want, you want some sales? These guys are supposed to know how to sell books, so screw it, let's do it!'

In the edition published in 1953 Avati depicted Holden in an overcoat, carrying a suitcase and wearing a baseball cap with the peak turned to the back. The copy alongside read: 'This unusual book may shock you, will make you laugh, and may break your heart – but you will never forget it.' Salinger grumbled that it was inappropriate to depict Holden because he had not been described in great physical detail in the book; it did, though, reveal that he was tall and skinny and 'wore a crew cut frequently'. This pictorial cover survived twenty-seven reprints in almost eleven years before Salinger, who said he 'hated' it, forced its removal. The original painting, oil on board and measuring 22 inches by 18.5 inches, sold at auction in October 2010 for an undisclosed sum thought to be around $30,000 – original artwork by Avati routinely sells for about a quarter of this amount.

Salinger's next target was the blurb. He had agreed to one for *Franny and Zooey*, contributing it himself under the tagline, 'The author writes'. He had a change of heart and this was removed from later editions.

As a literary hero, Salinger is a contradictory figure. Does he represent vanity or, alternatively, the purity of artistic vision? Would he have held so tightly to his standpoint if his books had not sold so well or would he have compromised in search of readers? And how would he be viewed if he were an author today – as an egotist or a refreshing advocate of self-determination? Much would depend, of course, on his popularity. The attitude of publishers to their authors, indulgent to intolerant, is obviously affected by their sales figures at any given time.

The great strength of *The Catcher in the Rye* is that it feels so exceptionally personal. The paradox, then, of the author wilfully hiding himself away is viewed as an outright betrayal of his integrity. Why would a 'friend' do this? Many have speculated, with some justification, that Salinger's wartime experiences, several of which were horrific, led to the man (Salinger) greatly changed from the boy (Holden Caulfield, his alter ego). All that Holden had, the hope and love of the world (even if inverted to appear as cynicism), had been lost to the darkness of conflict and its aftermath. In such circumstances, it was perhaps unfair to judge Salinger's reclusiveness against the 'message' of the novel.

This is where it all properly began, me and the books. The weekend of the reading of *The Catcher in the Rye* catapulted me into a new life and a new me. Joy is not a joyful enough word to describe how the book – and I knew instinctively – *other* books would make me feel. As before, when I was a Christian, I had found tranquillity: me and a book and the quiet. I was also animated and excited, lit up by these characters, these places, this feeling. And all this could happen while you were sitting in a chair, away from the world, wholly yourself and not having to speak to anyone or consider what they thought about you or expected from you. The peace of it.

CHAPTER SIX

There was a snag of some magnitude – books were proscribed in our house. My dad considered reading and writing to be predominantly a feminine pastime, much the same as, say, sewing or netball. Unlike today, when almost everyone can type, very few men back then knew their way around an Underwood 142. And Dad had no knowledge of nicotined men such as Ernest Hemingway, Norman Mailer or Jack London, who could drink prodigiously and thump a typewriter, a love rival or a barroom brawler with the same force. He was unaware that even the most wistful of writers, the likes of John Keats, for example, relished the occasional set-to (while at the progressive Clarke's Academy in Enfield, Keats was known to fight with older boys).

Dad didn't know any writers or anything about them. The men he knew worked with their hands, fixing cars, building houses or toiling at lathes. They married young. They played sports together, drank together. They didn't retreat to their bedrooms, choosing solitariness ahead of the street, park or pub.

His view was not alone in the world, of course, sometimes to extreme conclusion. Yukio Mishima, the Japanese author and poet, could only write after his father had fallen asleep, for fear of him ripping up his manuscripts. One of his father's 'cures' for this assumed effeminacy was to hold young Mishima close to passing high-speed trains and build up his resolve. My dad's version of this parental compulsion was an awkward, abrupt, shambling few lines, delivered in my bedroom and then left to dangle in the air, for a lifetime.

'Why aren't you out?'

'I'm reading this book.'

'Don't you think you should give it a rest?'

I'd fall quiet, unsure how to answer.

'It's not normal, a lad of your age on his own so much.'

Being normal was everything to my parents, much as it had been to Jeanette Winterson's mother, as related in the memoir *Why Be Happy When You Could Be Normal?*. Unlike my parents, the tyrannical Mrs Winterson (as she was known to Jeanette) at least had a relationship with books, albeit a bizarre one. She had read *Jane Eyre* to Jeanette as a child and, later, sent her daughter to Accrington Library with the order to bring home murder-mystery books, preferably by Raymond Chandler and Ellery Queen. When it came to Jeanette, Mrs Winterson banned her from reading fiction but permitted history books, specifically 'about kings and queens'. Mrs Winterson, when quizzed about her attitude to fiction by her spiky, intrepid teenage daughter, responded: 'The trouble with a book is that you never know what's in it until it's too late.'

I didn't see Grandad led away. I buried my face in Mum's coat. We went back to see him the next day. He'd spent the previous afternoon locked in a police cell. He wasn't wearing any shoes or socks and his face was blotchy with a ring of black around one eye like I'd seen in comics. As soon as he opened the door to us he began swearing and shouting about the bastard police. He led us through the debris of broken plates and newspapers spread across the floor. While Mum cleared up, he slipped me a pair of scissors from his trouser pocket.

'Here,' he whispered. 'If the police ever come for you, use these.'

There was no kudos in a rebel or artsy or bookish stance in downtown, run-down Rochdale: who do you think *you* are? My parents feared I'd be bullied, picked off by the pack. By undermining me, they believed they were helping me, saving me. They were adhering to a wider class code. Where middle-class children are decorated with self-worth and confidence, and encouraged to rise from the crowd and celebrate themselves, the working class are taught to kowtow, defer, and view talent or individuality as a vanity rather than an accolade. There is also anti-intellectualism at work, as if they are afraid of you becoming clever in case you walk away, leave them behind. Books are regarded as signposts to this other life.

Another time, on a further straying into my room, I *think* Dad hinted (in very clumsy terms) that my love of books might lead to, gulp, homosexuality. Or celibacy, at least.

'If you're stuck up here day after day reading you'll never get yourself a girlfriend,' he said. 'That's if it's a girlfriend you want.'

Again, it was well meant. A *normal* life was easy; it offered much less of the bruising that a parent feels by proxy for a child who strays from the conventional. But the counsel felt especially unnecessary because in all other respects I conformed to the stereotype of the good, earth-bound son: I had plenty of friends, I played for the school football and cricket teams, and I had that photo of Debbie Harry on my bedroom wall.

I feared confrontation, particularly with Dad. His disapproval could burn scolding hot. Many times I have wondered on the effect of his psychological hand grenades, so casually thrown. He wasn't consulting a book, a counsellor (*as if*) or an extraordinarily wise friend. He thought it, said it, and had done with it. Maybe this was how he saw the role of a parent, the belief that he was passing on wisdom in its purest form. But by doing so he often superimposed his thoughts onto mine, cauterising my natural, instinctual feelings, to leave me unsure and mixed up. I wanted to be liked, and often became his version of what he wanted me to be. How many decisions thereafter were my own or his, spoken and acted upon through me? I knew, though, sure as sure, that I wasn't going to give up on these books and my nascent attempts to write, no matter how undermined or unnatural I was made to feel. This was it, everything: me and these books.

Mum went in for a much more impulsive, visceral rejection of books. Library and second-hand books were dirty, the harbingers of germs. She'd heard long ago that a kid (somewhere) had contracted chicken pox from one. Or it might have been impetigo. And if the germs didn't cover you in buboes or make your skin flake away, reading books would leave you 'half blind'. When, at about the age of fourteen, I was prescribed glasses, I could almost smell the sulphur and hear the thunderclap as this biblical prophecy played itself out at Stephen Holt's Opticians, Oldham Road, Rochdale.

Beforehand, I had told Mum how I'd borrowed Ian Seeley's glasses for a few minutes and entered another world where everything was vivid and detailed.

'You just want glasses because all your mates are getting them,' she said.

'No, Mum. I want them because I can't see very well.'

'That's because you're always bloody reading.'

'I like reading.'

'Well then.'

She folded her arms. She told me kids would call me 'Four Eyes' and 'Specky'.

I was taken to the optician's to *prove* that I didn't need glasses.

In the waiting room she started chatting to a woman. Mum has a curt way of talking; it often catches strangers off guard.

'He says he wants glasses,' she said, pointing at me. 'All his friends are wearing them. It's the fashion nowadays, isn't it?'

The woman nodded. After a few seconds, the lady asked why I thought I needed them.

'I can't see the board at school.'

'Does it help if you screw your eyes up?'

I said it did.

'You're probably short-sighted,' she said.

'He's not short-sighted,' groaned Mum. 'He's having everyone on.'

The woman's son, a kid of about eight, was led into the waiting room by the optician. He'd been having a pair of glasses fitted. They had thick lenses that magnified his eyes. After his mum had taken hold of his hand and they had left together, Mum leaned over to me and announced:

'She's only jealous.'

As I expected, I couldn't read beyond the first few letters on the card. I scanned two or three lines down but was guessing at the rest; they were a blur. During the test, Mum pulled a chair up to the seat where I was sitting. I was aware of her shaking her head and heard the soles of her shoes scraping on the floor. The optician left the room to deal with someone in the shop. Immediately, Mum asked what I was playing at.

'Can't you see that? It's as big as your bloody head.'

When the test was over and he confirmed I needed glasses, she still didn't believe it. He explained that it happened to a lot of kids as they became teenagers. She pursed her lips and nodded her head. The gesture meant that he could think what he liked but he was wrong; he'd been duped. Back home, we argued. I asked how she'd feel if she couldn't see very well and was told she was making it up. I told her I was self-conscious about wearing them; it was something I'd never choose to do. And I couldn't stop reading books. I loved them too much. She cried. Mum always cried when she finally understood. She had only wanted the best for me; it was love, always, even if cack-handed. But then she rallied:

'You'll end up wearing them all your life now.'

I was baking with Gran in the kitchen when the doorbell sounded. Grandad was away having treatment at the hospital that they told me was called 'electric therapy'. She opened the door and I could hear her talking in the hall. A man appeared at the entrance to the kitchen in a smart jacket and trousers with turn-ups at the bottom. He took off his flat cap. Gran asked him to sit at the small table where I was spooning lemon curd into pastry cases.

'They look good,' he said. 'Are they for your grandad when he gets back?'

'Yeah, but me and Gran can have some today if we want.'

'This is Arthur,' said Gran. 'He's a friend of your grandad's. They work together at C&A in town.'

I'd often seen Grandad's fawn warehouseman's coat slipped over the back of a chair. He unloaded lorries and delivered parcels to the various departments in the store.

'Have you heard back from the hospital, Eveline?' asked Arthur.

'He's had one lot of treatment.'

She offered him a cup of tea and the kettle was soon whistling. Gran asked if they were missing Grandad at work.

'It's not the same without your John, you know.'

He smiled but struggled to stop it from slipping. His eyes were empty and sad. He looked at the table and brushed away a film of flour. He saw that I'd noticed his change of expression and gave me a wink.

I read voraciously, often more than a novel a week. I seemed to grasp instinctively a book's aesthetic worth. Gaudy and bright didn't appeal. I went for covers that were understated. I didn't care who recommended a book on the back, telling me it was great or riveting or that it would change my life – such an endorsement (unless made by Salinger, of course, and he didn't make any) would have put me off: I had my own mind.

I wasn't keen on authors' photos on books, even if on the flap of the dust jacket, part hidden, behind the door as it were. I have a writer friend and he has the same photograph of himself on most of his books. He is scowling in front of a brick wall, nibbling at his lips. It's easy to detect what his expression is conveying: 'Don't expect a gentle, joyous tale, dear reader. I'm going to assail your sensibilities, stir up within you irritation, anger, self-doubt and moral ambiguity, at least.' In a way, it's helpful of him to put his picture on there, getting his mate out with a decent camera on an ice-sharp winter afternoon (snow is visible in the background). When authors do this, you don't have to inconvenience yourself reading the first page to try them out. You can tell by the photo whether you're going to like their work or not, every time. Most readers are sly like this – they wouldn't be considering buying the book if they didn't fancy themselves as smart and observant, weeding out the mediocre, the desperate and the try-hard. They're looking closely at that picture, wondering whether to trust you and if they want to be in your gang or not. If you're sneering or cross-eyed or face-aching a faking smile, they're on to the next book.*

We each have our own checklist. I might have 3,500 books but I doubt, among the authors' photos, there is a bandana, cowboy hat, beret, pair of mirror shades, turned up jacket collar, fake tan,

---

* If a photograph of me is included in this book's packaging, I hope it doesn't offend. The one I have supplied to the publisher was taken most recently in a natural setting (a cafe) on a mobile phone. Honest.

ostentatious glasses, pout, wink, neckerchief, lobe-stretching earring or more than an acceptable dab of make-up (male and female).

Only occasionally has an author's photo brought me to a book, sealed the deal; more often it has repelled me. I suppose it's about what we imagine we see behind their eyes, whether it is a reflection of how they write and their subject matter. Above all, we are seeking integrity. Raymond Carver always looked how he wrote: sensible haircut, take me or leave me expression, a hard-working uncle back from parking the truck or enjoying a tipple in a quiet bar with pals, where the staff know his name and favourite drink. I hurried through the back catalogue of George Orwell and D.H. Lawrence because I was drawn by the design of their books and author photographs. They were both branded distinctively, the packaging reflecting the content, setting them down gently but assuredly as writers of gravitas. Lawrence, with full beard and centre-parted hair, is shaded to handsomeness in the monochrome shot and exudes serenity. This is at odds with his writing, which surges with restless indecision. Orwell is half smiling on his photo, as if reminding us that whatever is trapped within the pages, most often injustice, disappointment and drudgery, there is sporadic, cheery respite – probably, in his case, a favourite indulgence as revealed in various essays: very strong tea (drunk from a saucer, apparently), shag tobacco, beer, kippers and biscuits; presumably not all at the same time.

Many good books are shamed by their covers. The rebranding by Wordsworth of Fyodor Dostoevsky's classic novels featuring people with thumbprint heads is especially ghastly. Angela Carter has been failed by a hotchpotch of eccentric covers, placing an unfair blemish on radiant work. Virginia Woolf has also suffered several indignities, most notably when published by Harvest/HBJ in the mid-1950s and by Wordsworth (again) with a gaudy art deco theme in the 1990s. Books are *always* judged by their covers.

The best response to a cover, and one I've had many times, is the absolute resolution: I'm buying this book. Now, this minute. Where do I pay? The worst is an awkward hesitancy where a book passes from hands to rack or shelf several times. Book lovers recognise this malaise, the dithering, the alternating doubt and certitude, even the walking away and returning to the scene of the indecision. I've done this and often wondered whether I've been spotted by a store detective or a camera is being trained upon me. The tentativeness of a befuddled bibliophile can easily be mistaken for the furtiveness of a shoplifter. At such a juncture, a perusal of the blurb, even if for the third or fourth time, is essential: it might lubricate the brakes, let loose a decision.

The blurb, interestingly, has a categorical date of statute. The term was first used on a dust jacket at the American Booksellers Association banquet of 1907. Frank Gelett Burgess, a humorist and poet ('I never saw a purple cow, / I never hope to see one; / But I can tell you, anyhow, / I'd rather see one than be one.'), was promoting his book, *Are You a Bromide?*. He had set out a new meaning for the word 'bromide' as 'a sedate, dull person who says boring things'. The book cover, limited to 500 printed specially for the attendees of the AMA, featured a woman with voluminous hair, holding her hand to mouth as if hailing a taxi. Burgess introduced her as 'Miss Belinda Blurb in the act of blurbing'. More than a century later, the accompanying copy (blurb) is still sharp and funny:

Say! Ain't this book a 90 H.P., six-cylinder Seller? If WE do say it as shouldn't, WE consider that this man Burgess has got Henry James locked into the coal-bin, telephoning for "Information". This book has that Certain Something which makes you want to crawl through thirty miles of dense tropical jungle and bite somebody in the neck.

Blurbs were affixed to almost every book thereafter.

Despite being one of the first beckoning fingers to the reader, after the title and cover, the blurb is usually the last piece of business in the production of a book. Most authors struggle to relate what their book is about; they often fear this very question. They have spent hundreds of days, thousands of words and now, happily, they are convinced that the answer to this question is in the book somewhere, even if it is like salt in soup, indistinct but imposing flavour. Really, they would rather not forego nuance and shading to set down two or three paragraphs of summary. How is it possible without it feeling forced, reductive or even tawdry? This is not to understate its importance. All writers want readers, and a shoddy blurb is to forget to wash your face before a date: it reduces appreciably the chance of a relationship. Sometimes a good friend or another writer is the perfect remedy; they find in the work what an author has missed or they can distil it more succinctly.

Generally, most blurbs ring hollow amid hailstones of adjectives. A sample of such terms formed from a shelf of books within my easy reach reveals a tired glossary. In fact, they might have been computer generated, such is the repetition. For the record, listed alphabetically, they are: absorbing, acclaimed, accomplished, adventurous, astounding, bestselling, bittersweet, bold, brave, breathtaking, bumper, candid, compelling, delightful, delirious, edgy, engaging, engrossing, epic, essential, exhilarating, extraordinary, fascinating, fast-paced, gripping, groundbreaking, haunting, heartbreaking, hilarious, inspirational, magnificent, poignant, powerful, profound, remarkable, revelatory, scintillating, seminal, sensational, shocking, sizzling, surprising, terrific, thought-provoking, triumphant, unforgettable, unputdownable, witty and wry. At their best these adjectives stand as a code, a language within a language, and provide an approximate signal of what lies within.

Humour is highly subjective and I'm wary of books described as 'achingly funny', 'laugh-out-loud funny', 'uproarious' or 'a hoot': I'd be happy with a chuckle. Eyes are mentioned a great deal – an author having a sharp, good or observant eye for detail or a story is eye-catching or an eye-opener. There are many 'paeans to', 'meditations on', 'portrayals of', and an excess of authors undertaking metaphorical 'odysseys' or 'journeys'. Surely every book is relating a journey of some kind.

'Your grandad thinks the world of you and your sister,' said Arthur.

'I know,' I said.

Gran sat down.

'Do you ever see any of the lads from the hospital?' she asked him.

He and Grandad had worked together as porters. Grandad had a few pals who had each worked at the same places; they must have looked out for one another when it came to jobs.

'I still see Jan now and again. You know, the Polish lad.'

'John used to speak of a Jan but I never met him.'

'Did John ever tell you about that lady at the hospital, the one with a head out here?' He put his hand about six inches from his face and splayed the fingers.

'He did mention her now and again.'

'Well, that was Jan's job really. He was supposed to take in her food. They'd put her on a side ward, so she didn't frighten the other patients. He couldn't do it, though. It was upsetting him too much. John said he'd do it for him. Every day he went in there with a tray of grub and made such a fuss of her. The cancer had affected her sight and he used to stop for a minute or two and tell her what he could see from the window, whether it was sunny or not, who was passing by.'

Gran passed him the tea. As she turned the cup so the handle faced him, he shivered as if a draught had blown in from the veranda. He was looking away, almost facing the wall, hiding his face.

'Are you okay?' she said.

At first I knew little, if anything, about the books and authors I was perusing. Within weeks I learned to trust one particular publisher where the quality was consistently outstanding: Penguin. Unwittingly, I was setting down the foundation of my collection and personality as a reader. My loyalty to Penguin was such that the front covers almost became irrelevant as I turned the books over, searching for the little penguin in an oval outline, usually in the bottom left corner.

The logo had been drawn by Edward Young when only twenty-one and new to the firm. He was dispatched to London Zoo in Regent's Park where he sketched penguins for a day before settling on a design to fulfil the contradictory brief of being 'dignified but flippant'. On his return to the office, he remarked, 'My God, how those birds stink.' Young also devised the colour coding: orange for fiction; green, crime; red, drama; dark blue, biography; purple, essays; grey, world affairs; cerise, travel and adventure; and yellow, miscellaneous (often crosswords, pastimes or humour).

The legend behind Penguin, advanced by Allen Lane, chairman and chief executive, was that he saw the appeal of mass-market, pocket-sized paperbacks after finding himself without a book on a platform at Exeter St David's railway station in 1935. He was said to be heading back to London after visiting Agatha Christie in Devon. The few titles on sale were bulky and expensive, so he went without. The veracity of this anecdote has been questioned. Although he loved the *business* of books, friends claimed he hardly ever read. He was, though, aware of the value of a good tale to snag media interest. If a photographer asked him to pose with a book in one hand and a live penguin in the other or to sit on a chair indoors while wearing his best bulky overcoat, he would oblige to sell more books.

Most likely, Lane had noted the success of Bernhard Tauchnitz, a Leipzig-based company that had great success with English language reprint paperback editions called the Collection of British and American Authors. Another German publisher, Albatross (an influence on the choice of name for Penguin), further developed the model, having books of a standard size, uniform typography, non-pictorial covers and colour coding by theme of content – practices adopted by Penguin.

The book industry was initially wary of the Penguin business model. The launch price of sixpence per book (approximately the cost of a packet of ten cigarettes) provided only a meagre profit. Each had to sell 17,000 copies to reach break-even, a large number when some titles routinely sold a few thousand. Allen Lane remained defiant, insisting that he believed 'in the existence of a vast reading public for intelligent books at a low price'.

Among the first ten Penguin titles were *The Mysterious Affair at Styles* by Agatha Christie, *A Farewell to Arms* by Ernest Hemingway and *The Unpleasantness at the Bellona Club* by Dorothy Sayers. The landslide of support began when Woolworths ordered 63,500 copies to be distributed across its 600 UK stores. Within four days of being launched on Tuesday, 30 July 1935, more than 150,000 Penguins were bought, and the millionth copy was sold after only four months. Authors were generally supportive (though earning much less in royalties per book than hardback) because it granted them extra readers, in their thousands. J.B. Priestley referred to Penguins as 'Perfect marvels of beauty and cheapness.' *The Times* acknowledged that reading Penguin books had become 'a new social habit'. The publishing industry remained unconvinced. Jonathan Cape told Lane: 'You're the bugger that has ruined this trade with your ruddy Penguins.' Lane reminded Cape that he had granted republication licences to Penguin, without which he might not have been successful. 'I know damn well,' Cape responded. 'But like everybody else I thought you were bound to go bust and I'd take 400 quid off you before you did.'

By 1961, 250 million Penguin books had been sold. When the company was listed on the stock exchange that year, applications for investors filled twenty-six mail bags in a single day. A Penguin book had become part of the cultural fabric, as quintessentially British as red post boxes, black cabs, pubs and the Sunday roast. They also stood as idiosyncratic personal statements. The strong, clear branding made them easy to spot when carried or poking from coat pockets and it defined the owner as *bookish*, with all its positive connotations.

I knew nothing of this history, of course, though it could be discerned through the packaging of Penguin books, the confidence and clarity. I tumbled from one author to another, chasing down their back catalogue. As I did, I dreamed of how it would feel to be a Penguin author, to have your work framed in such a sturdy manner. The books had an aura of *substantialness*, as if they could go some way to inure the author from everyday mortality or at least make the passing to the other side less final. A book with your name on it, containing your thoughts and feelings (even if channelled through characters), lit up bright in Penguin orange, was a much better signifier of a life well lived than a few lines chiselled into a gravestone.

I dipped into the 'Brainy' box on a weekly basis. I soon became known to the stallholder, a middle-aged man called Raymond (never Ray, which was unusual in a town where almost everyone had a nickname or an abbreviated version of their name). He had black curly hair and his face was the colour of corned beef. He started to seek out books especially for me.

'Got a cracker for you,' he said. 'I've seen the film but I bet the book is just as good.'

He held up *One Flew Over the Cuckoo's Nest* by Ken Kesey, the Picador edition with Jack Nicholson as Randle McMurphy on the cover, laughing eyes and exploding hair. I bought it and asked how he'd guessed I would want it.

'You like your stuff a bit different, don't you? You know, arty-farty and that. There's only you and a couple of others who ever ask for anything similar.'

I asked who comprised my brethren.

'I'm not sure I should say,' he said, in the tone of a man who, really, I could tell, would very much like to say.

'Okay,' I said, baiting him by apparently not baiting him.

'Well, one of the fellas is called Ian. Odd-looking bugger, all bloody arms and legs. Always wears a raincoat, a dirty thing with bits of stains all over it. He likes his foreign stuff. What do they call him? Dotsandeffski, something like that. Some of the books he buys are about this thick.'

He held out his arms as if playing a concertina or pressing the sides of a loaf of bread.

'I kid you not, bloody massive they are, these books. No wonder he's got bottle-bottom glasses. I got him what I could, like, this Russian stuff and, oh, a Spanish bloke he kept asking about, Mario Vases Lager or something. Then, one day, he slips to the side of the stall, a bit snaky like, and whispers to me. I couldn't hear a bloody word at first so I made him speak up. Anyhows, he's only asking me if I've got any blueys.'

'What's a bluey?'

'You know, a porno. Someone must have told him I keep a few under the stall, like, for special customers. Well then – he never stopped mithering after that, did he? Every bloody week, he wants to get his mitts in the cardboard box with all these mags in. He soon gave up on those foreign doorstop books when he got the liking for a bit of crumpet. He's spent a fortune here.'

I asked him about the other shopper for 'Brainy'.

'Now then, Carl or C-c-carl, as I know him, on account of his stutter, is weird as well but in sort of a nice way. Thing is, with Carl, you think he's normal, he kids on that he is, but then he says or does something and you go, hang on, what's that all about? I've heard he used to be a schoolteacher but I can't see it myself.'

'What books does he buy?'

'He's a big fan of the bloke who was in that group – break on through to the other side.'

'Jim Morrison?'

'That's him. I bought up a collection from this lad and Carl snaffled the lot in one go, all this poetry and books about the group he was in.'

'The Doors?'

'Yes,' he said loudly, as if I'd named one of the most obscure bands that had ever existed. 'Bloody hell, you know your stuff.'

Biographies of the Doors and anthologies of Jim Morrison's poetry didn't sound particularly 'brainy'. I asked him what other books Carl had bought.

'I can't recall. See, it's not my thing really. Give me a Dick Francis or a Ruth Rendell and I'm a happy man.'

'You were saying that Carl was nice but weird.'

I was enjoying the conversation.

'Oh, yeah. Like, he came here the other week and asked if I had the key for the toilet, the private one that you can only use if you're a trader. I said he should have gone before he came out and he said he couldn't because it was broken. I asked him what had happened and without batting an eyelid, just talking normal, like, as if he was telling me the cistern needed attention or there was trouble with one of the pipes, he says it won't flush *because of the dead kittens*. Turns out his cat had had all these kittens and that's how he'd tried to get shut of them.'

I made a face.

'That's how I felt when he told me. To be honest, I think

he's had some kind of breakdown and could do with being reported to social services or somebody like that, but that's not my job, is it? I tell you what, his house must be full of books, even if it *is* a bloody mess. I've just remembered – he left me a list of stuff he wants me to look out for.'

He fished it out of the metal cash tin; it had been held down by a clasp and was written on what looked like the back of a bill.

'Keep it if you want,' he said. 'I've never heard of most of what he's got on there, never mind finding it for him.'

At the top, Carl had put 'Any book by or about' and it read: 'Joseph Pujol, circuses, Spike Milligan, Laurel and Hardy, UFOs esp. abductions, Aleister Crowley, Second World War, Kenneth Anger, Erich von Däniken, James Leo Herlihy, the Beats esp. Herbert Huncke, Jim Morrison/the Doors, Moors murders, Leo Tolstoy, Diane di Prima, Tony Hancock, the battle of Chamdo, Jules Verne, aircraft (civil), David Lean, Ray Bradbury, Thomas De Quincey, J.D. Salinger.'

So this was the gang I had joined. It had only three members: me; Carl, a kitten-killing, mentally ill, possibly ex-teacher in the throes of a breakdown; and Ian, a grubby, myopic, Dostoevsky-reading, porn-obsessive.

'It's a rotten business, isn't it, Ev? John being ill all the time,' said Arthur. 'I keep thinking about what he's going through at the hospital. We knew he wasn't well last week and things were getting on top of him. One of the bosses was on about a sticker missing off a box. It was a joke really but John got upset about it. He wouldn't listen to us; it was as if we weren't there.'

'That's how he gets when he's ill.'

'I keep thinking I should have done something, told him to go on the sick for a day or two, take a break. All this might not have happened then.'

'There's not a lot anyone can do when he gets that way on.'

'I'm sorry. You don't want me adding to your upset at a time like this.'

She said it didn't matter and that she'd tell Grandad he'd called and had been asking after him. Arthur had some fruit in a brown paper bag and asked Gran to give it to Grandad when she visited him.

On a bus ride into town I noticed a bookshop I had never seen before on the outskirts of the centre, amid the taxi ranks and boarded-up houses, where chip wrappers and discarded drinks cans chased each other like mad dogs across the pavement in the wind.

I got off a few stops early. I knew the area well because Alexander's was there, my favourite second-hand shop. I'd stopped at it many times, pressed up to the wire grille at the window, staring at the shiny things framed by fairy lights; they were left up all year round as if Christmas never left this speck of the world. A fly's compound eye was needed to see everything jammed in the shop. And it was all designed to make a life louder, brighter, happier: drum kits, guitars, stylophones, bikes, lava lamps, football games, piles of magazines, model aeroplanes, flags, mouth organs, fishing rods, microphones, records, snooker cues, table-tennis tables, amplifiers, postcards, record players.

At the entrance, hidden beneath the oilcloth, was a device to detect footsteps and trigger an alarm. The noise was so loud it made everything in the shop oscillate. Customers would cover their ears and then check for gunshot wounds. Old Alex was out from the back immediately:

'Yes?'

He always looked at everyone contemptuously, as if they'd done something horrible, such as posting dog dirt through his letterbox. His skin was yellow, presumably from spending too long under the fairy lights, and his cheeks were drawn and tense, as if he'd eaten his lips in retaliation for a secret they'd revealed years before. I called in and was thumbing through PG Tips card booklets (an old habit) when a woman entered with a lad aged about ten. She was carrying an electric guitar. Alex asked what she wanted.

'This bloody thing doesn't work.'

She said her husband had adapted a kettle lead and plugged it into a wall socket but they couldn't hear a thing, not a dicky bird. Alex's teeth did a kind of jig.

'You expected it to work without an amplifier?'

The woman said he hadn't told her nothing about no amplifier when he sold it to them – this wasn't on.

'Everyone knows you need an amp to hear anything,' he said. 'You could have blown yourselves to kingdom come.'

He refused to refund her money. She said she'd return later. With her husband. To sort him out.

'Bring half the street with you if you like, love.'

When she'd gone, I asked Alex about the shop a few doors down.

'Been here years,' he said.

'I've not noticed it before.'

'That's probably because it's always boarded up. I think he mainly sells at book fairs and has the shop for storage, opening when it suits him. He's a rum bugger.'

I wondered how rum could a bugger be if one of the rummest buggers in town had passed such a judgement. I soon found out.

I went up to the front door and looked through the window. It was so dark I could barely see inside and was still unsure whether it was open. I pressed down the door handle and entered. The room smelled musty. Walls were lined with shelves of second-hand books. Directly in front of me was a group of tables pushed together with trays of books on top. I instinctively leaned forward and began passing them though my hands.

'What you looking for?'

I traced the voice to a thin man of about forty sitting on a padded wooden chair. He was wearing a cardigan with a polo-necked jumper underneath, looking at me over a pair of glasses.

'I'm not sure,' I said.

'Do you have any money?'

'Yes.'

'Well, that's a start.'

He rose from the chair and stood a few inches behind me, looking over my shoulder. After I had perused a line of books, he patted it back into shape. I was sweating, runnels of water trickling down from my armpits. He sighed. I wanted to leave, never to call there again, but I also wanted to stay, to confront his intimidation. He moved away and stood in front of me on the other side of the trays. After a minute or two, during which I sensed he was aching to speak, he blurted:

'There's nothing in there for you.'

I had picked up *The Iliad* by Homer.

'There might be,' I said.

'Tell me an author you're looking for and I might be able to help,' he said.

This felt like a test. I couldn't think. Then I had an idea. I reached into my back pocket and pulled out Carl's list. I passed it to him.

'Do you have any of these?' I asked.

He frowned.

'Is this *your* list?'

'Yes,' I lied.

'Don't be silly,' he chastised. 'Aleister Crowley? Thomas De Quincey? And what's this? No one from round here reads Tolstoy, especially not twelve-year old kids.'

I told him I was fifteen, nearly sixteen.

'Well, you don't look it.'

I was still sifting through books as we spoke. The next to flip up was *Antigone* by Sophocles: this wasn't helping my case.

'What school do you go to?' he asked.

I told him.

'Well, I doubt very much you'll be studying Sophocles,' he said.

He chortled and rocked his shoulders as if he'd said the funniest goddam thing anyone had ever said, ever. I realised that I was dealing with this agonising experience by becoming Holden Caulfield, writing it all up in my head. I dispensed with any social etiquette – he didn't deserve any – and turned round silently as if lifted by a giant hand and marched out of the shop. In the hope of annoying him (I imagine he thought I'd slam the door), I closed it extremely gently. That'll teach him.

Grandad had several sessions of electroconvulsive therapy (ECT). He joked about it, claiming they'd 'wired him to the mains' (which they had, actually) and the lights had dimmed on every street corner in Manchester. He said it left him with a 'banging' headache and he could smell burning for days. He'd find himself wandering through the flat, convinced that Gran had left the cooker switched on or something was on fire.

I quickly exhausted Raymond's 'Brainy' box and noticed he was replenishing stock with a hotchpotch of books, the likes of Jean Plaidy, Alan Hunter, Jack Higgins, Miss Read and Sven Hassel. One Saturday, I challenged him.

'These don't really belong in here,' I said.

'I know,' he said. 'But I've got to put them somewhere.'

He was unpredictable, some weeks extremely friendly and then, on others, distant. He often brought the conversation around to sex and I'd given him the nickname (solely in my head, none of my friends knew who he was) Dirty Raymond. He told me, extremely matter-of-factly, about a trip he'd made to a brothel, or, as he called it, a 'knocking shop'. While he'd been there, a row had broken out. The girl wasn't sufficiently open-minded and when he complained, a 'spade' suddenly turned up threatening 'to punch his lights out'. Another time he asked me if I wanted to look in his 'special box' (the one containing porn magazines) and when I said it was okay, thank you, he said, 'Even clever lads have got to clear the pipework now and again.' These conversations had started to feel inappropriate, middle-aged man to fifteen-year-old boy.

Gran was never sure what to do; it wasn't the same as a proper illness. There were no spots or swelling, temperature or nausea, and no plaster big enough to cover it. She had to trust intuition but was conflicted when Grandad began losing his temper or acting strange. One minute she thought it best to call the police. The next, an ambulance. Or maybe she should ask for a neighbour's help or hurry to the doctor's and see what he advised. But while she was racing there, Grandad might hurt himself; he'd accidentally cut himself before on broken glass. Best to sit tight. He would tire soon, though he could become worse and then it would be her fault for waiting too long.

There was little expectation or pressure at school and almost no homework or preparation for exams, so I was free to absorb myself in books. I can recall days where nothing much happened but, paradoxically, *everything* happened because I was in a heightened state of awareness through a particular book. Over the course of a freezing day during the Christmas holiday I read *The Outsider* by Albert Camus. I had a cold. I stayed in my pyjamas all day. I felt like I was living a parallel life: part of me on the sandy streets of Algiers, drinking strong coffee at Celeste's restaurant; the other, slightly feverish in snowed-in Rochdale. Camus wrote exquisitely of the fig trees, the red sky, the old men sitting on chairs outside the tobacconist's and the trip to a nearby beach where the sea sent 'long, lazy' waves across the sand. More than this sense of place, there was a deeper geography at work in the short, sharp sentences and the rhythm of ordinary acts of living expressed until it became hypnotic. I loved this altered state of thinking induced by a book, how it transcended mere story or characters, to become elemental.

A few months later, more books read, the snow all gone, the sun was shining hard and bright on Rochdale and I found myself reading *Three Men in a Boat* by Jerome K. Jerome. It formed the axis to the year, the summer book to the winter of Camus. Now, via the novel, I was transported back a century, wearing a straw boater, striped jacket, floating languidly down the river, from Kingston-upon-Thames to Oxford and back, with Harris, George, J. (Jerome) and Montmorency the dog. I recall sitting in a deck chair in the back garden at my parents', one hand holding the book still, the other tearing strands of sappy grass at my side. As I made my way through the mannered text, hamper-full of japery, everything seemed to be ghosting to sepia. I even began to wonder if it would be possible to sail a skiff down the Rochdale Canal and from where I might purchase tinned pineapples – a favourite of the three men in a boat.

One night, there was a knock at the door after we'd gone to bed. I heard Gran's voice at the bottom of the stairs. She'd walked from their flat, a raincoat pulled over her nightie. Grandad had emptied the cupboards and made a pile in the front room of everything they owned. She said it looked as if he was going to set them alight.

'He's going to burn the block down,' she sighed.

I went downstairs. Mum said she didn't know what to do. If they rang the police, they'd take him away. A night in the cells might clear his head but he might return even angrier. If he resisted arrest too forcibly (and he usually did) he'd be taken straight to Springfield. Mum persuaded Gran that they should ring the doctor, even though it was the early hours. As Mum picked up the phone, Gran went to speak but Mum waved her away. Gran looked at me and shook her head. Whatever she had wanted to say, it was important. Mum apologised for waking up the doctor but said she was calling about her dad, John Duffy, and stressed it was an emergency.

One of the last books I bought from Dirty Raymond was another comic novel written at around the same time as *Three Men in a Boat*. The title ensnared me, and the fact that one of the authors had the Christian name Weedon.* I enjoyed *The Diary of a Nobody* by brothers George and Weedon Grossmith without pondering too much on how I related to the tale of manners and mishaps of Charles Pooter and his 'dear wife' Carrie residing at The Laurels, 'a nice six-roomed residence, not counting basement, with a front breakfast-parlour'.

Although I could trace a strand between my life and, for example, *A Kestrel for a Knave*, I didn't feel an overwhelming urge to 'see myself' or my environment reflected back in books and, likewise, there was no overriding desire to escape, to seek out the fantastical. I was also largely blind to class. This – whatever appeared before me on the market or at Boots or WH Smith – was all I knew, so I assumed it to *be* literature, which was almost wholly posh people writing about their lives, usually from long ago. Later, as I read more, the bloody truth of class was spilled by the likes of Charles Dickens (*Oliver Twist*), Elizabeth Gaskell (*Mary Barton*), Arthur Morrison (*A Child of the Jago*) and Robert

---

* His actual name was William Weedon Grossmith. Weedon had been the maiden name of his mother, Emmeline.

Tressell (*The Ragged Trousered Philanthropists*). These particular novels, written between 1837 and 1914, recognised that class was distinct and the line between them drawn red and sore. They also acknowledged that fate and class were inseparable. 'I encountered a place in Shoreditch [London], where children were born and reared in circumstances which gave them no reasonable chance of living decent lives: where they were born fore-damned to a criminal or semi-criminal career,' wrote Morrison in the preface to *A Child of the Jago*.

I was good at daydreaming, a state made more easily reachable with a book in hand, but the bark of real life was becoming louder and difficult to shut out. The cold war had intensified through the 1970s and we were approaching three minutes to midnight on the Doomsday Clock. The country was in deep recession, with more than three million people unemployed. Rochdale, in particular, was on its knees. Cheap imports had led to the close-down of the textile industry. Round-the-clock working shrank to a four-day week, to three, two, one, gone.

Mum lost her job as a sewing machinist but quickly found another that sounded impossibly glamorous. Overnight, without any training or even leaving the house, she became a 'fashion director'. This was the job title bestowed upon its 'associates' by Sarah Coventry, a company with its head office in New Jersey, United States. On a commission basis, Mum organised jewellery-selling parties at friends' houses. In the brochure it said she could be a millionaire within ten years and its folksy ideals were laid out sweet: 'We are founded on the principles of small-town, small-business America; hard work, quality products, complete customer satisfaction, and concern for others. The key to Sarah Coventry's success is that despite our size, we retain these ideals – caring and sharing.' Mum wasn't a saleswoman and neither were the others taken on. Most had been made redundant from the mills and were bored or feeling guilty that they were at home during the day, their husbands at work, children at school and, of course, they wanted to contribute once more to the household income. They progressed through their circle of friends, holding parties at each other's houses. Eventually, a few months in, they exhausted this hospitality and generosity. Other similar party-selling fads were for Tupperware (plastic kitchenware) and Pippa Dee (clothing); Mum had a try at both.

I came home from school earlier than expected one afternoon. There was an unusual smell in the house.

'What are *you* doing here?' asked Mum.

'The teacher's ill, so we've been let off last lesson.'

I walked through the living room to the kitchen. Boxes were piled high on the table.

'What's this?' I asked.

'My new job.'

'What is it?'

'Don't be nosey. I didn't want you to find out.'

'Why not?'

'Because I knew you'd have something to say, that's why.'

She was soldering together strips of thin black wire, presumably a component of a machine to be assembled later. She had done about fifteen and had them in a small pile. I asked how much she was getting paid.

'It's none of your business.'

I asked her a few times until she revealed she was on £1 for every fifty she soldered.

'Well, you've done fifteen, so that's 30p. How long has it taken?'

'Nearly two hours.'

'Two hours? That means you're getting paid 15p an hour.'

'So. I'll get quicker as I get used to it.'

I said I wouldn't work for such a small amount and she said

116

I was a spoiled brat and didn't have a clue what life was all about, not a clue.

When they came to collect the wire the next day, she handed back the boxes and told them not to deliver any more.

Mum told Grandad's GP:

'He's smashing things up at the flat. My mum's scared to death here. Can you help us?'

The doctor must have said it was very late.

'I know, I'm sorry.'

He told her she shouldn't be ringing him – it was a non-medical matter and she should call the police. In the end, Mum, Dad and Gran convinced each other that Grandad would probably get tired and fall asleep before doing any harm to himself or serious damage to the flat. In the morning, Dad called around and Grandad was asleep on the sofa. The pile of furniture had been pushed over.

We found out later that Gran had been trying to tell Mum that Grandad had visited his doctor a few weeks before, accusing him of 'carrying on' with Gran and saying that next time he was going to bring a gun with him.

The final piece of school business was a mandatory appointment with the careers teacher, Mr Swales. He was a tall bloke and most days wore check trousers. His nickname was Rupert, obviously. The room was bare, without any posters on the walls and only a few items of furniture. After a few seconds he closed the folder he was perusing and stared at me, as if surprised to find a kid there.

'Right, what can we do for you?' he asked, shuffling in his chair.

'I think I already know what job I want to do,' I said.

'Well, that makes a change. Go on, tell me.'

I said I wanted to be a writer.

'English is my favourite subject,' I volunteered.

'That's a good start.'

He rose from his chair and began pulling drawers out of a filing cabinet. He handed me two booklets, one about a career in printing, the other on technical authorship. I'd never heard of this before.

'It's when you write manuals for machines, things like that,' he said.

I was surprised he noticed my change of expression.

'Just read the pamphlet and see if it's up your street. I'll tell you this now – journalism is very difficult to get into. I think we've only ever had one boy from this school who got on the *Rochdale Observer*.'

I hadn't mentioned journalism; I'd said I wanted to be a writer.

'Nick, he was called, Nick something. His name will come to me later. And, I've got to say, he had quite a few O levels to his name, if I remember rightly.'

He lifted the paper on his desk and scanned it.

'What subjects are you doing in your O levels?'

'I'm doing CSEs.'

'Look, if you're one of those lads who doesn't like getting his hands dirty, have you thought about a career in retail? Marks & Spencer are looking for trainee managers. They're a good firm, they even have their own chiropodists who visit once a month and make sure everyone's got lovely feet.'

He smiled. Appointment over.

'Send in Craig Cheetham, will you?'

CHAPTER SEVEN

We didn't go far on our holidays, seldom more than fifty miles away or so. These days, a trip out to Morecambe, Blackpool, Southport or Anglesey – places we went to for our main summer holiday – would be regarded as a pleasant way to spend an afternoon. Or, if you set off early and packed enough butties, you could possibly call at two or three of them and be home before it got dark. It's difficult to imagine that we would spend a whole week there, sometimes two, and this would be anticipated all year, days counted down until we got to those red circles around dates in August on the calendar. We'd usually stay in either a caravan or guest house.

The hot summer of 1976 saw us break with tradition and have a holiday away from Lancashire and North Wales. We went to Torquay. The weather was obviously better in the south but it might also have reflected an improvement in our social status because afterwards we almost always took our holidays in Devon, usually at caravan parks where there was a social club; Mum and Dad liked to watch a 'turn' when they had a drink.

On the later family holidays of my childhood, every day felt much the same. I'd leave my parents and sister at mid-morning and head to the book and record shops. I'd walk miles to villages and towns on the seafront; it was impossible to get lost with the edge of the sea drawing a hard blue-grey line across the landscape.

Seaside towns in England are wonderful. The air is salty, turning sweet as it passes the candy floss and doughnut stalls. Old couples sit sipping milky tea from polystyrene cups. Shops at the seaside sell the unusual and the collectable. Over there, by the café with tea towels fixed to the wall instead of wallpaper, is a shop selling coins in little plastic wallets. Next door is one with glass cases full of seashells and vintage watches (who thought of such a combination?). If you want postcards or army memorabilia, turn left, walk down a passageway painted nautical blue and follow the hand signs on the wall to Uncle Tom's Cabin.

At the other end of the snicket is a pub, the Rope and Anchor (what else?), and in its car park, a Nissen hut, the roof carpeted by moss. A Colson Flyer is parked outside with a note taped to the spokes of the front wheel: 'Manufactured in Elyria, Ohio, US of A, this bicycle, a Colston Flyer, from appox [sic] 1935, was painstakingly restored by Mr. David Leach of Colyford, East Devon, over a period of three and a half years. NFS.' Fastened to the crossbar is a wooden sign with 'Bob's Curios' painted neatly on it with a string of dancing dandelions beneath. Venture inside and dust shimmers in streams of light from the windows. There are old maps; rusty tools; stuffed foxes; a church pew; hand pumps from a pub complete with perished tubing; a mannequin; driftwood and a table overflowing with invoices and programmes from productions held mainly at the Grand Theatre, Plymouth, in the 1920s. A sun-bleached handwritten note is inserted in a polythene bag placed on top and reads: 'Rare! Theatre bombed by The Nazis in March 1941, now demolished!'

Bob (I presume it is him) is wearing a waistcoat and has the crimson cheeks of a rural pub landlord. He shouts across to a customer who is picking up old spanners and puffing at them in a futile attempt to blow off pitted rust. There is no context to anything Bob says and he appears to know the spanner-blower so well that he can miss out the beginning of every sentence: 'That was him done for, then'; 'Always the same when you take that particular route' and, best of all, 'She had it coming, I suppose, doing what she did that time.'

These emporiums are not staffed by normal shopkeepers under normal economic conventions (i.e. for profit). They are enthusiasts, people who love being in the vicinity of the sea and seem as happy entombed by their wares as they are selling them. They will cheerfully wait hours, a whole day if necessary, listening to the radio or an Enya album, to sell a shark eye moon or Scotch bonnet shell wrapped in a brown paper bag.

'That'll be 10p, please.'

When Grandad was well and at peace with himself and the world, you were drawn into the happiness. He was tender with Gran. He'd sometimes put a newspaper at his feet and peel potatoes while sitting in the front room. His hands moved briskly and when Gran came in he'd joke or tease her. He'd pretend to spit out.

'Seen that?' he'd ask.

'What?'

'Look closer.'

He put his lips together again.

'There. See it?'

'See what?'

'I'm spitting feathers here, I'm that dry.'

He'd hold up his finger and mime the flight of a feather falling to the ground, moving it across in small curves. She smiled. He was asking her to make him a cup of tea.

'That's it, love, a nice cuppa and don't spare the sugar. It gets this lad peeling faster when he's had a couple of spoonfuls.'

His mood could change in an instant, though. He would suddenly put on an overcoat.

'I'm going out.'

'Where to?' asked Gran.

'Just out.'

When the door shut, Gran moved to the veranda and watched him walking away on the street below. She said she didn't know how long he'd be gone or what mood he'd be in when he got back. She moved quickly around the room, scuffing her feet as if the floor was hot and burning through the soles of her slippers.

Most of all, seaside towns have second-hand bookshops. They are usually found parallel to the seafront, three or four streets back, often — if you're very lucky — in a cluster of two or three. They are full of rooms and corridors, each lined with hundreds, maybe thousands, of titles. I was at my happiest in these dingy, claustrophobic caverns, climbing the rickety stairs, over the worn-out carpet, to the natural history section or the room heavy with old, yellowing comics, so parched that it felt as if they might turn to dust at your fingertips. There was invariably a room at the very back, a lean-to assembled from glass panels, beer crates and pallets where there were warnings to be mindful of the buckets left out to catch the rain. The markdowns were kept here, bundles of old magazines wrapped in fraying string — *The Strand*, *Home Notes*, *Stitchcraft* — and tatty hardbacks pocked by mould, sometimes so musty that it took your breath away; I'd often need several puffs on my inhaler to see me through. I'd seek out the patch of orange that denoted the Penguin section — it always seemed more substantial than in ordinary bookshops, those that weren't close to the sea. Within an hour or so, I'd return several times to the desk at the front of the shop, placing onto it the books I wanted to buy but didn't want to carry around and compromise my capacity to browse.

Over my first summer of truly, deeply discovering the joy of reading, two authors are most affixed to memory: W. Somerset Maugham and D.H. Lawrence. The only pointer to their most famous work was by inadvertently finding a well-known title or by reading the text on one of their others: 'Best known for . . .' or 'The author of the acclaimed . . .' Usually, this meant I would read a lesser-known book first and move to the more popular.

I started with *The Trespasser* by D.H. Lawrence, a study of adulterous love, played out by Siegmund and Helena. Lawrence knew this subject well; he had eloped with Frieda von Richthofen, the wife of his former university professor, Ernest Weekley. Lawrence evoked a dreamy, resplendent world with constant references to nature – 'the sea was as blue as a periwinkle flower' and 'women, like crocus-flowers, in white and blue and lavender'. He had you there, lying amid the summer corn, full up on desire and despair. Next, I read the more famous *Sons and Lovers* and *Women in Love* and, in the seaside bookshop, I sought less well-known titles that I had seen listed, among them *The Boy in the Bush* and *Kangaroo*. Curiously, I didn't seek out *Lady Chatterley's Lover*. I had been put off by the media clamour. In fact, I still haven't read it, although it hardly feels necessary when a new adaptation is played out on television every few years.

My introduction to W. Somerset Maugham was *The Moon and Sixpence*, the novel inspired by the life of Paul Gauguin, the French post-impressionist painter. I read it over a couple of days. Although occasionally long-winded (it seems more so, forty years later) and leaden with repetitive plot summaries, its elegant style was seductive. Maugham had been aware of his limitations and determined to play to his strengths: plotting, characterisation and relating the predilections of high-class society. 'I knew I had no lyrical quality,' he wrote in an essay towards the end of his life. 'I had a small vocabulary and no efforts that I could make to enlarge it much availed me. I had little gift of metaphor; the original and striking simile seldom occurred to me.' Edmund Wilson, the acerbic American literary critic, said of Maugham's work: 'It is such a tissue of clichés that one's wonder is finally aroused at the writer's ability to assemble so many and at his unfailing inability to put anything in an individual way.' After *The Moon and Sixpence* I moved on to the colossal *Of Human Bondage* (such an evocative title, albeit adapted from a section heading of Spinoza's *Ethics*).

At the time I knew nothing of Maugham's life story. To know it is to trace the soul that runs through the best of his work and also, puffed up by great wealth and prestige in his dotage (he had *thirteen* servants on hand at his lavish home, Villa Mauresque in Cap Ferrat), the hubris. He was born into privilege but his parents died before he was ten years old; he kept his mother's photograph by his bedside all his life. He was adopted by an uncle, Henry MacDonald Maugham, the vicar of Whitstable, who showed him scant affection. Maugham was of small stature, stammered and was bullied at school.

Before becoming an author and playwright, he trained for five years as a medical student; this informed *Of Human Bondage*. 'I saw how men died. I saw how they bore pain. I saw what hope looked like, fear and relief.'* Although he had a thirteen-year (largely unhappy) marriage to Syrie Wellcome, the ex-wife of Henry Wellcome, the pharmaceutical magnate, he later said he was 'three-quarters queer'. He had a thirty-year relationship with Gerald Haxton, a carousing American he met when they were

---

* *The Summing Up.*

both serving in the Red Cross ambulance unit in France during the First World War. He wrote in *The Summing Up*: 'I have most loved people who cared little or nothing for me and when people have loved me I have been embarrassed. In order not to hurt their feelings, I have often acted a passion I did not feel.'

In 1908, aged thirty-four, Maugham had four plays running simultaneously in the West End; no other playwright had known such exposure and popularity. Riches, fame and adulation hadn't quelled the bitterness and anger fomented in childhood and carried all his life. He was often bitchy and spiteful, disappointed with the world and the people in it. Acquaintances said it was visible in his face – the tired, withdrawn eyes and the arc of a mouth slumped to a perpetual frown. He fitted the maxim delivered in *Man and Superman*, the drama by George Bernard Shaw: 'There are two tragedies in life. One is to lose your heart's desire. The other is to gain it.' Maugham's redeeming feature was self-awareness: he addressed the issue of goodness and self-centredness across much of his work, as if seeking remedy.

On that particular holiday (Sidmouth, Devon) I was looking for Maugham's more obscure books, perhaps *The Gentleman in the Parlour* or *On a Chinese Screen*, or another collection of his short stories. I bought six books on the first day, using up most of my saved-up paper round money, two each by Maugham and Lawrence; *A Summer Bird-Cage* by Margaret Drabble and *August is a Wicked Month* (another terrific title) by Edna O'Brien. This meant I now had thirty-one books with me on the holiday – the new purchases and twenty-five others I'd jammed into two Tesco bags and put in the boot of the car. I was hoping for rain, obviously.

I could think of nothing more blissful than seven days in a caravan, rain lashing on all sides and a pile of thirty-one books. When Mum had seen the bags, she remarked that 'it was a lot of holiday reading'. I didn't say anything but, rather tetchily, decided I didn't like this concept of 'holiday reading' – it was reductive and made reading a measly component of a holiday, the same as a boat trip across the bay or a game of pitch and putt. In fact, reading *was* the holiday and I planned to do it in a more varied environment than at home. I might read under a tree in the park; deep in a wood somewhere; by the edge of a farmer's field; on the beach or simply sitting in a deckchair by the caravan, should the rain relent. I can sometimes see why Mum and Dad fretted about their middle aged 15-year-old son.

One of Grandad's regular outings with me was to visit Aunty Lizzy and Uncle Wright, who lived a few streets away. Their flat was furnished with large dark sideboards and bulky cupboards. Dotted around were numerous figurines of imps and Scottie dogs and busts of Winston Churchill. At the side of the open fire in the living room was a tall glass-fronted display cabinet containing rows of dolls they had brought back from holidays. It felt as if we'd walked into a strange cobwebby museum where all these small black eyes were watching every move. I clung to the bottom of Grandad's jacket until I was sure none were alive and out to get me.

The holiday plan was more, a lot more, of Maugham and Lawrence, a thorough expedition into as many of their books as possible. To glean a better understanding of Maugham I took with me *Somerset Maugham and his World* by Frederic Raphael, an author with a long Hollywood career writing screenplays for, among others, *Far from the Madding Crowd*, and, thirty years later, *Eyes Wide Shut*. On the first page of the biography, published in 1976, a paragraph begins by telling us that Maugham was born in the British embassy in Paris, three years after the siege of the city by Prussian forces. Raphael writes, using a bizarre analogy: 'The Prussians had returned across the Rhine, taking Alsace and Lorraine with them, so to speak, but Paris had recovered, like a beautiful woman after a rape.'

The other books were to function as snacks, a few pages

here and there to nourish the mind after a feast of Maugham and Lawrence. A new book, however, all fresh to the eyes and the touch, freighted with potential, was hard to resist. I began reading *A Summer Bird-Cage*. I immediately fell for its conversational style, as Sarah rambled about coming back from Paris to be bridesmaid at the wedding of her sister, Louise, 'an absolutely knock-out beauty', to Stephen Halifax, an author of four novels. Drabble was twenty-four and just out of Cambridge University when the book was published in 1963. I surmised that she had started it unsure of where it might lead but followed it home regardless; a perfectly fine approach to a first-person narrative, replicating life itself: who knows tomorrow? She acknowledged her influences in an article in *Reader's Digest*: 'While at university it was Angus Wilson and Saul Bellow and J.D. Salinger who showed me that novels could still be written about the modern world.'

As the reading plan had been abandoned and I'd already spent a day with *The Summer Bird-Cage*, I moved on to *August is a Wicked Month*. Again, it had been published in the mid-1960s by another woman pushing at the sides of her world, this time with more scepticism and guile, probably because O'Brien was nearly ten years older than Drabble.

Inside those plastic bags and later fanned out around me on the bed like numbers on a giant clock were books by other female writers whose work I would devour: Jean Rhys, Virginia Woolf, Muriel Spark, Monica Dickens, Mary McCarthy, Joan Didion, Mary Shelley, Charlotte Brontë and Doris Lessing. Back then, the demarcation of genders, races and nationalities of writers was barely referenced. I had seen that these books had strong covers, they *seemed* interesting and so I bought them; I had no other agenda. Thereafter, they would be judged on the writing and I'd read as many pages or chapters as I found engaging and enjoyable.

On a theme, I remember picking up books published by Virago Press — 'The international publisher of books by women for all readers, everywhere' – but putting them down again. The covers were awful. They usually featured a glum woman looking out of a window or, for a little variety, a glum woman sitting on a chair looking out of a window. Or else it was a woman (glum) carrying hay on a sunless evening, or a smudgy still life of flowers or fruit. They might have been excellent books, and one or two had great titles (*Mr Fortune's Maggot* by Sylvia Townsend Warner and *A Pin to the Peepshow* by F. Tennyson Jesse, for example), but they looked so determinedly unappealing, especially set against the golden orange glow of a Penguin.

I was looking for work over the summer and visited the job centre in Rochdale town centre, flitting among people hacking and muttering, smelling of (old) sweat, (recent) cigarettes and (last night's) beer. I rubbed my eyes, much as actors do in films to convey an incredible view or plot shift: 'Part-time job in book warehouse'. I stared again at the notice. A book warehouse? In Rochdale? The town didn't have an established independent bookshop but, bizarrely, secreted somewhere amid the streets and mills and kebab shops, was a warehouse *full* of books. I arranged to attend a job interview.

The Dickensian ring to 'Walter Heap & Son, Booksellers (Wholesale)' was apposite. The company was based in a drab building, red brick sooted to black, on the ginnel side of a main street in the town centre, affording a view of piled-up rubbish and falling-down outhouses that had once been lavatories. Lost souls wandered nearby; a drugs unit and homeless shelter were based across the road. As I approached the entrance to Heap's, I cycled past two lads I recognised from school. They had crisp bags fastened to their faces and were gorging on glue. They broke off from the sniffing to argue with one another but, try as they might, could only grunt and yell rather than form actual words.

*

Uncle Wright was much smaller than Grandad and his legs were slightly bowed, as if he were carrying something heavy on his back. He wore thick plaid suits. In summer he'd take off the jacket and reveal a ring of elasticised metal that looked like a watchstrap around the top of his arm; he said it kept his sleeve up. He had a scar in the centre of his neck and a coarse whisper of a voice. Grandad said he'd had trouble with his throat and 'rather than mess about' he'd asked the doctors to take out his voice box (I learned later that it was throat cancer).

I could tell when Grandad was anxious but it left him when he was with Wright. They would drink tea in the kitchen, sitting at a small table, and I'd be given a glass of lemonade. Every so often Wright would offer me a top-up and a biscuit. Lizzy usually stayed by the fire in the front room.

I padlocked my bike to the rusty drainpipe outside and pushed open the door set in a large wooden frame. The place had a distinctive smell of damp and fumes from Calor gas heaters dotted amid the aisles within a maze of stacked books. The interview was a formality; I don't think the allure of being among books was shared by many in Rochdale. I was taken on to work three days a week over the course of the summer. When I arrived each morning I had to report to Bill, the foreman. He was usually pressed close to one of the fires, his thin grey coat lifted at the back so the warmth could get to his backside; it was chilly despite being May. He was small and wiry, about sixty years old and bald apart from a snake of grey hair that ran from ear to ear above his neck. He had 'breakfast eyes' — one on the eggs, the other on the bacon — and you were never sure where he was looking. He'd start talking and I'd not realise he was addressing me.

'Sorry, Bill.'

'Are-you-with-us-this-morning?' he'd ask slowly.

One of my tasks was to brew up for the four or five people

who worked there. On the first day, after I'd handed everyone their drinks, I was told to 'listen up, laddie'.

'You're not reckless, are you?'

'No, Bill.'

'Good. I don't want you messing with these cups, see.'

'I won't.'

'There was a serious accident here once involving a cup.'

'What happened?'

'Someone nearly lost a bloody eye, that's what happened.'

About ten years earlier a lad called Phil had drunk his tea and motioned that he was going to throw the dregs into someone's face. The cup flew off its handle and hit one of the company's reps above the eye. He needed stitches and was off work for a few days.

'You see,' said Bill. 'Accidents can happen at work, just like that.'

Bill asked me another question:

'Do you know your dogs?'

'I'm not sure what you mean.'

'Do you know your dogs?'

I looked at the others, hoping for help. I didn't get any.

'You know, what colour they are,' said Bill.

'I know some,' I said.

'Well, you'd better learn more, then. You see, I like red setter but Tony over there goes for golden Labrador. And none of us like bull terrier.'

I realised he was talking about the colour of tea and its preferred strength.

'Don't bull terriers come in different colours?' I asked.

'They might, smart-arse, but I'm talking about those horrible white ones that look like they were born before they were ready. Do me a cup of tea that's a bull terrier and it's going straight down the sink.'

130

Although I was surrounded by books at the warehouse, they weren't *my* kind of books. The business served the market stalls of Lancashire and further afield. Pulp westerns were the most popular line and, after packing box upon box of them, the front covers of J.T. Edson's *Ole Devil and the Mule Train* and *Bad Hombre*, along with Louis L'Amour's *Mustang Man* and *The Man from Skibbereen*, were imprinted for ever on my mind. The female equivalent was historical romances, each with a similar cover – a man and a woman in Victorian fineries looking lovelorn. The rest of the stock comprised puzzle magazines and colouring books for children, along with an odd publication called *Funny Half Hour* which featured cartoons of people caught up in calamitous sexual escapades, usually involving doctors, handymen, vicars and strippers, sometimes all four.

Bill was a hard worker and mesmeric with a piece of string, a pile of books and a Stanley knife. He knew the location of every book and box file in the building. He was so keyed into the company's business – the arrival of deliveries, phone calls from reps – that he knew the time at all points of the day without looking at his watch. He thought the authors' names were ludicrous and performed the same routine every time it was his turn to package up the westerns.

'Do you think their mams and dads gave them these fancy, highfalutin names? Did they fuck!'

He'd shout out 'Bollocks' after each passed in front of his wonky eyeline. A typical outburst would go:

'Gunn Halliday, bollocks! Elmer Kelton, bollocks! Dale Van Every, bollocks! Gene Curry, bollocks! Todhunter Ballard, double bollocks!'

As I was leaving work one afternoon, Bill beckoned me over.

'You've put a shift in today, lad,' he told me.

'Thanks.'

'Would you like one or two books to take home with you?'

I realised this was a reward, a thank you.

'It's okay, Bill.'

'I thought you liked books,' he said, tilting his head. A couple of days earlier he had found me reading *Rabbit, Run* by John Updike, at lunchtime.

'You're not a snob, are you? Aren't these books good enough for you?'

'It's not that,' I lied.

'Look, sonny boy, these fucking books about gunslingers coming to town and shooting everyone up, they keep us in a bloody job. It's what people, *real* people, actually like. They bring in the money so publishers can put out all that deep and meaningful stuff. You know, writers contemplating their own belly buttons. I don't call them novels like every other bugger – they're navels. That's another name for your belly button, do you know that? I suppose you like stuff like that, don't you?'

I was thinking how to respond when he began talking again, nostrils flared.

'It's all a load of horse shit.'

Sheila was one of the reps. She was in her thirties, slim and attractive. She had red hair that fell down in tight ringlets. Bill said she looked like the actress Susannah York and was an 'English rose'.

'You should have seen her in that film, *Loss of Innocence*. She had skin like fucking porcelain, she did. Loss of innocence? Give her five minutes with this lad and I'd sort her out. No trouble, no trouble at all. I'd have her screaming in bloody ecstasy and begging for mercy at the same time. That's why I've gone a bit bald, you know [he was actually extremely bald] – it's all that rubbing my head on the pillow while I'm on the job. It's worn my hair away. Sheila's just the same as Susannah York, you know, even if she's getting on a bit. Beautiful, she is.'

When Sheila called in, the mood lifted behind her trail of perfume.

'Hello Sheila, my love,' sang Bill.

She fell coy around his quaint flirting. He whistled to himself and set about his tasks with even more relish and efficiency, cutting down on his swearing. After she'd gone, he imagined we'd all found her irresistible.

'That's a proper woman, that is. A classy piece.'

He told me: 'Don't even think about tapping her up. She'd have you for bloody breakfast.'

Most of the stock was kept downstairs. The first floor was practically derelict, with broken windows and missing floorboards. Pigeons flew across the eaves and small mounds of dust formed beneath slates that had worked loose. One day, a few minutes after Sheila had gone, I went upstairs to use the toilet. Bill was waiting for me at the bottom of the stairs. As I passed he pretended to cuff me around the back of the head.

'Hey, you've not been pulling it up there, have you? Don't be having any lurid thoughts about our Sheila.'

The C&A would become concerned if Grandad was off work for more than a few days. Gran called in with sick notes but they sometimes wanted to see for themselves. One of their visits coincided with a breakdown. Two people approached the flat in smart clothes, a man and woman. Grandad was on the veranda, hurling plates and ornaments to the wind.

'What do you bloody want?' he shouted down.

'We're looking for John Duffy.'

'What do you want him for?'

'We're from the C&A.'

'He's not here. He's run off with a fancy piece.'

Gran raced to the edge of the veranda to see who he was talking to. She couldn't make herself heard above the crashing of crockery, some of it striking the ground close to where they were standing. The lady living in one of the ground-floor flats must have explained that it was John Duffy who was shouting down to them. The pair began walking away, minding their backs as they went. Gran yelled:

'Do you want me to come down?'

The woman stopped and shouted that they had all the information they needed, thank you very much.

I didn't tell anyone that I wanted to be an author. I would have been viewed as deluded; *tapped*, as they say in Rochdale. Most families saw it as a duty above all others to keep their offspring earthbound. Any sign of being 'full of yourself' and there was a queue of parents, grandparents, aunties, uncles, near neighbours and passers-by all keen to put you right, fasten you to the ground. Even now, around these parts, if you ask about someone, the first commendation is usually that he or she is 'down to earth'.

I resolved to become a journalist, viewing it as a precursor to authorship; it would, I told myself, hone my writing, ensure I met deadlines and liaised with editors. Along the way, I'd also garner a broad experience of life. More pressingly, it would supply an agreeable answer to the recurring question – what are you going to do when you leave school?

Initially Dad had wanted me to join the family firm (basically him and one or two other subcontractors) but he had realised I had no real interest in or bent for manual work. On jobs with him as a kid, he told me regularly, half joking (possibly), that I was 'as much use as a double rupture'. Years earlier, my uncle Peter had served a formal apprenticeship under Dad. He told me: 'When I got a bollocking from your dad I didn't have to open doors – I felt so small I could go *under* them.' Dad had endured similar when he was young and assumed it was the only way: knocking you down to build you up. There was a lot of this about; it might have been a legacy of army life and the war years.

Once he'd accepted 'and Son' wouldn't be painted on the side of his van, Dad, and Mum, had no alternative career plan for me, though Mum hoped it would involve my wearing a suit and tie and having 'a decent haircut'. They deferred to others, so when I'd told Mum that the careers teacher had said it was unlikely I'd become a journalist and was perhaps more suited to retail management, she'd responded, 'Well, they know best.' They didn't.

The NCTJ (National Council for the Training of Journalists) liaised with unions and newspaper owners to supply the industry with a regulated flow of young talent. Five O levels and two A level passes were needed for the one-year full-time course. Candidates also had to pass vocational tests and an interview with a panel comprising senior journalists. Although I didn't sit O levels, I got top marks in five CSE subjects, which were equal to O level passes (albeit at low grades). As a 'CSE-er', I'd not been viewed as potential sixth-form material so there was no mention of my progressing to the school's prefabricated block, where I'd heard you could read the morning papers and listen to music at lunchtime, such was the exalted status. My standing as a CSE pupil also meant that the prospect of going to university was never mooted.

I learned that it was possible to do A levels at a nearby college in a single academic year, rather than the routine two. These courses attracted students who had failed maybe one or two A levels but wanted to study for them again, and more quickly. I chose history and sociology. I knew nothing of sociology's reputation for both radicalising people and being considered an easy option. Soon after starting I was told the 'joke' that passing sociology was about as difficult as tearing in half a piece of tissue paper.

At the first lecture ('What is Sociology?'), Rob Davies introduced himself as 'Rob'. He was a thickset bloke in his mid-thirties;

you could imagine it taking a while to walk all the way around him. Under no circumstances were we to refer to him as Mr Davies, he said. At all times, it was Rob. Not Robert and definitely not Bob or Bobby, but Rob. The room of about fourteen A level-failers and me nodded.

'Do you know why it's Rob and not Mr Davies?'

We shook our heads.

'Because I'm your lecturer, not your fucking teacher, that's why,' he snapped.

Fucking hell, did he just say 'fucking'? Although it was shocking, it was also a little bit funny because of the self-conscious and lispy way it was dispensed. We weren't to know but it was the first in a long line of melodramatic outbursts designed to shock and antagonise.

While answering *very generally* (as he emphasised several times) the question, 'What is Sociology?' he began chomping on a sandwich, not caring that bits were dropping to the floor. He was wearing a baggy shirt that almost reached his knees beneath a tatty corduroy jacket. Afterwards, he handed out sheets of paper. They contained questions such as: what is your father's job? Do you consider yourself rich or poor? Are your parents still together? Do you believe people are essentially good or bad? He said it was an attempt to get to know everyone as quickly and as intensely as possible. We dutifully filled them in but they were never produced or even mentioned again.

Mum answered the front door. I'd been playing with my toy cars when Gran, who had been reading a magazine at the kitchen table, bolted and ran upstairs. She'd walked out on Grandad two days earlier, worried for her safety. Mum was accustomed to these visits. Grandad would be alternately contrite and angry. He couldn't, for the life of him, think why she'd abandon him like this, leaving him to cook his own teas and clean the house. What was it all about?

When he found her, he'd bloody tell her. This time he was different. He was composed.

'Hello, love,' he said to Mum. 'I've got bad news.'

They walked through the hall and into the front room.

'It's about your mam. She's dead. She was run over by a car this morning.'

'She wasn't.'

'She was.'

'She wasn't.'

Mum didn't know whether to reveal how she could be so sure that her mother was alive. Grandad was insistent.

'It's no good trying to kid yourself, love. She's dead and that's the end of it.'

She couldn't carry on the pretence any longer.

'Dad, she's upstairs, here. Hiding from you.'

'Is she?'

He looked shocked, as if hearing that she'd returned from the dead. Mum left the room and shouted up:

'Mum, come and show Dad that you're still with us, will you?'

Gran came down, cursing.

'Why have you told him I'm here?'

'Because he thinks you're bloody dead.'

Grandad was relieved. He sat back in the chair.

'It's the police, Eveline. They came round this morning and told me they'd found you dead on the main road. They said you'd been squashed. They're bloody liars, they are.'

Gran went back home with him.

During lectures, Davies made us form a horseshoe shape with the desks around him. Sitting across from me I noticed a fair-haired kid in faded jeans and plimsolls. His cheeks were candyfloss pink. At lunchtime I saw him sitting alone at a table in the refectory.

I don't know why – it was a feeling I've had only a few times in my life – but I felt drawn to him, as if I had no choice in the matter.

'Can I sit here?' I asked.

'Sure.'

He said he was called Pete. We talked about music. He liked the right bands. I noticed he was eating a pizza with hardly any topping.

'That looks a bit boring,' I said.

'I asked for one without meat.'

'How come?'

'I'm a vegetarian.'

He was the first vegetarian I had met. I was intrigued, asking how long he'd been one, what he ate instead of meat. He said he travelled to college on his bike, a journey of about six miles. While we were sitting together, me leading the conversation, I had the impression that a part of him was elsewhere, already thinking about home perhaps and the journey there, whizzing through the streets, past the houses and through the traffic. He said there was a table-tennis table at his house and, a week or so later, we agreed to meet up for a game.

His house, more a mansion, was on the edge of town. The only similar places I knew were museums or doctors' surgeries. The main staircase was as wide as a room, flushed with light from a magnificent arched window. The ceilings were high with ornate coving, the doors made from thick, dark wood. Bookcases lined the walls and all around hung oil paintings: contorted faces; cleaved insects; crows by a roadside; telegraph poles scratched out against a rainy sky. I was surprised to find concessions to domesticity here and there – a television, a conventional kitchen, a ball of wool and knitting needles on the coffee table – and to realise people actually lived there, rattling around in such a large space. On subsequent visits I noticed the dust, the cracks in the ceiling, the patches of damp, a broken window in the attic room; it was as if the occupants had too much on their mind to fix up the place or no longer had as much money as they used to.

We became good friends. I'm not sure he noticed but we went together well, we fitted; a few people commented on this. We were roughly the same height and weight, though he was leaner because he ran and cycled. He was fair, I was dark. We had a similar taste in clothes. I spoke more, he listened. He always seemed slightly out of reach, which meant that to be one of the few allowed up close felt special, permitted. We came from different strata of society. While my family had spent summer holidays in a caravan at Blackpool, his had been in a tent in the Lake District, calling at museums and consulting their Wainwrights as they traversed the fells. His growing-up home had been a hushed place where people read books, or, up in the attic, painted naked men holding giant moths (one of the more striking oil paintings).

Around this time, I read *Birdy* by William Wharton and saw our relationship played out within its pages. I was Al Columbato, chatty and eager, and Pete was Birdy, introverted and two steps back from life. One of the recurring scenes in the book has Al visiting Birdy and trying to coax him out of himself, to join in and reach for happiness. Over the next few years, I would play this role frequently with Pete.

I arrived for the lecture five minutes before it was due to start. I put a small pile of books on my desk, sociology textbooks by Max Weber and Talcott Parsons, and, between them, *Down and Out in Paris and London* by George Orwell, which I had been reading on the bus. Davies tilted his head to see their spines.

'George Orwell!' he exclaimed. 'Don't tell me you're a fan.'

I said that I was, very much so.

'What was it G.K. Chesterton declared?' he said. 'The English love a talented mediocrity. That's our George, or Eric, as he was known to his mater and pater. He was a pious sod and don't get me started on his so-called rules of writing. What was that all about? What's he got against metaphors and long words? Why does he want everything to read like a fucking shopping list? Boooooring.'

Fortunately, others began entering the room and he was distracted, greeting most of them with a personal put-down: nod, 'time for a haircut'; nod, 'dodgy cardigan' and, nod, 'bit downcast today'.

My fleeting contretemps over Orwell was nothing compared to the tension developing between Davies and the Cohens, Rebecca and Sarah, two near-identical twin daughters of an ophthalmologist who, in tribute to their dad, wore glasses with ultra-thick lenses. They were extremely articulate and smart. They were also good-looking, and when Davies teased them you sensed a sexual undertone which, I'm sure, was wholly one-sided (his).

On one occasion he was piling up the profanities, as good as imploring us to start the revolution there and then. He was interrupted.

'Are you supposed to be doing this? Isn't it against the rules?' asked Rebecca.

'What rules?'

'College rules.'

'Rules are there to be broken.'

She shook her head.

'This isn't on,' she said. 'All the preaching you're doing. You're supposed to be teaching us sociology not the fucking *Communist Manifesto*.'

It was good that she had sworn. One of her fucks was worth twenty of his, an atom bomb after all the hand grenades. Go on, give him some more. She did. It was brilliant.

140

'I wouldn't mind but everything you say is so stereotypical. It's as if you're stuck in the 1960s with all this corny rhetoric. It doesn't mean anything. It's hackneyed. We're all at least fifteen years younger than you and we've heard it all before, everyone has.'

Halfway through her speech he'd started grinning. He asked if she'd finished her 'little outburst'.

'No, one more thing,' she said. 'Why are you flouncing around college indoctrinating us and not out there in the real world? Is it because we're considered easy – a pushover?'

'You've been got, Miss Cohen, thinking *I'm* the enemy,' he said. 'When I'm patently not the fucking enemy. The enemy is all around you but invisible to you. They've been getting at you since you were born, in insidious ways.'

I was talking to Grandad, undecided what to do one particular afternoon – work on my stamp collection or help Dad clear out the garage.

'Make your mind up. You can't be in two places at the same time,' he said.

It was, of course, an extremely facile statement but there and then, aged about nine, it affected me greatly. He was good at delivering these truths without any trace of sentimentality or ambiguity: there it is, accept it. I don't know what I had hitherto been thinking but it felt as if my world had narrowed instantly to this single track, one direction: I can only be in one place at one time. Surely there were ways of fragmenting yourself, being everywhere all the time. I knew not to say this aloud, how stupid it would seem.

(Maybe, since then, books have formed those surrogate other-lives or simultaneous-lives I thought were waiting for me. I can open a book and place myself anywhere in the world, with all kinds of people. So I can be in more than one place at any time, of a fashion.)

*

And we've heard it all before, everyone has. I hadn't. In fact, I had never met anyone remotely similar to Rob Davies, someone intelligent and charismatic who spoke in such a direct, confrontational manner, utterly sure of himself. No one in my family discussed politics or expressed themselves in this prescriptive, dogmatic way. Instead, they passed on cryptic maxims such as 'You'll find out' or 'He'll get what's coming to him' or, most often, they'd deflect a topic entirely, telling me to 'give it a break' or 'go and look in a book'. The few hours spent each week with Davies felt to be theatrical performances or sermons as much as lectures.

Davies's main theme was that the world was run by a cartel of families who owned the banks and for whom capitalism was a guarantee of everlasting and self-perpetuating wealth. Religion was a con – he often quoted Karl Marx: 'Religion is the sigh of the oppressed creature, the heart of a heartless world, and the soul of soulless conditions. It is the opium of the people.' The family was oppressive and an anachronism; children should be reared communally. Possession was theft. The police was a private army for the middle and upper classes. Monogamy and marriage were constructs, a means of facilitating social control. Sex was a gift to be expressed at will. Education was a tool of the state used to indoctrinate the masses into subservience. Crime was a natural but cancerous outgrowth of the capitalist system which worked for the benefit of elites against the lower social classes. War was caused by competition for resources and markets between imperialist powers.

This landslide of information submerged me so that I had to fight my way back up for air and breathe again. I knew I'd be left changed and nothing would be the same afterwards. Davies, bluntly and belligerently, smashed through the roof of the theatre of life, revealing the strings above and in whose hands they were held. Most of all, I remember feeling disappointed to learn that an unseen force held so much power over our lives and from here on I'd be burdened with the heavy knowledge that it was all a carve-up.

The sense of being overwhelmed, not quite myself, lasted for several months, perhaps a year. It was a lot to take in. Davies and his revelation of how the world was run. Three million people unemployed. Margaret Thatcher on a mission to disenfranchise the poor, the working class, the north and anyone standing in her way. She was seen unequivocally as *the enemy*, a manifestation of greed and stubbornness, and then, later, as the Falklands conflict escalated, a callous warmonger. That condescending smile, the spray-on hair, the faux husky voice — we knew no woman among our extended families or down the street and round the block who looked or sounded as she did. She seemed to have been assembled in a laboratory where scientists had forgotten to install the vital human elements of compassion and humility.

The threat of nuclear war was omnipresent. 'Nuclear explosions are caused by weapons such as "H" Bombs or atom bombs.'* Coming to your town soon: mushroom clouds, bodies snagged in barbed wire fences, Hiroshima, Nagasaki. 'They are like ordinary explosions only many times more powerful.' Marches and badges, films and documentaries. 'They cause great heat and blast. They also make a cloud of deadly dust.' I'd often wake up fretful, imagining that a car door slamming on the street was the aftershock of a fallen missile. 'When you hear the four-minute warning.' Protect and survive. Stock up on tins of food. Stay indoors. Hide under the table. 'The risk is as great in the countryside as the towns.' I was worried that we would soon be stockpiling rings drawn from the fingers of the dead, and comforting wide-eyed

* Extracts from Home Office pamphlet warning of impending nuclear attack.

women, as we'd witnessed in scenes from *The War Game*. Later, if we survived (which was highly unlikely), we'd have to bury still-born, malformed babies. There didn't seem to be anything worth growing up for and it was relentless, suffusing you with despond-ency, your life placed in a polythene bag. I spoke with Pete about it; he understood.

'You've not got to be too over the top about it,' he said. 'Try to maintain perspective. Sometimes it feels physical with me. It's as if it's pressing on my chest or my head and it's difficult to bear. It always feels worse when I'm indoors. I've got to get out and do something, even if it's stuff like gardening.'

Davies set the chainsaw ripping through everyone's belief system, left them feeling wrong-headed and wretched. The Cohens put up a game defence but it was futile. Sometimes his speed of thought, depth of knowledge and precision of expres-sion became hypnotic and left the class near catatonic and paralysed, as if put under a spell by a witch doctor. We began to wonder: why was this man, assembled from kryptonite and dynamite, teaching A level sociology in a scruffy northern provincial town?

'He's a fuck-up,' Sarah Cohen told me in the refectory one lunchtime.

She was playing with the sleeve of her jumper, stretching it and wrapping the loose threads at the cuff tightly around her fingers.

'What do you mean?'

She said his dad had been a major or captain or 'something big' in the army. He'd never really cared about his kids and treated them as if they were his platoon. They had to clean their shoes until they could see their reflection in them and were beaten if they were naughty. This was why Davies had such a big issue with authority.

'How do you know all this?' I asked.

'My dad had a receptionist who went to the same school as Davies.'

I'd never considered Davies having a life outside college; he was so much part of it. What did he do at night? Where did he go? Until that point, I'd thought charismatic rebels merely existed, on their own, not needing the comforts the rest of us sought: family, lovers, friends, somewhere to live. The information about his dad changed everything. It was the first time I'd properly looked at someone from round the back, their history, to see them more clearly. I'd always assumed the anger of clever people was righteous too, born from the injustice they saw around them and not because they came from a dysfunctional family or as a consequence of incidents from years before.

Grandad's favourite walk was across wasteland that formed a grassy slope between two main roads leading to railway arches. Rusty bicycles, prams and even cars lay abandoned. Newspapers, blown by the wind, were caught around the stems of saplings. Dotted everywhere were pools of rainwater discoloured by engine oil, lying dark and flat in furrows of soil. He called it Indian Country and would send me a few yards ahead to look for Red Indians hiding in the tall grass.

'Seen any?' he'd shout.

'Not yet.'

'Well, don't give up. They could be anywhere.'

We'd sometimes find old comics and read them sitting on a box or a tatty discarded sofa. The paper, rained on and then dried out in the sun, had a brittle feel, so you had to open the pages carefully to keep the comic intact.

By great fortune, we all saw Rob Davies on television and afterwards everything was different, his authority diminished. It wasn't actually Davies; it was Anthony Sher playing Howard Kirk as good as impersonating Rob Davies in an adaptation of *The History Man*, the novel written by Malcolm Bradbury. Apart from having a much more substantial frame and lacking a horseshoe moustache, Davies *was* Kirk.

Such was the exactness of the portrayal, we sought corroboration from each other the next day, as if to prove we hadn't dreamed it. Kirk, a self-proclaimed Marxist, is a sociology lecturer at the fictitious Watermouth University. He is a bully and a manipulator, espousing liberalism while practising indoctrination. He loves himself above all else and uses his sovereignty to prey on female students, measuring liberalism and hipness by their willingness to embrace sexual emancipation, to his benefit of course.

Kirk's nemesis is a near-comic creation, George Carmody — an earnest, polite, jacket-and-tie-wearing student with a side parting and kindly demeanour. Or, alternatively, in Kirk's estimation, 'a neo-Nazi'. Carmody addresses Kirk as 'sir' and is told, through gritted teeth and with fire-fierce eyes: 'I am not *sir* — I don't want your deference.' As a seminar on 'Conflict Versus Consensus Theory' progresses, Kirk goads Carmody relentlessly, while other students, eager for Kirk's approval, giggle at his every shard of sarcasm. Carmody snaps, shouting: 'It's all right to have a conflict model as long as we don't conflict with Doctor Kirk.' We had seen this same scene played out many times between Davies and the Cohen sisters. We also recognised the dogmatism, the arrogance and the narcissism personified by Kirk.

As the course progressed, Davies's impact was reduced. The truth tablet of how society was structured could only be handed down once; afterwards it became a process of acceptance. Unlike Kirk, Davies could at least laugh at himself and, over several months, he transformed into human form, flesh and blood.

*

Down the years, I learned that many others, usually on the cusp of adulthood, had met their own version of Davies/Kirk. These were magnetic men or women who had grown up through the 1960s, been mis-sold idealism and hope, and were left with disenchantment seeping to fury. Many found work in academia, where subjects as broad as sociology gave them scope to merge the personal with the professional. The depiction of Kirk in *The History Man* as such an egregious, conniving figure was said to have cemented the stereotype of the 'lefty lecturer' and even influenced government policy towards universities. As a subject of study, sociology was dealt such a blow that it remained maligned for generations.

CHAPTER EIGHT

I fell in with a group of *like-minded* (we used this expression all the time) friends, mainly from college, each of us influenced by punk and with an irresolute view of the world, alternating between acute cynicism and giddy hope. We were new to going out, hiding in the back rooms of pubs, daring the oldest-looking among us to put on his best deep voice to see if he could wheedle a round out of the landlord. We had most success in the Lincoln Inn on Oldham Road, about a mile or so out of town. It was a dive (a new word I'd just learned) with about five or six regular customers, old men dotted here and there on their favourite chair at their favourite beer-sticky table.

Towards the end of our first visit, Ernie, the landlord, popped into the side room. He'd spotted us.

'Look, lads, I'm fine with you having a pint or two but as soon as one of you starts playing silly buggers, you're all out, okay? I keep a quiet pub, no mither.'

One night in there, I was wearing a Jam badge.

'Fucking great band, the Jam,' said a man sitting two tables away. He was wearing a donkey jacket, cement dust on his shoulders and in his hair.

I told him I wasn't keen on the Jam's first two albums but loved everything from *All Mod Cons* onwards. We spoke for about two hours. He listened carefully and traded opinions about books and music and culture, Bob Marley to Throbbing Gristle, *Eraserhead* to Henry Miller. As he got up to leave at the end of the night, he gave a little speech standing over our table.

'We've had our day, my generation. I'm thirty-two years old. Well fucking past it. It's up to you lads to carry the baton, believing in what you're doing. Punk is your starting pistol, bang! Get up and do something with your lives, something you'll enjoy or if you don't enjoy it, at least make a difference.'

Sometimes Rochdale wasn't a bad place to be.

On a walk, me and Grandad came to a building site. A tall black man put down his shovel.

'John, how are you?' he shouted.

He had worked on the railway with Grandad.

'Who's this little fellow?' he asked, pointing at me. I was about six years old at the time.

He bent down and held out his fingers. The grip was loose, his hands dry. The skin on his palms was lighter than on the rest of his body. I shook his hand and took a step backwards. They talked for a few minutes and I kicked at stones lying on the pavement. An ice cream van pulled up against the kerb a few feet away.

'Do you want one?' asked Grandad's friend.

After pub closing time we started visiting Indian restaurants, usually the Koh-i-Noor on Drake Street.

'Shall we go for a curry?' someone would ask, last pint downed.

'Yeah.'

The Koh-i-Noor was a few steps down from the pavement and, on busy Saturday nights, it felt as if we were descending into the rowing quarter of a moored galley where rum had been flowing all day and everyone was now milling around, looking for their friends, items of clothing or asking where the toilets were, please. One or two were actually eating food. Without alcohol shearing the edges this scene might have been intimidating, but with life made rubbery and supple, it was a heaving, beautiful mess of fun and shouting and even singing. One night, every time a new party arrived at the door a group of women banged on the table and sang to the tune of 'Another Brick in the Wall': 'Some more pigs here for the trough'. They went through a list of food items on the 'We don't need no . . .' section, including chicken dansak, lamb bhuna and prawn masala. Even the waiters were laughing, conducting them with ladles borrowed from the kitchen.

I'd never eaten Indian food before and was astonished by the sumptuousness – the ornate cutlery, embroidered napkins, the thali laden with rita raita, onions, yoghurt and chutney, the samosas, steaming rice and then all kinds of new flavours, overflowing. I'd stare at the drapes on the walls, the sparkly elephants and dancing ladies while, all the time, the hypnotic jing-jing and forlorn warble-wailing of sitars, tablas and flutes played in the background. I loved the etiquette, the waiters rubbing down *warm* plates as they placed them on the table, the food arriving on a two-tiered wooden trolley, the individual dishes announced and then left on strip warmers through the grill of which you could see lit oil candles, and then afterwards segments of orange to nibble and, finally, touch-hot, lime-scented towels to wipe down your hands.

The reading continued apace while I was doing A levels. I was making my way through new discoveries, among them Graham Greene, Truman Capote, Carson McCullers, Bernard Malamud,

Oscar Wilde and Anaïs Nin. At the same time, I was spending most weekday nights taping John Peel's show on BBC Radio 1. Punk had evolved into new wave, though it was also known as post-punk, alternative, college rock (more so in the US) and, later, indie. The records Peel played were minimal or crash-banged full of instruments. Some had the vocals so loud that the music was barely audible. Others were without choruses or verses, everything mixed up. It was the sound of people finding instruments (or sometimes fire extinguishers and beer trays, anything at hand) and doing what they wanted with them – playing them upside down, ripping the strings off, setting them on fire, putting bass strings on a normal guitar, throwing a snare drum against a wall. These were soundtracks written for imaginary, never-to-be-made films and anyone anywhere could be a small-town David Bowie – mysterious, vital. Except that Bowie, the same as others from the early 1970s and earlier, were now viewed as the Establishment, the old wave. This irreverence was crucial. Kick over the statues.

The lyrics and subject matter of the songs were eclectic, too. Authors and artists who I had considered personal to me were being sung about or quoted widely. The list of bands with literary references was endless; I felt dusted by intellectualism by merely being aware of these groups and their influences. The Cure had a song, 'Killing an Arab', based on a pivotal scene in *The Outsider*. They also had a track called 'Charlotte Sometimes', the title of a book from 1969 by Penelope Farmer about a magical cedar tree. The Fall took their name from the Albert Camus novel of the same title. Joy Division found theirs in the novella *House of Dolls* by Yehiel Feiner, about his time spent in Auschwitz. Eyeless in Gaza were named after an Aldous Huxley novel. Korova Records (the label of Echo & the Bunnymen and the Sound) was inspired by the bar in *A Clockwork Orange* where Alex and his droogs called to drink special 'milk' supplemented with drugs. Gary Numan was an avid reader of Philip K. Dick, William Burroughs and J.G.

Ballard. Gerald Casale of Devo wrote 'Whip It' after reading *Gravity's Rainbow* by Thomas Pynchon. Josef K took their name from the protagonist of the Franz Kafka novels *The Trial* and *The Castle*. If seemed as if everyone was gorging on music, literature and films, and all of it was leading to somewhere special.

As he waited at the ice-cream van I looked at Grandad's friend from behind. His trousers rose above his ankles and there was more chalky blackness where his socks ended. He passed me a cone. I was hot from the walking and the sunshine. The ice cream looked delectable.

'I didn't want raspberry on it.'

'Lick around it,' said Grandad.

They tried to coax me. I refused to eat it. Eventually Grandad's friend threw it away, pushing it down by a wire fence surrounding the site. I looked back as we left and saw the ice cream dabbed with loose stones and grit, melting dirty white into the soil. We set off walking again and Grandad was quiet for some time. He then began talking incessantly, hardly stopping to draw breath. It didn't matter that his friend was a different colour than us, he said: I should have taken the ice cream. I should never do anything like that again. Didn't I care about his feelings? He had children of his own, lovely kids. He could have saved his money and spent it on them; he didn't have a lot to splash around. I wanted to run back to the building site and cry my apologies. He kept saying, 'It's too late now.' My chest was aching from trying to stop myself from crying.

We started making C90 mix tapes. Pete was especially keen and it was widely agreed that his choices were the coolest; he was the first to discover REM, one of those rare bands that *everyone* loved. On mine, I always included a track by Crass; I had bought their records on Kenny's recommendation. Of all the groups spawned by punk, only Crass had stayed loyal to its original DIY ethos.

Their loud, frenzied ranting was a shout out for life. Avowed anarchists, they were screaming blue murder at meat eaters, fascists, liberals, misogynists, religion, bigots, capitalists, the media, communists and the Clash:

> They said that we were trash
> Well, the name is Crass, not Clash
> They can stuff their punk credentials
> 'Cause it's them that takes the cash.'*

Crass wore black clothing and were part-army legion, part-missionaries as they moved through Britain in a knackered van, performing at scout huts and shabby pubs, where they sang and shouted about all manner of injustices and forces of oppression. Afterwards, shell-shocked kids were left walking their home towns, deafened by the noise, dumbfounded by the enlightenment: *so that's how the world works.*

More to the point, Crass were an obvious addendum to my wider reading and seeking. They were an intellectual force, their values and philosophies drawn from the counterculture of the 1960s: existentialism, the Beat poets, Woody Guthrie, surrealism, French literature, communal living and horticulture. I was inspired.

I bought a guitar from Alexander's and formed a 'group' with David Johnson called Untermensch. The name, German for 'subhuman', was drawn from a Sven Hassel novel; as an act of solidarity and defiance we were aligning ourselves with the lowest caste in society. Within two weeks, and despite being unable to play my guitar or even tune it – I made 'manicured noises' instead

* 'White Punks on Hope'.

– we had released an 'album' on cassette, recorded live on an Aiwa Stereo TPR 901K cassette player (it was essential to have a decent machine for your taping) in David's parents' garage.

Most of the songs were about nuclear Armageddon – 'Last Person on Earth', 'Neutron Bomb', 'The Grave', for example. That summer, there were riots in most of Britain's towns and cities, beginning in Brixton, London. We immediately supported fellow insurrectionists with the track 'Brixton Riots', which lasted about twenty seconds:

> Brixton riots.
> Police are starting it,
> Brixton riots
> Police are loving it,
> Brixton riots,
> Out of sight!
> Brixton riots
> Britain's alight!

I remained infatuated by Crass. I bought their records (monochrome artwork, dark surreal cut-up imagery, interlocking poster that folded down to become a record sleeve), studied the lyrics and went to the concerts. These were the equivalent, almost, to 'happenings', with banners and banks of television screens showing videos of crash test dummies, marching armies, Holocaust victims, stills of Myra Hindley and Ian Brady and, inevitably, the explosion of nuclear bombs: bleak *in extremis*. Pete wasn't sure about Crass although we usually shared a very similar taste in music.

'I like a few of the songs, especially when it goes a bit reggae, but I can only listen to them for so long,' he said. 'There's something too much about them.'

'Too much?'

'They don't ever let up with the gloom.'

'But you love Joy Division!'

'There's a kind of euphoria in Joy Division. "Love Will Tear Us Apart" is a fantastic pop song. They'll still be playing it on the radio in fifty years time,' he said.

Crass didn't have 'fans' in the conventional sense; it would have suggested deference and contradicted one of their principal slogans: 'There Is No Authority But Yourself'. They had a lot of slogans. One evening I was chatting with Mum, explaining how the family was a regressive and anachronistic institution waiting to be toppled.

'I don't know what you're talking about,' she said.

I tried to explain.

'Who did you say was filling your head with all this?'

'Well, I've been influenced *slightly* by this band I'm into and a lecturer at college.'

She smiled.

'Why are you smiling?'

'They've too much time on their hands, doing all that thinking. I wish I had enough time to get my housework done and spend the rest of the day coming up with crackpot ideas.'

'It's not crackpot.'

'It is,' she said, dismissively. 'There's something not right with them.'

During the final weeks before my A levels I revised at my grandparents', in a small room intended for the storage of stepladders, old tins of paint, vacuum cleaners and brushes; it was very similar to where Harry Potter lived at Privet Drive, Little Whinging. I managed, just, to fit a tiny table and chair in there. I spent hours in this windowless room filling notebooks with revision. Everyone, friends and family, kept telling me how this was an extraordinary level of commitment but it came naturally; I enjoyed it.

As a child, when I stayed at their flat I'd sleep on a camp bed in the same room as Gran and Grandad. He'd tell me about the other people living in their block of flats: the Smalleys two floors down who had eleven kids (at the last count) and, across the landing, Mrs Whitfield, at least ninety years old and owning about thirty budgies. It felt as if we were part of a comic strip, all these little stories going on above and below us.

I took a day off from revising to undertake the NCTJ test and interview. The test was based on a list of facts about an accident at a railway level crossing that I had to write as a newspaper story. I also had to spot the 'angle' – it was the train driver's last day at work before retirement – and show that I could prioritise and condense more than 1,000 words of information into a lively 400-word article.

I was confident I'd done well and was set for the interview that afternoon with a panel of three journalists. I had a plan. I fully expected that I'd be asked about my local paper – the course was designed specifically to provide trainee journalists for local papers, after all. I knew the *Rochdale Observer* extremely well and, much as I'd done with A level past papers, I'd studied it meticulously. There was nothing I didn't know about the *Rochdale Observer*, even down to the nickname staff gave to 'A Word in Your Ear', the editor's weekly column: 'A Turd in Your Beer'. I had prepared a critique of the paper and was going to spend up to fifteen minutes outlining how it could be improved.

The formal greetings over, they asked about two people everyone mentioned when you said you were from Rochdale: Gracie Fields and Cyril Smith, the town's gargantuan Liberal MP, posthumously disgraced as a paedophile.

'Before your time, Gracie,' said one of them.

'Just a bit,' I said. 'We still like to keep our aspidistras watered, though.'

This was high wit, especially for a sixteen-year-old. Gracie's best-known song was 'The Biggest Aspidistra in the World'. They all laughed. How easy was this? They asked how I thought I'd do in my A levels and I mentioned the room at my grandparents'.

'So you're studying in a cubbyhole?'

'I suppose I am, yes.'

This level of dedication must have impressed them greatly – what a chap. I knew it was coming, here we go.

'The *Rochdale Observer*, that's your local paper, isn't it?'

'Yes.'

I was looking forward to this; my exposition on the *Rochdale Observer* allied to the future of the local newspaper industry itself.

'Do you read it?'

'No.'

I was waiting to be asked the obvious supplementary question: 'Why not – why don't you read the *Rochdale Observer*?' This was to be my start point. Instead, the question was repeated in a different way:

'You *don't* read your local newspaper?'

A sensible person would have noticed the incredulity in the tone of this question, if not the import. Unfortunately I was unprepared for anything other than the follow-up question of why I didn't read my local paper. Instead of saying, 'Let me tell you why I don't read it' or similar, I became, stupidly, suicidally, entrenched.

'No,' I said again.

There was muttering among the panel, providing a vital few seconds during which I could have volunteered my pre-prepared discourse. Defiant (and brainless) to the end, I said nothing. Here, on a plastic chair in a room in the humanities department of Preston Polytechnic, sat the boy-man so desperate to be a journalist en route to becoming an author that he thought of little else, did his A levels in a year (revising in a windowless room) and refused to countenance any other job, even one that offered free chiropody.

To be clear, saying I did not read my local paper at such a forum was the equivalent of a trainee car mechanic unable to distinguish the bonnet from the boot of a car or an apprentice roofer revealing a fear of heights.

'How do you think it went, son?' asked Dad as I climbed into the car afterwards.

'Not very well.'

Two days later – *two days*: how sure they were of their assessment – I received a letter revealing that, regretfully, I had not been 'successful in my application' but, on the proviso I passed my A levels (which I soon did), I was a reserve for the calendar-year course that began in Sheffield in January. I imagined everyone was told this to sweeten rejection.

Life went on. I was in my first relationship. I had my books. I had the band. We had quickly recorded our second 'album', a C90 with a single extremely long track on each side: 'Factory Workers' and 'Alienation' – subjects we knew bugger all about, of course: we were world-class empathisers. We had strummed unplugged and untuned electric guitars while the television, radio and vacuum cleaner were on in the background, recreating, we hoped, the cacophony of the factories and mills around us (those that hadn't been shut down in the recession). David had groaned and yelped into the recorder, with passion. Twenty copies, individually numbered, were run off by placing two recorders next to each other.

'The deterioration in sound quality adds to the post-industrial authenticity,' I said.

'That's precisely what I was going to say,' said David.

Pete bought two copies, one for himself and another for his brother; it felt odd taking money from a pal, but he insisted.

We began crafting songs with at least a vague structure that we might possibly be able to play more than once. Most of these were based around two or three strummed strings of a guitar, rather than the routine six. Conventional playing, the type learned from Bert Weedon and *Play in a Day* books, was viewed as abhorrent. Enthusiasm and originality was the mantra and we scoffed at anyone spending hours learning to play *properly* – we mimed being sick after saying the word.

'When you get good on an instrument you become a slave to the conventional.'

'Definitely,' I agreed. 'Proficiency is a disease.'

We set up a fanzine named after the band, printed on the college duplicator. There was a 'community lecturer' whose job was to assimilate the college with the local populace – mums and toddlers, pensioner groups, charities and, in our case, teenagers peddling civil disobedience. He was called Bill Healey and he had a bushy beard and a wardrobe generous in tartan waistcoats and corduroy trousers. 'Look, lads,' he said, after perusing our first issue. 'I don't want to impinge on what you're doing and get all, like, you know, Big Brother on you, but all these swear words – would you mind spreading your "fucks" out a little bit? If they're all in one place, we might get a few complaints.'

A synthesiser was needed to add ghostly trails of sound evoking a nuclear winter; it was all the rage. We agreed on another edict: no auditions.

'Your audition is who you are, how you live your life,' said David.

I had someone in mind: my next-door neighbour, Terry. He was a few years older than us and worked at an engineering works. Through the wall, I'd heard him playing a synthesiser. We met up and told him, sincere as hell, that the social and political philosophy was as important as the music. In short (and he could make notes if he wished): educate yourself, celebrate yourself,

159

banish ego, do something, speak out. And, of course: fight capitalism. Terry listened, nodding his head while fiddling with rolling papers and shreds of tobacco. When David used the word 'project', Terry held up his hand.

'I like that word: project. Do you know what I say? Zero tolerance for apathy. It's what this fucking town needs. It shouldn't be music for its own sake. Anyone can do that. It's about using this that matters.'

He banged his forehead with his knuckles, hard.

I told Grandad I was afraid of ghosts. He said it was the living I should watch out for; they were far scarier. As I drifted into sleep he'd tell me about the stars and planets and how the moon had a magnetic pull that caused the tide to go in and out. Looking all that way down from up there, he said, we were dust, so small that we didn't really count.

We agreed to meet at the Spread Eagle in town. It was mid-December. Terry was early, smiling broadly at the bar and waving a pint glass as a greeting. We drank the first pints quickly, as if they were water. The place began filling up. Giggling girls, their perfume sharp and sickly, ordered Cinzano and lemonade before ambushing tables, bags at their feet, puffing on cigarettes. Lads entered in streams, following the leader, passing heavy glasses along the row to swill down in greedy mouthfuls. They seemed oblivious to the cold, their thin white shirts unbuttoned, sleeves rolled up.

'Look at them, the wankers,' said Terry cheerfully. 'It's like a cattle market in here.'

We scoffed and imagined the record and book collections of the people around us.

'Where's the individuality, the expression? Where's the poetry? They all look the fucking same.'

Terry made the sound of sheep baaing. Four pints later:

'Let's go to a club. There'll be more of this lot to laugh at,' said David.

We trooped out into the night. Snow had started to fall. The streets were swarming with people, everyone shouting, everyone pissed, taxis swerving to avoid them. A burger van was parked close to the club entrance and two or three people waited while the vendor, a scrawny bloke in National Health glasses, pulled steaming onions from a vat of hot water and placed them on muffins. A couple meandered by, hardly able to walk, holding each other upright. Outside the club, a queue had formed. Bouncers flirted with the girls, smiling, throwing back their shoulders. We all agreed we couldn't be bothered waiting.

'Let's go and get some kebabs,' said David.

We stopped off for the food and took the quickest route back, through the Ashfield Valley estate. We became aware of a group of lads on the path about two hundred metres behind. Nothing was said but we must have each decided subconsciously that we weren't going to speed up but would amble on, letting them catch up and pass us by. They did this. All seemed fine. After they had gone a few yards ahead, they stopped abruptly. We could see now that they were skinheads and numbered about fifteen. A shout went up from within the group and they charged at us. We ran up the snowy banking. Our chances of avoiding a beating depended largely on our footwear. I covered the ground faster than time itself. I have a memory of being on the path and then another of looking down from the top of the hill, about sixty yards away. I saw David slipping again and again as if caught in a tumble dryer. At one point, as the ground briefly allowed him traction, it looked as if he'd evaded his pursuer but a hand reached out and pulled at his hood, causing him to fall backwards to the snow. He was then lost to the pack as they set about kicking him. I couldn't locate Terry for a second or two but then saw a figure close to the path curled into a ball; he'd barely had time to run before they were on him. One or two were still kicking him but it looked as if they were about to join the rest around David.

I ran for home, which was only a few hundred yards away. Our house was in darkness but I saw that the downstairs light was still on at Terry's. His dad answered the door. I told him what had happened. He rang the police. He started putting on his shoes and coat, and while he did so he admonished me.

'The best thing you could have done for those lads was hide in bushes nearby and then follow the gang to wherever they were going.'

I was speechless and thinking that if he hurried up, we could probably get back and catch them, there and then. Minutes later, David turned up at the door and then Terry. They were both the same colour, somewhere between yellow and green. David was sick on the lawn and holding his stomach, groaning. Terry had been wearing a thick coat and said it had saved him from getting badly hurt.

'I pulled it over my head and waited for them to stop booting me,' he said, matter-of-factly. 'It didn't go on for too long.'

The police arrived and quickly left in their van to look for our assailants. They were soon at the front door again, saying they hadn't seen anyone but we should make statements at the station the next morning. After a sleepless night, we did as we had been asked. We were led to the desk of an officer.

'Did you do anything to goad them?' he asked.

'No.'

'You weren't shouting or carrying on?'

'We were just walking home.'

'Didn't you think to get a move on when you saw these lads behind you?'

'Not really, no.'

I noticed that he was barely writing anything down. David said it:

'You're not writing down what we're saying.'

'I am,' he said, defensively.

'You're not.'

'I'm making brief notes. I'll expand on them later.'

When we were leaving he told us he'd 'keep us abreast of the investigation every step of the way'.

'We won't hear from them again,' said David, as we made our way down the stairs at the police station, having to stop occasionally while Terry caught us up — one of the gang had stamped on the back of his knee and he was wincing at every step.

We didn't hear from them again. I had the impression that, as young men, we were expected to know the dangers of being out on the streets after dark; we had shown 'contributory negligence'. The only outlet for our anger and frustration was to make a statement as a band. We rehearsed in a room above a working men's club on a busy main road. We taped most practices and played the cassettes as we walked home afterwards along the canal bank. In the darkness, framed by trees and heading towards the twinkling lights of the nearby estates, we were often surprised at how good it sounded. At the next practice we wrote 'Ashfield Valley Headkick'.*

'It's the sort of stuff you'd hear on Peel.'

This was the benchmark. This was the everything.

* Available on YouTube.

163

CHAPTER NINE

On Christmas Eve 1981 I received a letter offering me a place on the NCTJ calendar-year course at Richmond College, Sheffield. I was told I'd receive another letter 'soon' with details of possible places to stay; it arrived on the morning I was due to start the course. Dad drove me over. I registered at the college and briefly met the other students before getting back in the car with Dad to look for accommodation, crisscrossing the city. We were met at every door by a shrug of the shoulders and shake of the head – it appeared as if all the rooms in the city were taken; most students had moved in during the late summer to undertake academic year courses.

Finally, long after darkness had descended, we came to a maisonette on a council estate in Gleadless Valley. I was surprised to find they had a couple of rooms available. It was late. We were both tired. On the spot, I agreed to take the box room; the other, they told me, was 'full of junk' and would take a day or two to clear. My new landlord and landlady were a middle-aged couple, John and Joan Lomax. Dad lingered awkwardly and kept asking if I was okay. I could see he was emotional, leaving his seventeen-year-old son with two strangers in a peculiar house in an unfamiliar city. After the earlier resistance to my writing and reading, he had become my greatest supporter. When he left, I looked out onto the street from the window and I realised I had no idea where the college was or where I'd even catch a bus to it.

The NCTJ had chosen a handful of curious outposts for its courses: Harlow, Preston, Darlington and Hastings among others. Richmond College was based in a suburb to the east of Sheffield, among a maze of council houses. We were three miles from the city centre and even further away from the next university student. The others at Richmond, all from nearby, were taking diplomas in hairdressing, secretarial skills, business studies, joinery and mechanics. There was no infrastructure for those from out of town – no freshers' week, student bar, concert venue, societies and not a single social gathering unless one or two of us drifted into the Richmond pub for a game of pool at lunchtime. The plan might have been to make the NCTJ course as vocational as possible, as if you'd moved there for a job; it certainly felt that way.

Most of our group were postgraduates and one or two were in their mid-twenties, turning to journalism after trying other work. I was the youngest. The others had a poise and reserve, and I sometimes felt like a yappy dog around them, too open with my views, too eager for approval.

During the first week we were each interviewed and filmed with a small handheld recorder – the first I'd ever seen. We watched the videos back on a large television that had been wheeled into the room. I appeared on screen, slumped in my chair, working very hard at nonchalance. 'What do you want to be?' I'm asked. I smile and flick the hair out of my eyes. 'A novelist,' I reply.

Afterwards, as I was leaving the room, the lecturer beckoned me over.

'You do know, don't you, that this isn't really a course for aspiring novelists? It's very much geared towards the newspaper industry.'

I said becoming an author was my *long-term* aim. I reassured him that I was extremely keen to become a journalist; this wasn't a complete untruth. I doubt the conversation stayed in his memory for more than a day but it remained with me for years. What had earlier seemed a short footbridge, journalist to author, suddenly stretched wide. I shouldn't have let it feel this way, of course. I was far too sensitive. Afterwards, I thought of the scores of novelists who had started out in journalism: Charles Dickens, Mark Twain, Ernest Hemingway, Joan Didion, Hunter Davies, Susan Sontag and Michael Connelly among them. David Nobbs, one of the UK's bestselling authors at that time, had worked as a reporter at the *Sheffield Star*, a few miles from where we had been standing.

We were walking alongside a fence bordering the railway. Grandad stopped and tugged at the wire mesh, lifting a section from the ground. Grass and weeds were entangled around the bottom, holding it down like strands of stretchy glue. He kicked at these, scraping his foot along until it was completely free.

'Go on, get under there.'

I bent down and scurried through the gap.

'Right, you hold it up for me,' he said.

I held the wire as tightly as I could, my teeth clenched and my hands clutching it to my chest as if hitching up a pair of trousers. As he bent down he asked me to make sure he 'didn't cut his old bald head'. I put my hand on it to guide him through, making sure he didn't rise too quickly and graze himself on the sharp edge. He stood up when he reached the other side and wiped the dust and grit from his hands.

'Are we allowed here, Grandad?'

'No bother.'

'What if someone comes?'

'Tell them you're with John W. Duffy and he used to work here.'

When I signed to stay at their house, John and Joan told me they smoked two or three 'ciggies' a day, but it was more like two or three dozen. Ashtrays overflowed and packets were left all over, jammed down the settee, up Joan's sleeve. She was overweight and wore what she called 'tent dresses', which were cotton and usually floral patterned. John had been unemployed for years and was coat-hanger skinny with a long face and bedspring eyebrows. I never saw him in anything but a vest and washed-out tracksuit bottoms, which I think he slept in. They had a small mangy dog called, without any irony, Princess. The television was left on most of the day and when someone came on who John didn't like, invariably a Conservative politician, he'd move to the edge of his chair, yelling abuse.

'Tell your pals about us,' Joan would say. 'There's room for more, you know. One or two, anyway. We might be last on the list because we're a few miles from the college but we shouldn't get overlooked.'

She believed the geography was against them, not that they lived on a rough estate or were a bit odd or that most students no longer wished to live with middle-aged people they didn't know as if it was still the 1960s; it wasn't so bad for me because I went home every weekend. Joan reminded me of my mum or gran except you always felt there was some badness waiting to go off with her or John because taking in students, having to share their personal space, had been forced upon them; their benefits didn't provide enough income. Joan often spoke of better times.

'You should have seen John when he'd leave for work in a morning, proud as punch,' she said.

Her eyes became watery and I told her not to get upset.

'Thanks, love. You do something with your life. But listen on — never trust anyone.'

The only other student staying, briefly, at John and Joan's was Neil. He was doing the journalism course after completing a degree. He was twenty-two years old which, to me, made him impossibly worldly. He had the bedsit attic room, the biggest in the house. He liked his own company and rarely ventured downstairs, apart from one disastrous night. Joan, as usual, had gone to bed early, leaving me and John on our own in the front room. Completely unbidden, he asked me what kind of girls I fancied.

'I'm not mad keen on skinny girls,' I said.

'No,' he said. 'You want a girl with some flesh on her who'll make your ears pop.'

I said I liked girls that were good company and easy to talk to.

'That's what you've got mates for,' he scoffed. 'Talk to *them*, instead. It's best to be with a woman who gets your sap rising. You'll stand anything if you continually want to tup them, though they can drive you bastard-mad if they're forever flirting with other blokes. You see, I made a mistake with Joan. She's a lovely woman, don't get me wrong, good with the pan and a decent companion but, God bless her, she's not the prettiest flower in the garden, is she, and especially now she's chubbed up. If you're not engaged down below, you soon start to get bored and that's when the bickering starts, like with me and her arguing over nowt most of the time.'

At that moment, Neil entered the room.

'I thought I'd watch a bit of telly,' he said.

He sat in an armchair, his long legs stretched out across the carpet. He began talking to John about football. Neil said one of the funniest things he'd ever seen at a football match was when Willie Donachie scored an own goal for Scotland.

'It was as if he'd placed it away from the keeper on purpose, so he had no chance of saving it,' he said.

'I remember that goal,' said John. 'But it wasn't Willie Donachie.'

'I'm sure you'll find it was.'

A game of verbal tennis ensued: he did, he didn't, he did, he didn't.

Neil changed the angle of delivery:

'It *was* him. John, get that prehistoric brain into gear, will you?'

He was smirking and didn't notice John glowering. Some badness was about to go off.

'I'm not having this in my own house,' boomed John. 'Being spoken down to by a little shit like you. [Neil was at least six feet, two inches.] You can pack your bloody bags, you can. Now.'

'You're joking. This is a joke, right?'

'I'm not bloody joking, no. I'm not chuffing having it, you sitting there telling me Willie Donachie scored that own goal when I know for a fact that it wasn't him.'*

'Where's he going to go, John?' I asked.

'That's not my problem, is it? He should have thought about that before he tried to make a fool of me . . .'

It looked as if he was going to cry, but a second later he spat:

'. . . in front of my own fucking wife.'

---

* Willie Donachie scored an own goal for Scotland in the ninetieth minute against Wales in a home international match played at Hampden Park, Scotland, on Wednesday, 17 May 1978.

'But she's upstairs in bed,' I said.

'She can hear, can't she? She's not bloody deaf.'

I saw Neil at college the next day. He seemed surprisingly upbeat for someone who had spent the night at the YMCA.

'Great news, I'm sorted!' he chirped. 'Really sorted.'

I asked what he meant.

'I've been offered a room in a house sharing with two girls. And they're top crumpet.'

I wasn't sure whether I envied him or not. I knew John and Joan's was a disaster but there seemed something heroic about trying to sleep in a box room next to the lounge, the telly blaring, hearing them coughing and spluttering and sniping at one another, and Princess yapping away night after night while young thugs threw cans at one another on the street outside. All perfect material for a budding writer. And better, surely, for shaping the soul than an easy threesome in a candle-scented semi-detached on a tree-lined street across town. Who knows?

Grandad led the way to a small brick building on land beside the railway lines. He said he used to sit in it with workmates when they had butties and drank tea from flasks. He pushed at the door. It was locked. He scooped up the chain and tried to lever open the padlock.

'No, it's not having it.'

He stepped back.

'Anyway, this is the place.'

The door was a washed-out green colour. The hinges had rusted brown and specks had seeped into the wood, forming the shape of dandelion heads. Someone had painted a giant love heart on one of the walls and coloured it with blotchy white paint. The paint was fading, the brick visible like bones beneath skin. Underneath were two sets of initials: 'JL+AH'.

'Do you think he still loves her?' he asked. 'We used to wonder who'd be daft enough to do this. If he didn't get caught on the fence, a train might have whacked him. It must have been true love, that's all I can say. I bet she left him the week after!'

Pete first tried to kill himself while away at university. He'd gone to study at Bristol and I'd heard from his mum and brothers that he 'wasn't doing great'. I called on him a few days after he had returned home. His mother answered the door and led me to his room. It was a sunlit day and I noticed how different the house looked in sunshine; it lifted the place up, suspended it in the air. Pete was wearing a light-blue denim shirt and pale jeans, the healthiest nearly-died person you'd ever seen. He was going to be fine, he said. The counselling sessions were booked and the wounds across the inside of his arms were healing. He showed them to me. They were like notches on a prison wall counting out days.

'Why did you do it, Pete?'

'I don't know.'

I looked around and was surprised at the bareness of the room: no pictures, a small tower of coins on the windowsill, a few clothes folded on top of a wooden bedding box.

He gave up university and a month or so later he started work as an instructor at an activity centre; it seemed the perfect job, with his love of the outdoors. Within days, he met and fell in love with Lauren, an American student on his drystone walling course. I saw him soon afterwards and he was so happy I thought he might levitate. It was as if his body was wrapped in fairy lights flashing on and off in shifting thumbprints of colour. He moved and spoke quickly and was rubbing his hands together and wiping them on his jeans as if afraid of catching fire. I envied his fervour, how he could give so much, floods of himself, but I was also a little troubled by it; this high was too high.

Lauren was sixteen and, according to Pete, the prettiest,

171

cleverest girl in the world. I met her a week later. She was tall and boyish with fierce brown eyes, wearing a loosely stitched jumper pulled out of shape and almost reaching her knees. She didn't look me in the eyes or ask anything, answering most of my questions with 'sure', 'cool' or 'gross'. That first night, the three of us went to the pub. Lauren had never been in a pub before and was probably the first American to visit Pete's local. It was busy. She wandered off. Pete kept rising from his seat, concerned. I saw her talking to some of the lads in the pool room. When she came back she was trailed by two or three of them and they backed up in the area between the tables as if queuing for something, not sure what. She sat down beside Pete and kissed him passionately for about thirty seconds, full on the lips. The men-in-waiting drifted off.

Back at the house after closing time, Pete's brother Geoff, home from university for the weekend, was sitting in the kitchen reading a book. He was enthralled by his brother's new girlfriend and began asking her questions: did she like England? What was it like in New Jersey? What music was she into? How long was she staying? She answered at first but then reverted to body language – a nod, a shrug. She was bored.

'What do you think of our pubs?'

She pulled an 'I dunno' face.

'We've got some peanut butter. You'll probably like some of that, won't you?'

She asked where it was.

'In the cupboard.'

She walked past him, opened the cupboard door and took the jar from the shelf. Screwing off the lid, she dipped in her fingers, scooping out a handful.

'Well, mind my manners!' said Geoff, smiling.

She froze. And stared at him. She carried on, nostrils flared, top lip raised.

'It was a joke, come on . . .' he pleaded.

She didn't move.

'. . . a joke, I didn't mean it.'

'Fuck you,' she screamed, slamming down the jar as she left the kitchen.

Pete ran after her and returned a few minutes later. He tried to explain:

'You shouldn't have said that. Americans have a different sense of humour. How was she supposed to know it was a joke?'

The journalism course was rigorous and comprised thirty-six hours of lectures a week, divided into four sections: shorthand, law, public administration and general journalism. Every few weeks we had an 'outing' which we had to write up as a feature. One was a talk at Sheffield University given by an author called Stan Barstow. I was familiar with his name but unaware of his work. At the end, he invited questions from the audience. He was bombarded with abstruse queries, few of them about his latest novel (*A Brother's Tale*).

'Can we get back on track?' he pleaded.

The request went unheeded. The same huddle of people, each in their early twenties and archetypal university students – striped scarves, duffel coats, greasy hair – continued to harass him ('Like a dog with a bloody bone,' as our lecturer said afterwards). They wanted to know how he saw the future of *the novel* and whether it was a writer's duty to please and appease the reader or confront him or her, to pierce the consensual 'now' in the furtherance of the very art form itself; expression as agitation, as it were. I struggled to follow this philosophical approach and realised how vocational our course was in comparison. Barstow constantly ran his fingers through his thick grey hair and, between sighs, tried to summon satisfactory replies. It was hopeless.

'That's a sop, if you don't mind my saying, Mr Barstow,

intended to deflect the question rather than answer it. There is no elucidation or resolution offered whatsoever.'

'Well, I'm sorry about that,' said Barstow, shaking his head.

There were two oil drums next to the hut, almost as if we had been expected. Grandad lifted me onto one and climbed onto the other. A breeze lifted a plastic sheet fastened over a stack of pallets nearby. He asked if I wanted a sweet. Wherever he went, he carried with him a small paper bag of mint imperials or Uncle Joe's in his jacket pocket. He'd crack them loudly between his teeth. Over the years this had left him with a mouth full of dirty yellow stumps. They were broken and twisted and if you asked he'd swivel one nearly all the way round with his finger or pull it partially free so it sprang back into his gum. If anyone scolded him for making too much noise as he cracked and chomped, he'd say:

'This here is a busy fellow. He can't be doing with all that bloody sucking. He wants to get down to the flavour as quickly as he can.'

He'd set about the sweets with renewed vigour, smiling at every wince from those around him.

Rain began to fall. I stuck out my tongue and caught a few drops. They tasted slightly sweet.

'You're not bothered about a bit of rain, are you?' he asked.

I shook my head. After a few minutes the sun reappeared, tapping us on the shoulder. The rays of light chased away the rain. Steam rose in twisting columns from the cabin roof. I could feel the heat against my face, tingling. Across from the trees was a knoll that fell away sharply. I noticed, for the first time, iridescent purple among the green; the sun and the rain had coaxed colour from a patch of scrubland. Grandad saw it, too.

'Lovely, aren't they?'

'What are they?' I asked.

'Rosebay willowherbs.'

'Are they flowers?'

'People say they're weeds but they're as nice as anything you get in a garden or they sell at a florist's.'

They were tall, higher than I stood, with long stems swathed in purple petals.

'You find them all over the railway,' he said. 'People call them fireweed because they spring up wherever there's been a fire. You see them down entries too, anywhere with a bit of dirt.'

I could see them along the side of the tracks and between the outbuildings and piles of sleepers. They were even growing out of walls, wafting in the breeze as if waving to us.

I wasn't altogether sure about Barstow. He was a little fond of himself but his books sounded interesting. A few days later, I bought the one that had been most talked about between the jousting: *A Kind of Loving*. I was drawn in from the first paragraph where the protagonist, Vic Brown, twenty years old, is chatty and questioning, sure of himself and then shadowed by doubt. The obsessive nature of first love – on this occasion for Ingrid Rothwell, a typist who works at the same place as Vic – is swiftly laid out and leads the story. I knew the vernacular well. Men were 'blokes'; girls were 'bints' or 'birds'; a mother was an 'Old Lady' and something became 'summat'.

The novel, Barstow's debut, had been published in 1960 and, as I soon discovered, was of a genre dubbed 'kitchen sink realism' because it featured working (or unemployed) people in their natural environment – down the pub, in the backyard, on street corners and, of course, gathered in their kitchens, bickering or making up as the kettle boiled.

During the 1950s and 1960s the creative industries had noted the rise of intelligent, educated writers of working-class origin (drawn chiefly from grammar schools) and offered them patronage to reach the huge but largely untapped market they represented.

These authors and playwrights who held a cracked mirror to life in post-war Britain had been given the catch-all classification of 'angry young men'. They were drawn mainly from the north of England and the Midlands and saw the literary value of setting work in their home towns and featuring people similar to those with whom they'd grown up. They were eager and passionate for change, although the categorisation was somewhat of a misnomer. Most were in their thirties – not particularly young – when published, and depicting working-class life in an authentic way was enough for them to be viewed unilaterally as 'angry'. Also, unlike, say, the Bloomsbury Set or the Beat Generation in the United States, it was an unconnected grouping, both politically and socially, most of whom did not know one another.

John was watching the television in the living room. Through the partition wall, I could hear it was a succession of news pieces about the Falklands War. He banged on my door and shouted through:

'There's a film coming up you might like. It's called *Look Back in Anger*.'

I'd heard of *Look Back in Anger*, the film based on John Osborne's play of 1956, but I wasn't sure about watching it with my landlord.

'Joooooaaan,' he shouted downstairs. 'Get some tea mashed, will you? And bring up a few malted milks.'

While watching the film I had that rare experience of being happy and also being acutely aware that I was happy, and so the minutes felt rich and special. I knew it was a film I'd return to many times. John was quiet. I wasn't sure if he shared my enthusiasm. At the end, before the credits had even finished, he asked:

'What did you make of all that, then?'

I was careful not to appear cocky or antagonise John; it was his house and I didn't want another Willie Donachie episode. But after watching a film so powerful and brilliant, I felt emboldened.

'It was incredible.'

'Why?' he asked, slapping his thigh.

'The intensity of it, the use of language—'

He cut me off:

'No one talks like that in real life. What was that word he used, pucie-something?'

'Pusillanimous. It doesn't matter. It's not claiming to be real life. It's a piece of work, taking you off to somewhere else, making you think.'

'What did you make of Richard Burton [Jimmy Porter]?'

'He was a volcano in human form.'

'But what was he on about?'

'That doesn't matter, really, but I suppose he was ranting against conventionalism, marriage, privilege, society—'

He spoke over me again:

'I thought he were a pillock. He had no reason to go on at that lass like he did. He was bored and looking for a fight.'

He looked down at his copy of the *Daily Mirror*, probably checking what was coming up next on the telly – discussion over.

Afterwards, when video tapes became widely available, I watched the film often but, each time, became increasingly irritated by the gratuitous nature of Jimmy Porter's temper. It was selfish, born of meanness and frustration. Maybe Osborne's cultural mission was to kick down the doors, stir it up. More accomplished and focused stories, set similarly against the grit and gravel of life, were to follow, in novels by other relatively young writers. I read most of them.

The band, expanded to a four-piece, began to rehearse in a barn on land attached to Pete's house. The huge garden was ringed by rhododendrons, with outhouses and pergolas which became sheathed in clematis and Russian vine in summer. Pete said they had awoken one morning to find a tramp sleeping there. When they stirred him he apologised and said he thought it was a park.

Pete told us to help ourselves to biscuits, tea, whatever was in the fridge. No, it didn't matter if we smoked or drank in the house; his mum wouldn't mind (his dad had died a few years earlier).

'We're liberals,' he joked. 'Anything goes!'

We were rehearsing one evening, unaware that Pete had arrived home from London where he'd accompanied Lauren to the airport. His mother came into the barn and motioned to me. The band stopped playing.

'Could I have a word?'

Grandad had an excitable mongrel dog called Smokie. We took him for a walk down the canal. The towpath ran alongside factory walls but after a mile or so it opened into an expanse of scrubland. On the other side of dust-blown bushes we came across a group of kids sitting on a ripped mattress. They had made a ramp by propping a door against an empty oil drum. They looked exhausted.

'We've been doing gymnastics,' said the smallest.

He had very short hair and a dirty face. He was wearing shorts and a pair of baggy grey socks. Grandad sat down on a wooden crate.

'How do you do gymnastics?' he asked.

Another boy, standing away from the others and holding a stick loosely in his hand, said:

'See that there? Well, what we do is, right, we get that oil drum, put the door on it, run up it and dive onto that mattress. You've just got to watch for them springs sticking out. They're really sharp.'

Grandad asked if he'd show him how it was done.

'I can't,' he said solemnly. 'I'm just too knackered.'

The little kid spoke up.

'I'll show you, mister.'

He ran a few yards from the ramp and began preening himself, bowing and holding his hands in the air as if accepting applause.

'Stop showing off,' shouted one of the others.

He made a couple of false starts and set off. Smokie hadn't expected this sudden movement and ran over, barking and jumping. The kid panicked and kicked out.

'He's going to bite me. Get him, mister, get him off.'

Grandad shouted Smokie over, grabbing his collar and holding him tightly at his side.

'You're all right now, son,' he said. 'He won't bite you. He gets excited, that's all.'

The boy took his run-up. His body fell stiffly on the mattress and he bounced. Grandad laughed and clapped. The kid pulled a funny face, sticking out his tongue at the others. When he came back over, he moved to stroke Smokie but stopped a few feet away:

'Is he friendly?'

'Yeah, he loves kids.'

'Not for his tea, I hope!'

Smokie licked the back of the boy's hand and left a wet trail.

'Yuk. Will I get germs now?'

'He thought you needed a wash.'

The other kids began stroking Smokie and tickling under his chin. Smokie settled and Grandad let him loose. The kids were scampering about, beckoning Smokie to follow them and stopping in their tracks to test his reflexes. They threw sticks and he chased after them, tripping over himself and skidding in the dust. After a while he lay down panting, his tongue hanging out of his mouth. The smallest kid lay beside Smokie and turned to face him. He *reached out as if about to give him a hug. Smokie bolted upright and shook fiercely. A few specks of dust went into the kid's face.*

'Hey, I didn't want a shower,' he yelled.

Pete's mum had heard noises in his room. He'd not answered her shouts and she'd been unable to open the door. I knocked quietly and pushed. Papers and books were jammed at the bottom. I shoved them aside and they scraped on the polished wooden floor. I switched on the light. Drawers had been levered from runners and thrown to the floor. Books and records were everywhere. A magazine was torn into shreds lying next to bits of cardboard. I looked closer and saw that they were plane tickets and a passport, scattered like petals in a storm. He had also attacked his tape collection, unspooling lengths that had fallen like the guts of a dead animal over the bed and around the room.

Pete was lying face down in the middle of the bed. I spoke his name and wasn't sure if I heard a murmur or not. I sat next to him and reached over, patting his shoulder. The denim of his shirt was soft, the flesh beneath sinewy. I persuaded him to sit up in the bed. He was tearful but brushed away the dampness with the palm of his hand. He said he was fine now and would clean up the room and then reassure his mum it wouldn't happen again; it was the pressure of being apart from Lauren. I pointed out that he'd ripped up his airline tickets and passport, which would make it even more difficult to see her.

'I know,' he said.

'Why have you done that?'

He looked about him, at the mess of it all, as if surprised to find it there, like he was taking the blame for someone else's actions.

'I don't know.'

The novel *Saturday Night and Sunday Morning* by Alan Sillitoe, published in 1958, matched the ferocity of *Look Back in Anger* but there seemed to be a *point* in the fury of Arthur Seaton, the principal character. He'd identified the enemy, at least: 'They [employers, the government] rob you right, left and centre. After they've skinned you dry you get called up to the army and get shot to death.' Not that Seaton was prepared to align himself: 'I'm me and nobody else. Whatever people say I am, that's what I'm not . . . I'm a bloody billy-goat trying to screw the world, and no wonder I am, because it's trying to do the same to me.'

Arthur Seaton was the first literary celebration of fag-end charisma coalesced with sexuality and savvy. He was further cemented in the nation's consciousness through his portrayal by Albert Finney in the film, for which Sillitoe wrote the screenplay. By 1961 the book had sold more than a million copies in the UK, for which, in the Pan paperback edition, Sillitoe received a royalty rate of a penny per copy.

'I remember at one point having £4,000, which was quite a whack in those days. I didn't really give a toss about the money as long as I could go on writing,' said Sillitoe.

The novel affected me hugely. Fresh from reading it, I tried on Arthur Seaton as I might a new coat. The sloshing down of pints at the weekend in pubs similar to those frequented by Seaton, from the Derby Inn to the Merry Weaver in Rochdale – smoky, loud, packed – suddenly had a higher standing. I adopted the belligerent, defiant, sure-of-myself attitude, too: the world kept at arm's length, nothing and no one allowed in, just me and the beer. As I supped, I was scripting it as if living two lives in one: me and this Arthur Seaton bloke, a part share of the same body and brain. At every step and with every pint, I was making imaginary notes for future novels. It didn't last. By the third or fourth hangover, I'd had enough. Friends were beginning to ask if I was all right, that I didn't seem myself.

I hadn't been seeking a role model in Arthur Seaton – he

wasn't particularly likeable – but my *becoming* him was both testimony to an absorption in reading and an obsessive nature. I was relatively shy and undemonstrative so it suited my personality to occasionally adopt characters from books. I effectively became them without anyone usually noticing and it set loose a safe and secret internal dialogue and world of imagination. And if I wasn't a particular character at any given time, I was constantly narrating my own novel, visualising what I was thinking as if written down – how best to describe events, people and feelings. There later came a point, sometime in my thirties, when I stopped doing this, considering it juvenile and a futile reverie. I remember the sadness of the first day I felt this way. A little of the hurt and loss has remained; as if I'd given in to getting old.

A year after the publication of *Saturday Night and Sunday Morning*, Sillitoe repeated its success with *The Loneliness of the Long Distance Runner*. He made Colin Smith, the novella's anti-hero, a cauldron of resentment. His hostile tongue is burning from the first page when he announces: 'Cunning is what counts in this life.' He is clear, always, that life is 'us' and 'them' with a tall fence between. The 'them' is the staff at Ruxton Towers, the borstal where Smith is sent for breaking into a bakery, but it could easily be the police, the school, the state – whatever stands in his way. Sillitoe draws poetry from the soil. He writes of 'phlegmy bits of sunlight' and Smith smelling 'green grass and honeysuckle' as he embarks on another early morning run. The borstal governor, meanwhile, is a 'half-dead gangrened gaffer'.

John Braine, another 'angry young man', turned to writing while suffering from tuberculosis. He mapped out *Room at the Top* at Grassington Hospital, a sanatorium of 200 beds where the sick were sent to breathe 'medicinal' air blown across the Yorkshire Dales. He was explicit about his approach to the book: 'To be shockingly original with your first novel, you don't have to discover a new technique: Simply write about people as they are and not as the predominantly liberal and humanist literary establishment believes that they ought to be.'*

Joe Lampton, the protagonist of *Room at the Top*, railed against the system but did not want to tear it down. He was aspirational, in search of 'an Aston Martin, 3-guinea linen shirts, a girl with a Riviera suntan'. While rooted amid the northern working class, the novel was a traditional morality tale: how many compromises were needed to reach the room at the top and could integrity survive the climb?

Two more novels of the same era also based in West Yorkshire were *Billy Liar* by Keith Waterhouse and *This Sporting Life* by David Storey. Waterhouse was raised on a council estate in Hunslet, an industrial district of Leeds. His father, a greengrocer, died when Waterhouse was four years old, leaving the family, in his own words, 'ridiculously, almost unbelievably, poor'. He left school at fourteen to become a clerk to an undertaker, an experience that provided material for *Billy Liar*. The main character in the novel, William Fisher, is a nineteen-year-old fantasist living with his parents and grandmother in the humdrum fictional town of Stradhoughton. He retreats to Ambrosia, an imaginary kingdom. Back in the real world, Billy is caught between the affections of three very different girls, Rita, Barbara and Liz. In the final scene, which differs significantly from the film version, he buys a ticket for the 1.35 a.m. train to London, where he plans to become a comedy scriptwriter. He walks from the waiting room to the ticket barrier with 'the sensation of a water-tap running in my stomach'. He doesn't board the train. He turns back and heads for home, relieved to be returning to Ambrosia.

*

* *How to Write a Novel* by John Braine, 1974.

David Storey, born in Wakefield and the son of a miner, wrote eight hours a day to 'replicate the rhythms of working-class life'. He had the idea for *This Sporting Life* after an incident during a rugby league match. Storey had signed for Leeds on £6 per week and was playing for the A team*:

> I was in the second row, with a player who was playing out his last days. At one moment the ball was at my feet and I realised that if I picked it up I'd get my face kicked. And I hesitated just that amount, and he didn't, and he got his face kicked. He came up with a very bloody mouth, not knowing what had happened to his teeth. He turned to me and said: 'You cunt.' The guilt induced by that was enormous, which was what prompted me to start writing about it.[†]

In the novel, Arthur Machin receives this very kick and the opening pages trace his search for a dentist willing to open the surgery out of hours and remove six damaged teeth. *This Sporting Life* was rejected by more than a dozen publishers before acceptance by Longmans, Green in 1960, when Storey was twenty-six years old. He had previously written six unpublished novels, working on them while travelling on the train from Wakefield to London, where he was studying art at the Slade[‡] before taking up a job as a supply teacher.

The work of the angry young men (or 'kitchen sink' writers, which broadened the classification to include excellent women writers such as Shelagh Delaney and Lynne Reid Banks) was

* The back-up team to the first team in rugby league.
† *Guardian*, interview 2004.
‡ Now the UCL Slade School of Fine Art.

heavy with dialogue and a sense of time and place, which made them ideal to transfer to film. A new generation of British film-makers, each under forty, had reached eminence and were keen to reflect the realism of the books. They also attracted the finest young actors of their day – Tom Courtenay, Albert Finney, Richard Harris and Julie Christie among them.

I read the books by each of the movement's main authors, approximately 150 titles. Generally, they relayed their lives, cloaking it flimsily as fiction. In simplistic terms, they wrote of childhood, first jobs, moving to London, marriage, parenthood, failing relationships, illicit affairs and divorces. There were occasional triumphs (*Saville* by David Storey, *The Jealous God* by John Braine and *The Desperadoes and Other Stories* by Stan Barstow, in particular) but few had the vim of the early material. They were fortunate to be of an era where publishers viewed their commitment to an author as career-long rather than a handful of books.

I recognised the settings and the people. A good deal of the appeal, however, was nostalgic. The principal characters all seemed to be, at the same time, both twenty and forty years old – burdened with energy and attitude but also already middle-aged and fixed in place. Much of it was dated: the sexual reticence, the deference to parents, the heavy industry, the schism between generations and the insularity of lives. I learned more about my mum and dad's world than I did mine.

CHAPTER TEN

Notices of job vacancies began to appear on the pin board in the common room at college. The geographical spread was wide, from Aberdeen to Plymouth, and it was assumed we would accept a position no matter where the newspaper was based or the salary. The notion that you might hold out for a job in or near your home town seemed to be viewed as conceited or even cheating, as if your first job was a type of national service, leaving your family and friends to spend two or three years at the *Pocklington Post* or *Falmouth Packet*.

I succumbed to this prevailing viewpoint and, after successfully completing the course, found myself on a train heading to Cardiff. I was due to start work at a news agency, joining a team that found stories to sell on to newspapers. The journey took almost five hours but passed quickly because I was absorbed in the John Steinbeck book *The Winter of Our Discontent*. I was giddy with the thrill of discovering an author new to me and was continually breaking off to anticipate his other books listed at the back, many with stirring titles: *To a God Unknown, Of Mice and Men, The Grapes of Wrath.*

Rain lashed against the train window, forming snakes of water. Tickets, please. Night fell. We are now approaching Cardiff Central. I was elsewhere, deep in the novel, reading about storekeeper Ethan Allen Hawley in New Baytown, on the coast in New York State, as he traded integrity by measures, persuaded by the everyday nature of growing corruption across the United States.

Maybe the book, in offering several exquisite hours of distraction, had blindsided me to what I was doing. I was homesick immediately, missing my parents, friends, girlfriend, band and books. The owner of the agency, a kindly, middle-aged man, placed me with Geoff, another young staff member, in a first-floor flat in a Victorian property. The villa stood tall by the roadside but was showing signs of age, scuff marks on the wall and threadbare carpet at the entrance. The flats were positioned at the end of short corridors and it reminded me of the layout and feel, though not as shabby, of the accommodation in *The L-Shaped Room* by Lynne Reid Banks: 'One of those gone-to-seed houses in Fulham, all dark brown wallpaper'. I had a few days of uncertainty and then, shiny bright, I resolved: I'm going home. I rang the college; they had insisted we kept in touch as we started our working life. The lecturer told me you had to push the boat out sometimes in life, everyone takes a while to settle, opportunities like this don't come along too often and no one said it would be easy, son.

I left Cardiff after five days, absolutely sure it was the right decision. On the last day, as I stared down from the bay window to the street below, watching workers fast-walk towards the city centre beneath spiky, leafless trees, I realised it was the first time I had seen Cardiff when it wasn't dark or raining.

I finished *The Winter of Our Discontent* on the journey home and, although the book itself has no particular relevance to Cardiff and what happened there, it is the single item with which I associate the whole episode. To merely look at the cover (the Pan version, which shows Hawley in his grocer's smock examining a handgun) is to be taken back — the ache for home, the indecisiveness, streets I didn't recognise, someone else's house, people I didn't know, everywhere unfamiliar and, most of all, the pointless 'challenge' of it all when, most likely, I'd find a job closer to home within a few weeks.

The boys each took turns jumping on the mattress, asking Grandad if he thought they had done a good dive. He gave them marks out of ten.

'That's an eight and a half or maybe a nine.'

One asked if I wanted a go but I said I was okay watching. I felt a bit shy. Smokie had befriended the little one and every time he wandered off between jumps, he followed.

'Your dog likes me, doesn't he?'

'I think you're his soul mate,' said Grandad.

'What's one of them?'

'You know, like a best friend. Would you like a dog of your own?'

'Course I would.'

'Do you want Smokie?'

'But he's your dog.'

'I know but you two seem best pals.'

'Really? Can I have him? Honest to God?'

The others had stopped jumping and were staring.

'If you promise to look after him, you can have him if you want.'

'Honestly?'

'Honestly.'

Grandad tied Smokie to the handle of the upturned door with his lead.

'When we're a long way off, let him go and our scent will have worn off. He'll stay with you then,' he told them.

They were open-mouthed except for the little one, who couldn't stop smiling and patting Smokie on the back. When we got up to leave, Smokie pulled hard and barked loudly. We could still hear him whimpering from about half a mile away. As we reached the point where the canal bank met the road, Smokie caught us up, panting and excited. The lead was dragging on the ground behind.

Two months after leaving Cardiff I was offered a job as a junior reporter at the *Middleton, Moston and Blackley Guardian*, five miles away in north Manchester, the area where I had lived as a boy. The pay was £81.85 per week; in Cardiff it had been £69.88 (I've kept the letters of employment). The office, previously a car showroom, was on a side street in Middleton town centre. I pressed the bell on the counter.

'Hello, I start work here today.'

I was led to the editor's office, a small box at the back of the building separated from the newsroom by a sliding door. He stood up. I thought he was going to salute.

'Hello, son. All bright-tailed and bushy-eyed, are we?'

Jack Crosby stared at me, making sure I'd got the joke. He was tall and uncannily similar to the actor Walter Matthau, with the same jowly, baffled expression.

'Yes.'

'Right then, let's get cracking. Oh, before we do – do you know what my ambition is?'

Had he got our roles mixed up? Wasn't the editor supposed to ask this of the trainee? Besides, he looked to be about fifty, possibly sixty; it was getting late for unfulfilled ambitions.

'Well,' he began. 'What would make me happy, wonderfully happy, would be a nice quiet job as a car park attendant in Ilfracombe, somewhere like that. Have you ever been? The car park is on the cliffs, with a little flight of steps to the beach so holidaymakers can trip-trap down with their picnic baskets. Beautiful little spot, it is.'

He stood up and began miming winding tickets from a roll, putting money in an imaginary bag tied to his waist.

'Remember, I'd have a proper coat on, like they wear. "Here you are, sir. Here's your change. There's some room by the bottom end, just past the Volvo. Hope the weather stays fine for you." Have you ever heard any Rachmaninov or Rimsky-Korsakov? [Talking to me now, not imaginary holidaymakers.] Piano Concerto No. 4. Have a listen — it will take you away from yourself to somewhere else, up with the gods.'

I joined a team of seven reporters, a deputy editor and Jack. The office was piled high with telephone directories and old copies of the paper. Along one side was a row of dented green metal filing cabinets containing cuttings of stories. The room was swathed in smoke; most of the staff had a pen in one hand, a cigarette in the other. Rattling typewriters caused the tables and floor to shake. Although a trainee, I did the same as everyone else, a mix of the mundane to the extraordinary. I covered the local magistrates' court, inquests and council meetings, and called on the police, fire and ambulance services.

'Anything for us?'

Most days there was 'nothing doing' but on others there was a lot of living and dying. I covered all manner of stories: young car thieves careering into a reservoir wall ('Three Dead in Horror Smash'); a fifty-three-year-old 'mother of four' finding her husband suspended from the loft by a rope ('Hanging Tragedy'); the secretary of the chrysanthemum society predicting a good turnout at the autumn show ('Hoping for a Blooming Success'); the Najib

Hamed Appeal raising cash to send six-year-old Najib, 'stricken by a rare cancer', to Disneyworld ('America Here I Come!'); and the head teacher at St Joseph's School revealing that intruders had caused extensive damage when they broke in and left the taps running in the toilets ('Vandals Wreak Havoc').

On one of my first trips to the magistrates' court, a lad I knew from school was in the dock. Mark Shepherd had attacked a sex offender while serving time at Strangeways prison. The court heard how he'd struck the victim over the head with a metal tray in the canteen, causing him to need fifty stitches. When the magistrates adjourned to consider their verdict, Mark beckoned me over. As I reached the dock, there was only Mark, a police officer and me in the court.

'How's it going?' he asked. 'Working for the paper, then?'

'Yeah, started last week.'

'Good on you, pal. You were always into writing and stuff at school, weren't you?'

I nodded. He was extremely polite and for those few seconds it was easy to forget he was a sociopath. His sentence was extended by six months.

Jack was a worrier. His greatest fear, and one he mentioned most days, was displeasing 'the directors'. He spoke of them as if they were sombre Dickensian characters with distended bellies and mutton chop sideburns, kicking orphans down the street. On the few times they visited from head office, I was surprised to find they were fairly young, calling everyone by their first name, interested in what we were doing. Another perpetual grumble from Jack was that it was better in the old days when you had time to check facts thoroughly, telling a good tale to whatever length you wanted. It was all bloody wallpapering now, he said, sticking in free puffs from PR companies in London, getting your ear bent on the phone by toffee-nosed girls with names like Pandora and

Henrietta. Recipe pages and gardening columns weren't journalism. Claptrap like that belonged in magazines. No, he said, people around here bought the *Middleton, Moston and Blackley Guardian* to read about their next-door neighbour growing giant sunflowers or their old schoolteacher getting caught in a public toilet with the manageress from the Co-op, trousers round his ankles.

I was often sent to review productions staged by amateur dramatic societies. They were usually poor but the worst was a rendition of *Viva Mexico*, a 'comedy musical in three acts', at the Simpson Memorial Hall, Moston. I was the only person under sixty in the audience. We were sitting on rickety chairs in the dusty upstairs room. The script made reference to 'young, handsome banditos' but these roles were played by four old blokes whose make-up looked to have been applied with a blunderbuss. They coughed and wheezed through the dance routines, which amounted to turning around slowly, holding a sombrero over their heads and shouting *olé*. During the interval I won a raffle prize, 'kindly donated by one of the loyal and committed patrons of the Players' – a length of fuse wire wrapped around an H-shaped piece of cardboard. The old folk clapped and woo-wooed as if I'd won free drinks for life.

A hushed conversation between Mum and Dad in our living room usually meant that Grandad was ill again; he'd had one of his regular breakdowns. His restlessness was quelled finally by medication. Heavy doses of tranquillisers left him muddled and sleepy, old before his time, nodding gently in response to unspoken questions. His body shape changed. The tautness about his arms, shoulders and trunk left him and the flesh turned soft and pulpy. The energy was gone, the prize fighter punched out. The faces of his family revolved as if on a carousel and he struggled to match the name with the face and the relationship.

'What are you to me?' I'd ask playfully.
'We're brothers.'
He was so sure of himself, he often added:
'Don't ask daft questions.'

I was lucky, despite Jack's laments, to enter local journalism when it was still a relatively buoyant industry. The paper was thick each week with classifieds and adverts from traders, estate agents and car dealers – businesses which, a decade or so later, defected en masse to the internet. We were well staffed, and even had a de facto 'rest day' every Thursday. This was the day the paper was printed and, with Jack out of the office overseeing this, we spent most of the time drinking tea and chatting.

If Jack returned early he'd embrace the relaxed Thursday mood and invite you into his office. This was usually so he could pontificate on his favourite subjects, which he thought marked him out as cultured: opera, wine, Latin and, as I had discovered on that very first day, classical music. I was summoned one afternoon and he pointed to a small badge on his lapel that read 'Opera North'.

'You won't know much about opera, will you?' he said. 'Me and the wife went to see *Béatrice et Bénédict* last night by Hector Berlioz – have you heard of it? And him?'

I said I hadn't and, desperate to avoid fifteen minutes of him telling me every detail, I blurted:

'Nice badge.'

'I know. It was fastened onto my lapel by a very, er, very, er, a . . . by a . . .'

He had been pulled up a few times for his non-PC, out-of-date phraseology and was struggling to find the vocabulary acceptable in this modern age (1983). As a newspaper editor, and one who paraded his mastery of grammar, it should have been a relatively easy task. He was still struggling ten seconds after starting the sentence. He finally made it:

'. . . by a bosom-titted girl.'

I was delighted when Jack asked me one week to 'put the paper to bed' – overseeing the final part of the production, making sure the stories fitted on each page and inserting any late news items. This was done at the offices of the *Rochdale Observer*, the principal newspaper in the group. When I arrived, the 'proof' pages were on boards around the room. The compositors were sticking down stories, breaking off to shout over to me that an article was too long or short for the allotted space. I'd ask them to cut a particular sentence or paragraph or, if a story needed extending, add a word or two as a text break. I had to sign off each finished page before it was taken to be printed. This was a considerable responsibility and I had quickly earned respect. I was nineteen years old. I was feeling pleased with myself. A phone rang. One of the compositors answered. It was Jack on the other end of the line. He must have asked if he could speak to me.

'Never heard of him,' said the compositor.

Jack decided that the best way to help locate me in a room of about thirty busy people was to summon all his powers of description. The comp put down the phone and bellowed:

'Is there a little lad here wearing glasses?'

I had one or two chats with Jack where I said the paper should appeal more to younger people and regenerate our readership. My idea for a pop column was met with frostiness. He remained fixed on the page he was laying out, the marriage section, scribbling where the pictures were to be inserted. I tried one last gambit:

'It'll take up a fair bit of space.'

He put down his pen, leaned back and tapped his metal ruler on the edge of the desk. Nothing made him happier than filling space; it relieved the pressure of having to find material, whether news pieces, features or photographs. The deal was done.

'Could I have the copy nice and early each week?'

I had my pop column. Jack named it 'Pop Focus' and accompanied the text with a ghastly stock illustration of a rocker in a leather jacket playing a V-shaped guitar. I wrote to record companies requesting review copies. The first to arrive was the double live album *Nocturne* by Siouxsie and the Banshees. I had no idea of protocol and, for a few weeks, imagined that I would have to return it. As each day passed and I didn't receive a phone call or letter from the label, I realised it was mine to keep, once reviewed. This felt an incredible privilege.

'So these records are yours now, then?' asked Pete. 'It's the kind of thing you dream of when you're a kid.'

At his best, Pete always maintained this childlike view, pleased with the world and thankful for relatively small offerings. With all the new releases I shared with him, his mix tape collection was ever expanding.

I wrote to Rough Trade and about a week later received the single 'What Difference Does It Make?' by The Smiths. My record player was on top of a chest of drawers in my bedroom. I had to stand by it to put a record on the turntable or pick up the arm and play it again. I stood there for nearly two hours, playing the song and its B-side, 'Back to the Old House', repeatedly. The next day, I bought the band's previous two singles, 'Hand in Glove' and 'This Charming Man', disappointed that I had let them pass me by on release.

The connection I felt with The Smiths, and Morrissey in particular, was remarkable. As is often said of our heroes, it felt as if he had lived a life parallel to mine and was not only reporting back from it but kneading the highest art from unlikely material. This was made more poignant by the fact that for some time the distance between our growing-up homes (Blackley and Stretford) had been a mere eight miles. We had walked the same, or similar, districts:

When you walk without ease,
on these streets where you were raised
I had a really bad dream
It lasted twenty years, seven months, and twenty seven
    days*

Morrissey had gone to what he referred to as the 'sadistic and barbaric' St Mary's Technical Modern School, where, in five years, 'education had no effect on me whatsoever, apart from in an adverse sense'.[†] He left school without any qualifications but passed three O levels at Stretford Technical College, one in sociology. He referred to himself as a 'back-bedroom casualty' – the place where he read and wrote avidly, and how this was viewed as 'an illness' among the working-class community in which he was raised. He had wandered a great deal, as I had with Grandad, nowhere in particular but thinking while drifting, across wasteland and cemeteries. I knew intimately of all he spoke and sang about.

Occasionally Grandad rediscovered the fidgetiness of old and he'd begin hunting for the door. If he found one unlocked he'd trip out and roam. He no longer recognised the confines of paths and roads and stumbled through gardens, across parks, over barely accessible woodland. The police or a family member would find him, often late at night. We'd recognise his hunched form and the shuffling gait that the drugs had brought on. He was conspicuous in his suit, clambering through thick grass, tree branches catching his head and causing small cuts on his forehead. He was sunburnt in the summer, his skin pinky and sore. In winter he was shivering, his clothes sodden.
    'There he is, over there.'

---

* 'Never Had No One Ever', from *The Queen is Dead*.
[†] Interview with Nicky Horne on *Ear Say*, Channel Four, July 1984.

Grandad would climb into the car and sit on the back seat next to me and my sister. Small twigs, bracken and leaves would be around the bottom of his trousers, his socks rolled down to the ankles.

'We've been worried sick about you. Where have you been?' asked Mum, almost as if she believed he'd found the lucidity of old out there.

Morrissey's situation differed from mine in that he had an ally: his mother, Elizabeth. She was just twenty-one when he was born, a factor he mentioned in interviews by way of explaining their closeness. She worked as a librarian and was an animal rights activist and vegetarian. Unlike his teachers, she recognised at a very young age his sensitivity, originality and passion, and nurtured it assiduously. She recommended scores of authors, from Charles Dickens to Oscar Wilde, and played him music by relatively obscure figures ranging from the Italian-American soul singer Timi Yuro, to chart performers Marianne Faithfull, Cilla Black and Sandie Shaw. She encouraged his individuality and sanctioned his reluctance to succumb to a conventional job. She ferried meals, paper, notebooks, novels and a typewriter into that back bedroom. In the various biographies of The Smiths and Morrissey it is suggested that she over-focused on her son to compensate for her failing marriage to Peter Morrissey; they separated when Morrissey was seventeen.

The heavy boot of conformity was crushing in the early 1980s. Unemployment was high and self-worth low, especially among young people. Accept what you're offered, boy, no matter how measly. How lucky you are, was the message. And then Morrissey appeared, fully formed, this lanky, lisping hero, dressed in a big girl's blouse, wearing National Health glasses, beads around his neck, warbling and grunting and singing quite beautifully on *Top of the Pops*.

The Smiths were perfect in every way. The music was all of everything: sad, euphoric, clever and catchy. The lyrics, funny and intelligent and poetic. They were also direct and comprehensible, evoking wonderful imagery while offering homilies to self-empowerment and self-belief. Morrissey endorsed the outsider, the quiet-but-clever kid, and he made him cool. He had none of the reticence and deference that is painted heavily upon the working class. He dared to have his say and did so eloquently and brilliantly, sometimes proffering an outrageously spiteful view but then falling coquettish, twinkling his sapphire-blue eyes, pursing his lips, smiling a smile of which he knew the power and beguiling effect. The words he uttered were drawn from the end of the rainbow – 'charming', 'elegant', 'marvellous'; no one had spoken this way since Oscar Wilde had opened a crate of ale with Max Beerbohm and Reggie Turner a century earlier.

When I saw Morrissey, either on stage or in interviews, I thought: I could be that. Many others clearly felt the same, which is one of the reasons The Smiths were so popular. We were kidding ourselves. His incredible talent aside as a singer (and he is a fantastic singer, no matter what they say) and lyricist, we couldn't *be* Morrissey principally because we weren't brave enough to be so true to ourselves, so sure of ourselves. To him, whether innate or instilled by Mother Betty, it came naturally, easy. He owned himself wholly, unapologetically, and by doing so he changed lives, reclaiming confidence and art and culture for the masses and wreaking savage revenge on the naysayers and the conformists. We could dream and we could win!

The news cycle of the year quickly became routine at the paper: Christmas fairy (a kid from a local school decked out in clip-on wings and lifted up in a small crane) switching on the town-centre lights; Pace Egg play on the market car park at Easter; droughts or downpours in summer (and at least one teenager drowning in an abandoned mill pond or reservoir); Halloween parties; civic bonfire; Remembrance Sunday; anti drink-driving campaigns and then, again, that Christmas fairy.

'Here you go,' said Jack. 'Do me a couple of hundred words to go with the pictures.'

He passed me the black and whites of the little girl-fairy waving from the cherry picker, making her way up to the illuminated stars, candles, donkeys and Santas strung across the lamp posts outside the Arndale Centre. The rain had made the pictures a little fuzzy; everyone had their coats on and hoods pulled up. I wondered if I'd get away with it. I dared myself. I paraphrased Morrissey's lyrics from 'William, It Was Really Nothing' in my intro to the story: 'The rain fell hard on a humdrum town but nothing could drag down the fun at the annual switch-on of the Middleton Christmas lights.' It ran in the paper as written.

Almost everyone became at least a little bit Morrissey. I bought a flowery shirt and shaped my hair into a quiff; this was curious because the quiff belonged to my dad's generation and had always been viewed as faintly comical. And here I was now, at the mirror with the Brylcreem. I was also trying to bring a little bit of Ian McCulloch (of Echo & the Bunnymen) to the sculpting. At discos I danced like Morrissey; we all did. The knees were bent slightly; the arms slowly falling, windmilling or held aloft as if pointing; the occasional thrust of the hip and then the whole body twirling. No one had danced like this before and now everyone was doing it, as if it was innate and had been waiting within us all along.

I wasn't much of a guitarist but hearing Johnny Marr play made me approach the instrument in a completely different way. In Untermensch I could bang out a rhythm by strumming ferociously but, remarkably, I had never thought to pick individual strings. Marr did this extremely fast and with panache, and it forged that distinctive Smiths sound known as 'jangly'. Within two practices I had ditched the barre chords and fuzzbox and, such was the change in sound, we renamed the band the Monkey Run.

Unlike many, I didn't view The Smiths as dour or self-pitying. In every song, no matter the frankness of its message, there was a comeback or a joke, a love of life. And I adored (a very Morrissey word) the attention to detail: the branding of the sleeves with their literary, cinema and pop star portraits, the font used on these sleeves and on the labels in the middle of the vinyl. Everything counted.

Most of all, with Morrissey, I had discovered someone with similar taste. We had read the same books, watched the same films. He brazenly and extensively picked out lines or couplets and inserted them into his lyrics. On that very first song I had heard by The Smiths, 'What Difference Does It Make?', Morrissey was paraphrasing Ray Smith, the protagonist in *The Dharma Bums* by Jack Kerouac, and also borrowing lines from Shelagh Delaney ('The devil will make work for idle hands to do' – *Sweetly Sings the Donkey*).

He clearly had a pen and notepad by his side at all times because films, especially ones from where Morrissey might harvest material, were rarely shown on television and very few people had video players in the early 1980s* – they were extremely expensive and so desirable that people often put a plaster over the red 'on/off' light at night so burglars didn't target the house. In order to discover lines such as 'a jumped-up pantry boy who never knew his place' ('This Charming Man') and 'All those

* 10 per cent of the UK population had a video recorder in 1982 and 30 per cent by 1985.

people, all those lives, where are they now?' ('Cemetry Gates'), he was watching, presumably late at night or in the mid-afternoon (which was when non-mainstream films were often shown), *Sleuth* (1972) and *The Man Who Came to Dinner* (1942) while scribbling frantically.

As his fame grew, this kleptomania became more manifest; it appeared as if almost every song featured a borrowed line or two, sometimes a complete theme. Not that it mattered, of course. He was doing the research on our behalf, allowing us to use The Smiths as a portal to all these esoteric but interesting books, films and plays. Who else was doing as he did? Who could match his commitment and passion?

When he went missing, Grandad had no understanding of how far he had walked. To him, each step was the first. After finding him, over the next few days his muscles would stiffen and he'd struggle to leave the armchair. He'd complain that he was aching but couldn't recall what had caused it.

Police brought him home once and said they'd found him in a block of flats, trapped in a lift. One of his legs was covered in bruises.

'We think he got it stuck fast in the lift door, love,' the officer told Gran.

'Did you, John?'

'Why are you fussing about all this?'

'Because your leg's black and blue.'

'It's not.'

'It is.'

It was.

I was so consumed by Morrissey, so trusting of his taste, that I followed many of his recommendations. I had already read a good number of the literary works, among them Shelagh

Delaney's (he plundered heavily her play, *A Taste of Honey*), but I checked out with added enthusiasm Elizabeth Smart,* Jack Kerouac, Noël Coward, John Betjeman, Oscar Wilde, John Keats and W.B. Yeats.

He appeared extremely conversant with contemporary feminist literature, possibly under the counsel of his mother or, more likely, his close friend, the cut-up artist Linder Sterling. In interviews he mentioned two sturdy books written in the mid-1970s specifically about women in the film industry: *Popcorn Venus* by Marjorie Rosen and *From Reverence to Rape: The Treatment of Women in the Movies* by Molly Haskell. These, and other similar books (*The Handbook of Nonsexist Writing* by Casey Miller and Kate Swift), were cited by Morrissey in the *NME*; it was an interesting statement of self. He *may* have read them or merely leafed through them, or they could have been the nearest books at hand. Perhaps he was being playful; he often contradicted himself or was mischievous in interviews. Most likely, he was chiselling out the persona, the public branding of Morrissey, hoping to be perceived as radical, enlightened, the sensitive boy holding high the placard on behalf of womankind. By anyone's definition, these books were *heavy going* and very few were reading them in Manchester, unless advised by their lecturers.

The Wedding Present were a band I featured regularly in 'Pop Focus'. Although the group had formed in Leeds, where each member was studying, David Gedge (singer/guitarist) and Pete Solowka (guitar) were from Middleton. I first interviewed David at his parents' house. He was amiable and superficially easy-going but, clearly, extremely focused and determined, as we all were in and around bands at that time. If everything was going well in our

* I would later publish a book by her son, Christopher Barker.

various groups, it was a shrug of the shoulder, a nonchalant, we-got-lucky shrug, but if the gigs and momentum were stalling, the panic, the frustration, grew to the point of being overwhelming. The prize – recording your own music, acclaim, touring the world, radio airplay – seemed within comparatively easy reach. A good review in the *NME* or a few plays on John Peel usually had the effect of attracting agents, promoters, managers and record labels to bands and often, literally within weeks, a career in music was launched. It's what we all wanted.

The NCTJ lecturers had been unequivocal about our career path: two or three years on a local weekly newspaper and then a move to a daily, where the five or six deadlines each week (few published on a Sunday) presented a greater challenge.

I moved to the *Oldham Evening Chronicle*. Despite being only six miles from Rochdale, I had barely visited the town before. I knew it best from scenes in the film version of *A Kind of Loving*, almost all of them swathed in fog. Vic Brown (played by Alan Bates) was shot in various locations in Oldham – by the allotments at the rear of Oldham Edge; crossing the iron bridge near the railway sidings at Mumps and dashing along the cobbles of Rock Street, holding close the lapels of his overcoat to shut out the cold.

That had all happened in the early 1960s, but the town and the paper still had the feeling of a dreary monochrome long-ago. The office, I quickly discovered, was staffed by malcontents, especially the aged subeditors who might have carried knives as much as pens, such was their hostility. Soon after I'd started there I became aware of someone behind me, his shadow falling over my typewriter. He threw down the copy I had submitted about an hour earlier.

'Did you *go* to school?' he thundered.

The newsroom was arranged into two rows of reporters, each

at a typewriter. They could all see this playing out. I asked him what was wrong.

'You can't fucking spell "restaurant", that's what's wrong.'

I apologised and returned to the story on which I was working. This was a mistake. I should have got out of my chair, faced him and said I was sorry I had spelled the word 'restaurant' incorrectly but, in future, if I were to make a similar mistake, he should inform me in a civil manner and certainly not humiliate me in front of my colleagues. I should then have walked across to the news editor who had witnessed this and ask that, next time, would he consider defending his young reporting team from these unnecessarily spiteful attacks. Over the two miserable years I was at the paper, I learned that bullies prosper only when given the consent of the bullied. I should have stuck up for myself.

The news editor, face set to gloom, was ever eager to crush enthusiasm and initiative. He was moody and this acted as an internal weather system for the office: if he was happy (which was infrequent) we could all bathe in the sunshine of his joy, but if he was morose our working days were spent under an umbrella. I think he had a particular dislike of me. Soon after starting at the paper, my girlfriend ended our four-year relationship. She'd met someone at work that 'she just had to be with'; they were married within six months. I wasn't sleeping well – perhaps he detected a low mood in *me* and felt I wasn't dedicated to the job.

The Smiths released the album *The Queen is Dead* and, again, it felt as if Morrissey had spied on my life. 'I Know It's Over' was the song of the break-up and 'There Is a Light That Never Goes Out' was the recovery and the start of a new relationship. At this point, the Monkey Run were at their most successful. Our single, 'I Want the Blood of a Civil Servant', had been regularly played by John Peel. We'd recorded a session for BBC Radio 1 and supported the Stone Roses* on a delirious night in Manchester. We had also forged a tenuous link with The Smiths, featuring a photograph of Morrissey (with his permission) on our second single, 'Falling Upstairs',† released on our own label, Intense Records. Maybe I wore my happiness too brightly and it was this that irked the news editor.

When he reached into the past for his stories, Grandad often came to streets and people long gone. One of his favourite subjects was their old neighbours, the McGurrans. They were always swearing and fighting, 'knocking seven bells out of each other'.

'The women were worse than the fellas,' he said. 'Ma McGurran would be waiting at the back door for Paddy. He was five feet nowt but, bloody hell, if he thumped you, Christ you'd know about it. Anyway, he's coming round the corner half-cut, she's going up the bloody wall and there's three kids crying because they've had the last of the biscuits he's pinched from Crumpsall Biscuit Works. All hell breaks loose and he's trying to throw her in the river and she's screaming for the police. Next morning they're right as rain, larking about in the backyard, singing and blowing kisses to one another over the washing like a pair of lovebirds.

'Paddy used to sit with me in the back yard, having a cup of tea and playing his penny whistle. He only knew two bloody songs

---

* The International Club, Manchester, on Friday, 26 February 1988. Ticket price: £3. There was an element of strong-arm surrounding the Stone Roses but the band members were friendly and supportive; Ian Brown shared his special throat 'medicine' with our singer, Jim, who had a heavy cold. We played a solid gig ('barnstorming' according to *Sounds*) but the Stone Roses were exhilarating.

† Available on YouTube.

– "Come Out, Ye Black and Tans" and this awful hymn, "I Watch the Sunrise", which would set him off crying, getting all soppy about Ireland. He was mard,* really, like a lot who let on that they're tough guys.'

Many of my ideas for articles were quashed or I'd be told to do a 'blob par' – basically a few lines of copy. I resorted to getting by, watching the clock, wishing for the weekend. One day, I received a tip-off that revived my enthusiasm. I was told a suspected war criminal was living in Oldham. I did some research in my own time which, in pre-internet days, meant knocking on doors, consulting the electoral roll and perusing telephone directories. I found out his name, that he was either Ukrainian or Lithuanian, and where he lived, within a few streets.

Unusually for a regional newspaper, the *Chronicle* rarely put local stories on the front page, preferring to lead with national news. I was sure my forthcoming piece would instigate a change in policy, for one edition at least. I briefed the news editor and he nodded, not making eye contact. I asked if I could be taken 'off diary' (relieved of any scheduled jobs) for the afternoon to 'nail' the piece. He agreed. After lunch, I slipped on my jacket, put my notebook and pen in my pocket and slid my chair under the desk. I'd told one or two colleagues about the story and they looked over; one gave me a thumbs up – this was a big one. The news editor noticed and beckoned me to his desk.

'Don't piss yourself in all your excitement, kidder,' he said.

I didn't interview the man but managed to write a piece based on information from his daughter, neighbours and contacts

---

* Mard is northern English slang for someone considered to be delicate, easily frightened.

I had at *Searchlight*, an anti-fascist organisation. My story ran on page twelve without a byline. The episode made me realise I had to leave the paper. The frustration and sense of demoralisation tired me out and left me unable to concentrate. I had stopped buying or reading books. I'd set aside time and start reading but, a few pages in, like clouds drifting across the sun, thoughts of work, the exasperation, came to mind.

In the week I began looking for a job elsewhere, the news editor wrote a profile piece on the new leader of the council. It was witty, intelligent, well schemed, every sentence happily married to the next. He was a miserable sod but he could write. I shared this view with another young reporter.

'That's the problem with this lot,' he said. 'They're all pretty talented, or used to be, but they've hung around here for too long. They've all got bitter and twisted. Old Tom, the sub – he was a friend of Cary Grant! He interviewed him years ago in Manchester and they've stayed in touch ever since. No wonder he's pissed off, subbing stories about a new lollipop man starting at Grotton or a chip pan fire in Derker.'

I realised that I was among grown-up Billy Liars – men (for they were almost all men) who hadn't got on that train to London or anywhere else out of Oldham. And they didn't have Ambrosia as a fallback.

At least once a month, usually when we were out walking, Grandad would ask if I wanted to hear a poem. It didn't matter whether I did or not, really. He'd start:

> *There's a one-eyed yellow idol to the north of Khatmandu,*
> *There's a little marble cross below the town;*
> *There's a broken-hearted woman tends the grave of Mad*
>   *Carew,*
> *And the Yellow God forever gazes down.*

He'd recite all eleven four-line verses.

How could he remember scores of words and yet, an hour or so earlier, he'd asked whether I was his brother and guessed that the year was 1958?

'He was a Manchester lad. He lived in a little terraced house in Hyde Grove, Ardwick Green.'

He told me this every time he recited the poem. I didn't mind; it was lovely hearing him speak.

'Who was that?' I asked, knowing the answer.

'James Milton Hayes. He fought with the Manchester Regiment in the First World War. He was a normal lad – his dad was a gas fitter. He wrote it for the music hall and became an actor himself. He was a bloody fool, though.'

'Why?'

'He was too humble. He told everyone it wasn't a proper poem and this meant they all took the mickey afterwards, doing what they call spoofs. He should have kept his mouth shut, passed it off as clever-arse. That's what a toff would do.'

Me and Pete decided we'd rent a house together. In cities, especially in and around university areas, the notion of two young people of the same gender living together was perfectly normal. In Rochdale, especially at that time, we were viewed with extreme suspicion.

'Two lads in the same house, what's that all about?' asked one landlord.

The hysteria over AIDS was at its height and, despite reassurances that it was extremely difficult to catch, landlords were worried.

'You're not a couple of rear admirals, are you?' asked Fred Worsley, whose firm had about fifty rental properties dotted around town.

I told him we weren't and, to my shame, dropped my voice to a deeper register as I added, 'Definitely not', as if emphasising my manliness and, therefore, heterosexuality.

'How do I know you're telling the truth?' he asked.

For a second, I wondered if I should fetch my girlfriend to vouch for my straightness. Or had he devised some sort of test of his own? This was stupid; I'd had enough.

'Look, we've both got jobs, we can afford to pay – do you have a house we can rent or not?'

He offered us one of the most squalid properties on his books, saying the rest had tenants 'pending'. The small terraced house had mould on the walls. Windowsills had rotted to the texture of cinder toffee; you could push a pencil through at certain points. I moved in but Pete barely did; he had so few possessions anyway. One evening, I put down my dinner plate and it soon had tiny insects crawling over it. We had to leave for a week while the house was fumigated.

Once we returned, I decided to make the place more homely. I had made my way through the books of Sylvia Plath and was besotted by a piece of prose called 'Cambridge Notes' from her anthology, *Johnny Panic and the Bible of Dreams*. I considered every word to be so truthful and beautiful that it deserved to be commemorated in more than just a book. I set about framing it. I had never done this before, or since, with a piece of written work (or much else – I have no artistic ability). I smeared light-blue paint onto paper, set multiple photo-copied images of Plath around the edges (à la Andy Warhol) and laid the text in the middle. The piece begins, 'What I fear most is the death of the imagination . . .' and ends '. . . I must be stoic till then.'

I hung the picture on the front room wall, next to Pete's poster from *Paris, Texas* (his favourite film). In my every house move since, this Sylvia Plath montage has accompanied me. I put it in a place of prominence to force myself to stop and linger, take it all in. Look and learn. See that every word is earning its keep but also sparked hot with mood and meaning. And it is also a summary of self (my/our best self: inquisitive, searching) and a petition to keep on going this same way, to remain ravenous for more of everything. When people call round for the first time and ask what it is, why it is there, I tell them to read it and they'll understand.

Collyhurst flats were knocked down and the residents dispersed to various council estates in Manchester. The move worried Gran because they had lived in the flat for decades and, throughout everything, Grandad had always remembered his home address of 34 Regency Street. Most days, he spent an hour or so writing it down alongside his name on newspapers or bills, anything at hand.

After they moved I was trusted with teaching him the new address. Mum and Gran went shopping for the afternoon and left me to it.

'Grandad, you now live here – Kinmount Way.'

'Kinmount Way,' he echoed, nodding his head.

'Let's write it down.'

He jotted it down in lines one after another, 'Kinmount Way', again and again.

Applying a 1-2-3 rhythm to each syllable, I drummed it into him for about two hours and it seemed to be sticking.

'Where do you live, Grandad?'

'Kinmount Way – you've just told me.'

'That's right, Kinmount Way.'

This was easy.

I joined the *Halifax Evening Courier* to run its district office in Hebden Bridge, a valley town in the Pennines about 12 miles from Rochdale. This new job in a new town freed me from what I had become at Oldham – I would now speak my mind, stick up for myself.

Pete visited Lauren in the United States a few times, including an occasion when he made another suicide attempt. He'd arrived

210

there to discover she wanted an open relationship. She'd fallen in love with a poet from her home town. She was sure if Pete read his poems he'd understand. Back in England, Pete met Natasha, a nomadic, independent soul. She was the same age as him and wasn't so dim as to ask that he share her with a poet. He spent most nights at her place and, in the six months we rented the house, probably slept there about twenty times. Some of those nights, though, were special as various friends showed up waving cans of lager and bottles of wine. *The Queen is Dead* was on repeat and, for those few hours, we owned the world.

One weekday evening, we'd just finished tea and Pete said: 'Do you ever think what it would be like to have kids?'

I was twenty-two.

'Not really – do you?'

'I reckon it would be really good.'

I've often wondered why he said it, how it came to mind. I'd never heard anyone mention having kids before; it seemed so unselfish and mature, thinking of other little lives.

I felt Pete was at his best, his strongest, when we were together. Then one day everything changed. I came back from work and realised he was upstairs in bed. The door was closed to his room. I pushed it open. He lay face down on the bed. I could tell he wasn't asleep. On the floor were ripped-up concert tickets. They were for the Go-Betweens; we had talked excitedly about the forthcoming show for weeks.

'Pete, come on. I know you're awake.'

He didn't respond.

'Please, Pete, answer me.'

I had drawn him back after the tempest at his mother's, but not this time. I realised that my imagining I could always talk him round had been a vanity. His body was there next to me covered in a few sheets but he was somewhere else, drilled down deep below the house, into the soil and rock beneath, unreachable.

I cursed that he should suffer this, a sickness that blackened you all over until there was nothing left but a shell on a bed, stapled down fast. If only we could take turns, I thought, and pass it to one another like a medicine ball, making us leaden and tired but only until it was our turn to toss it aside. I stroked his hair. As I did, I imagined his smile; it was contagious, you had to smile back. You did so even to *think* of it, when you weren't with him. And his giddiness and fidgetiness. He could, at times, seem so light, as if made of air. But not today. I got up and closed the door quietly. I was hopeful, of course, but I wondered for how long someone could stand such pain.

CHAPTER ELEVEN

The Wedding Present became extremely popular, recording John Peel radio sessions and featuring regularly on the covers of music papers. I wrote to Omnibus Press, a music book specialist, and suggested I should write a book about the band. I received a reply that, as is often the case with life-changing occurrences, had a tone of supreme nonchalance. Chris Charlesworth, the commissioning editor whose name I had seen in dozens of rock books, wrote: 'Funnily enough, The Wedding Present were mentioned at a meeting this week as a band we might take a look at.' He asked me to submit a piece of about 1,000 words and finished: 'We'll take it from there.'

I did as requested and a few weeks later signed a contract to deliver the manuscript in four months, for which I received an advance of £2,500.* At the time, my weekly wage at the paper was about £300. I handed in my notice at the *Courier*. I had been there just over a year. As much as I enjoyed the job, I had made a covenant with myself, almost from reading my first book: I would one day become an author. I left local newspaper journalism with barely a glance over my shoulder. I could always return, so I thought.

As respite from Grandad's tutorial, I switched on the television. We watched a horse race on World of Sport.

 'Which one's ours?' he asked.

 'All of them,' I said, feeling chirpy.

 'Don't be bloody stupid,' he said. 'You can't back them all in the same race.'

 'You're right,' I said, rebuked. I waited a second or two.

 'Grandad.'

 'Yes.'

 'Where do you live?'

 'Kinmount Way,' he replied.

 Every four or five minutes I kept asking, unable to believe I'd got it through to him. I altered the question slightly.

 'Where are we?' I asked.

 'What do you mean, where are we?'

 'What's this address?'

 'Kinmount Way.'

 I went upstairs to use the toilet. On the way back, I looked through the window on the landing. I stopped in my tracks, unable to believe what I'd seen. There, fastened to the wall opposite, was a street sign and it read: Kinmount Walk. *I'd been teaching him*

---

* A publishing advance for a book is paid in three stages: on signing the contract, delivering the manuscript and publication.

Kinmount Way. I would now have to start all over again, though I wondered whether it was possible to make such a subtle reset. I was crestfallen.

'Where do you live, Grandad?' I asked, on returning to the living room.

'34 Regency Street, Collyhurst, Manchester.'

I split up the Monkey Run. As the principal hustler, the knock-backs were hurting too much and I was riven by jealousy seeing other bands secure greater success. Our early demo tapes had been engineered by Clint Boon and he drove the van to our BBC Radio 1 session. Within a year, his own group, Inspiral Carpets, with a sound not dissimilar to ours, were being played on daytime Radio 1 and signed to Mute Records, the respected independent label.

The snideness and downright hostility had become wearisome, too; everything always felt like a battle. At one venue I asked politely where we should store our equipment before sound-checking. 'On the stage, where do you fucking think?' was the reply from the promoter. Whenever we were the support act we were subject to bullying and piss-taking – it came with the territory. At another concert, the sound engineer deliberately sent squeals of shrieking feedback through the onstage monitors while we were setting up. The effect of this is formidable; it almost knocks you from your feet and causes immediate nausea, deafening you for the next two days or so – there goes the gig. I also felt, at twenty-four, that it was a cultural obligation to bow out. I couldn't imagine any of the post-punk generation carrying on much longer than their mid-twenties; it seemed to contradict the whole ethos. I was wrong, of course, and the 'rules' were altered or flouted to accommodate ageing. I should have known as much.

The day before I told the others of my decision, I went for a walk on the moors. At times of turmoil or confusion, Rochdale people often 'take to the moors'; there's a lot to recommend it.

As I set off, my body ached as if bruised by the vexation of it all, being so close but nowhere near – a few days after supporting the Stone Roses we had played to about thirty uninterested people in an upstairs room in a pub in Todmorden. All that effort, tapes sent out, photocopying press releases, lugging the gear, making lists of people to phone back. What was the point? I returned from the walk with a clear head. I was going to give my all to the writing.

Thank Yer, Very Glad, the biography of the Wedding Present, was a faithful account of the band's story until that point. The reviews were good and Chris Charlesworth invited me to London to discuss another commission. Everywhere was painted golden by an unusually bright spring sun. I sat on a bench in Soho Square. Pigeons cooed at my feet. The Spanish chestnut trees were starting to bud, small but bountiful smudges of light green across the branches. I was early and left the square to walk the streets, past people drinking cappuccinos at tables on the pavements, past theatres and restaurants, pubs and private members' clubs, sushi bars and strip joints. I could smell perfume and aftershave, garlic and coffee, and everywhere sparkly people were shouting from cars or mopeds and greeting one another, hugging tight. How long had this been going on, lives lived so free and easy? They knew nothing of this in Rochdale.

The reception area of Omnibus Press was wide and glass-fronted. A grand piano was next to the foam seats where I was asked to wait. Almost as if he'd been expecting my arrival, a thin, Hispanic-looking man appeared and began playing 'New York, New York'. I smiled at him and he nodded back. I thought at that very second: I will remember this for the rest of my life.

Charlesworth had an unusual hybrid of an accent. He'd been brought up in Yorkshire but had spent several years in the United States and now lived in London. He shook my hand.

'Have you heard of Marianne Faithfull?' he asked.

Everyone had heard of Marianne Faithfull. All the same, he ran through her incredible life story as if, that week, I'd had several offers to write biographies of cultural icons and he was on a mission to have me write Marianne Faithfull's ahead of the rest. He stressed that it would be a 'serious' book, published first in hardback and stretching to about 100,000 words. I would be granted an unusually long time – by Omnibus's standards – to complete it: six months (which is actually a very short period to complete a book of such length, requiring extensive research). I was flattered. I agreed.

I was too young to bring a personal perspective to Marianne's story and had no real awareness of her music or the times through which she'd lived. I was out of my depth. I began the research a year or so ahead of the introduction of the internet, which became widely available in the late summer of 1991. I treated the book as I would a (very) long news story and set about it industriously, combing directories for phone numbers, travelling to various locations – Norfolk, Reading, Ormskirk, London – anywhere with a link to Marianne, no matter how tenuous. I read voraciously about the 1960s, probably more than fifty books in total. I called on people unannounced. I walked down the street where Marianne had grown up. I spoke to her former neighbours. I met people in cafés and pubs. I spent a pleasant few hours walking the grounds of the peculiar Braziers College in Ipsden, Oxford ('a school of integrative social research'), chatting with her father, Glynn Faithfull. I sat on the grass in the grounds of her school, St Joseph's. I stood in the car park at the Progress Theatre in Reading and imagined it was 1960 and thirteen-year-old Marianne might appear from among the privet hedges and houses, on her way to rehearsal with the youth group.

Pete took a job as a warden at an isolated youth hostel in the Lake District. I visited for a party. He was fit from running and cycling and appeared to have embraced the responsibility of the role. It was extremely remote, though. When the last light was switched off at the hostel, no other could be seen in any direction. Pete said he didn't mind; he wasn't lonely. He had his favourite videos to watch – *Paris, Texas* and *Repo Man*, and his cassette tapes. *Tallulah* by the Go-Betweens had been on repeat most of the winter and he was still playing the first album by Happy Mondays.

'Manchester is really taking off,' he said. 'All those bands we used to see at the Boardwalk are getting raved about in the *Guardian*.'

A few weeks later, on a Sunday evening, my dad shouted upstairs to me that Geoff, Pete's brother, was on the phone. Geoff told me he had some very bad news. Pete had hanged himself at the hostel. He was twenty-five years old. Before the act, he had destroyed everything he owned: photographs, books, letters, records – as if it wasn't enough to die, he also had to remove from the world all evidence that he had existed.

Grandad began following Gran everywhere. He was a yard behind, stopping when she did, looking in the same direction. If she went to the toilet he grew fretful, wanting to know her whereabouts. He couldn't dress properly any more and sometimes put his vest over his shirt, his shoes on the wrong feet. Gran made it one of her many duties to dress him impeccably. She was with him all the time, sometimes mildly scolding. She reminded him to wear two socks: one on each foot, please. The simulation of normality was a tribute to her devotion.

He began to go into hospital regularly. The doctors were vague when Mum and Gran expected something categorical. They fed on any scant information they were given, as if naming the condition was part-way to making him better. At different times the doctors said he'd had a breakdown or a stroke, and that he was a manic-depressive or schizophrenic or that he suffered premature senility.

Under the regime of taking numerous prescribed pills, he did literally break down. He was supposed to swallow them with water but chewed them as if they were toffee. Gran said she'd tasted them herself once and they were bitter.

The book, *As Tears Go By*, was named after Marianne Faithfull's first single and was a desperately earnest and ambitious failure. I had been cowed by the gravitas of the subject matter and the book's framing – hardback, tasteful typesetting and high price. Before starting it, I had been reading Thomas Hardy and making my way (slowly, it's an extremely long book) through *Vanity Fair* by William Makepeace Thackeray, and the better known works by the Brontë sisters. This had influenced my writing, which meant the authorial voice belonged to a haughty older gentleman, possibly Hardy or Thackeray. He might well have worn a cloak. And, unlike the rest of us, he didn't, for example, 'go upstairs', but 'defected to the uppermost portion of the residence'. While, amid the malapropisms, it was a workmanlike read, there was no real *point* to it beyond a presentation of information. The best biographies are much greater than a rerun of a life. They are spiky and score-settling, pulling the hair of their subject, or they are fast and slick, played out for entertainment value above all. Or, if the work is more detailed and languorously paced, it can be novelistic, a winding path of words through the story of a life.

I was offered other books. These were much more in the tradition of Omnibus – information drawn from existing sources, usually the music press, and presented as a new, single body of work. The contract was often for two months with a one-off payment rather than royalties; this diminished the author's role and reinforced the 'hack' element. Under this arrangement I did books on Prince and Bruce Springsteen. I used the pen name John W. Duffy. I lent my real name to books on two groups for whom I had no real enthusiasm, Queen and Simply Red. I turned both into robust pieces of journalism. Still, I was no nearer to becoming a novelist than on the day I'd started the NCTJ course.

My dad had a lock-up for his electrical gear. The two-storey building was in an unadopted alley that led from a pub to a working men's club at the back of shops. I converted the upstairs into a writing den; it was a tiny, dusty space that was difficult to heat, even with a portable Calor gas fire turned up full. Outside, litter and drugs paraphernalia was strewn everywhere. Every day, at about 4 p.m., empty plastic containers were positioned at the back of two adjoining Indian takeaways and staff would peel scores of onions; presumably it didn't make their eyes water when done in the open air. From my window, I'd often see blokes unsteady on their feet trying to dodge the glass and dog shit. If they veered towards the wall, arm held out, I knew what was coming next. Despite just leaving the pub where the toilets were next to the door they had walked through, they would piss in the alleyway.

One time, a lad in a hoodie appeared while I was looking down. He was scanning about him furtively. He took a can of spray paint from his pocket and began shaking it. He positioned himself in front of one of the containers supplied by Biffa (note spelling), the waste management company – its logo and name were in large letters on the bin. I wondered what he might write, perhaps his unyielding love for someone, the name of a football club, a political statement or, more likely, another loopy, star-spattered slogan similar to those that filled up most of the rest of the alley. I guessed wrong. His message to the world (this grubby little bit of it) was: 'Bollocks to Bifa'.

There were three bolts on the inside of the lock-up door and once these were slid across I felt cocooned. Although a dump, it was a perfect retreat. No one visited and, aside from the odd graffiti 'artist' or drunk, there was nothing to see – the view across from the window was a brick wall and a huge vent pipe shared by the takeaways.

Most days I worked on a pop column of reviews and news which I syndicated to four or five local papers. The payment I received was meagre; the demise of newspapers had begun. When I'd worked full time on them, often writing stories of companies closing and the ensuing redundancies, not once did I consider that newspapers themselves might also shut down. Most had been around for more than a hundred years and what could possibly replace them or reduce their status and importance to a town? They were much the same as the sea, shadows, mists and trees in the John Betjeman poem 'The Hon. Sec.':

> A gentle guest, a willing host,
> Affection deeply planted –
> It's strange that those we miss the most
> Are those we take for granted.

Initially the internet robbed newspapers of advertising revenue and later, via electronic devices, the medium became a more efficient supplier of news. And it was free. Twitter, Instagram and especially Facebook further diminished the demand for newspapers. These allowed anyone with sufficient self-regard to set up a de facto 'newspaper' dedicated solely to themselves. No longer did they need to buy a paper to see their children's name and picture in there, winning the 30-yard dash at school sports day; they could post it on their Facebook page. Much of the world around us is now filtered through this group of shrill, untrained correspondents. Charles Bukowski had it right: 'The problem with the world is that intelligent people are full of doubt, while the stupid people are full of confidence.'

As I worked away in my den, newspapers were shedding staff, amalgamating or, a few years later, closing down completely.

Those lucky enough to keep their jobs in a shrinking profession were predominantly desk-bound, perusing the internet for stories. This meant the wonderful tour of duty I had undertaken was no longer available. No more cups of tea and a piece of cake with golden wedding anniversary couples; no heartbreak inquests or horror smashes; no have-a-go heroes or sneak thieves; no cot deaths or miracle births; no arson blazes or summer droughts; no council meetings or cheque presentations; no pools winners or, even, Christmas fairies. During my six years in papers, I had learned to get along with everyone and mixed with scores of eccentric colleagues – newspapers were often receptacles for life's misfits, chasing down stories while undergoing divorces, illicit romances, homelessness, alcoholism, mental illness and all manner of issues, sad to happy.*

I often faxed ideas for stories to national newspapers, almost always to no response. I was a passionate football supporter with a deep knowledge of the game (going all the way back to my collecting football cards as a child) and had an idea for a piece which I thought might suit the sports pages of a broadsheet. Within fifteen minutes, both *The Times* and the *Independent* expressed an interest; this was unprecedented. I sensed instinctively that my life was going to change again.

As *The Times* had, by a few minutes, made first contact I submitted the article to them; four days later it ran along the top of the back page, without a word changed. I phoned and thanked the man who had faxed me, Keith Blackmore, the deputy sports editor. Within a week or so I had joined, on a freelance basis, its

* Set in the 1940s, *My Turn to Make the Tea* by Monica Dickens is a superb account of life at a local newspaper. She based it on her time at the *Hertfordshire Express* in Hitchin.

'They weren't sure you were still here,' I told him.

'I think they've forgotten about me actually. I'm not bothered.'

During our conversation he often repeated the word 'wondrous'. He sang it much like a child would, having newly learned it. A lot was wondrous: being able to work as a writer; Barnsley FC's promotion and living in Sheffield rather than London. We discussed football and writing. He enthused about the view from the window, some trees and a stretch of grass. He talked about his journey to and from the office, the people he nodded or spoke to – how he often wondered about their lives: what did they do all day, where did they go at the weekend? I felt at ease, at home. Within half an hour or so, neither us felt a particular need to speak. The silences were okay. I had a feeling I'd only had a few times before: I liked being *near* him. I left and knew with absolute certainty that we would become friends.

At the end of the football season a publisher collected the pieces I'd done for *The Times* and compiled them into a book, also called *Life at the Top*. The cover was a pastiche of the Penguin version of *Room at the Top* by John Braine. Barry Hines wrote a short but evocative foreword. *The Times* repeated the commission the next season, when I supplied a weekly bulletin from a club in a converse situation to Barnsley. Manchester City had fallen to the third tier of the football pyramid, their lowest ever position. The season afterwards, I wrote about a club I had been passionate about since a boy, Rochdale AFC. A book was again published based on each of these seasons, *Blue Moon – Down Among the Dead Men with Manchester City* and *Life Sentence*, respectively.

While I was travelling the north of England conducting interviews with footballers and watching matches, a good part of me was often in Italy. An impulsive purchase of *The Wayward Wife* by

Alberto Moravia had led me to hurry through his other work. This was a rare occasion when I bought a book *despite* its cover. In fact, it was so hideous (the Penguin edition: a messy scribble of a bug-eyed woman cradling her head in her hands) I was intrigued. The covers of Moravia's books often misrepresent the fascinating work that lies within. Many are tacky and semi-pornographic while others are bland, telling nothing of the content. The Penguin titles feature line drawings but are inconsistent, sometimes suggesting depth, other times, whimsy. The same books sometimes have two or three different titles: *A Ghost at Noon*, for example, is also known as *Contempt* or, in Italian, *Il Disprezzo*.

No matter, Moravia was like a great friend waiting to be met; this happens maybe two or three times in the life of a reader. He was — across scores of novels — obsessed with the nuances of human behaviour, pondering on what was really meant by a character's apparently offhand remark or a barely discernible smile or sneer, or the way someone walked or positioned themselves while standing or sitting. He was especially interested in sexual relationships, ever looking for their downfall, helping the reader see the precious detail — the kiss retreated too quickly, the eyes widening to overstate a curiosity in what was being said, thereby perversely revealing a waning of interest, love fading to indifference. Most often, the setting was the beach or café in a coastal town, a seagull's cry overhead, sand blown from the promenade and shimmering across the town square as the boyfriend or husband is told: the love has gone.

Moravia, born in 1907, wrote more than fifty books, a mixture of novels, short stories and essays — enough to fill at least a shelf. Be warned: immediately after reading him, the first two or three days or so, his work is so infectious that it is difficult to avoid emulating him in your writing (and thinking), so that subclauses shake hands with semicolons in long, meandering, perfectly structured sentences, where fatalism, fear and, occasionally, sequestrated joy is suffused. I am wary of sharing him with others because I can see that he does not have a universality of appeal. His writing is arid and overwrought and intense, which means the pace is torpid, much the same as the hot, slow cappuccino days he describes. One friend, to whom I'd lent a Moravia novel, gave it back within a couple of days and said 'there's too much moping'. There is, I concede, a lot of moping and often no real 'story' (though many of his books have been made into films by directors as noted as Vittorio De Sica, Jean-Luc Godard and Francesco Maselli).

Another caveat in recommending Moravia is to be wary of his stories written from a female perspective. While the ambition is to be commended (it comes off best in *Two Women*), it can sometimes feel gauche, as if he's pushing at the limit of an otherwise considerable talent. 'Raped', for example, a short piece from *Lady Godiva and Other Stories*, has a discomfiting undertone and has not aged well. His forte is in sifting detail, the recognition of a tiny but crucial feeling or characteristic that has hitherto brushed your life but gone nameless or unexpressed. In providing this new part of you or helping you recognise similar in others, Moravia is presenting the ultimate gift of an author: a different way of seeing.

Afterwards, I moved on to other Italian writers such as Cesare Pavese and Italo Calvino. Again, their work is superficially narrow and they face inwardly, concerned with thought and contemplation rather than action or high drama. Reading in my car, I was sometimes so absorbed that I had to dash to the grounds to be in time for the kick-off.

Occasionally Grandad stirred himself and tried to recall the years that his children and wife were born, the names of his sisters:

    'Now then,' he'd say, putting up seven fingers. 'There's Louisa, Clara, Lizzy, Carrie, Laura, Ruth, Irene.'

He could remember them but didn't know whether they were alive or dead. I reminded him once that Carrie had died.

'Carrie's dead?' he whispered. 'She can't be.'

'Don't you remember?'

He shook his head. His face fell sad as if he'd learned of her death for the first time. She had been dead for years.

'Still, she can't come to any harm now, can she?'

Within the space of a couple of years I became a father to two boys. *Everything* changes, of course, when you have children but it's important that you hold on to enough of yourself to remain recognisable. That means doing what you do, what you like, even if it's done less often than before and on a compromised basis. With a pushchair in one hand and the palm of a three-year-old pressed tight to the other, trips to town centres, specifically bookshops, are achievable. Sadly, it's not 1954 any more and you can't claim the 'fresh air is doing him good' when you leave a toddler parked up outside a shop. The alternative is to clasp the three-year-old to your side and either hold the little one in your arms (making browsing difficult) or, slightly better, strap him to some part of your body.

My bookshop/children nadir came in the exquisitely named Hatchard & Daughters in Haworth, West Yorkshire (Brontë Country!). As we entered, the soundtrack was pastoral, a soothing flutey, chimey number, best listened to while wearing baggy pants. The CD (this was before iPods became popular) must have been compiled on a one-for-me, one-for-you basis, presumably between a parent Hatchard and a daughter Hatchard. Next up was 'Firestarter' by the Prodigy. The mad, disjointed rhythm was enough. We'd not got to 'I'm the trouble starter, punkin' instigator / I'm the fear addicted, a danger illustrated' and the youngest was kicking out madly, almost launching himself out of the child carrier on my back. Disorientated and bookless, I found myself back on the cobbled street outside the shop. This was hopeless. I had an idea. I'd source my books from elsewhere. I'd give libraries another go – they had become fervently child-friendly since I'd last called in to peruse their Bancroft Tiddlers.

Over the years, I'd monitored the news and was aware that the statistics were dispiriting. Library usage had declined by nearly a third since 2005* and 800 branches had closed in the past decade† – one-fifth of all libraries in the UK. The internet had robbed them of their primacy as 'gateways to knowledge and culture'‡ which meant that, at a stroke, mobile devices as small as a phone provided instant access to match the information offered in the best-stocked libraries in the world.

Among my friends I know of only two who regularly (once a month or so) call or *called* at a library. This is typical; only 5 per cent§ of the UK population visit a public library on a weekly basis. One pal went solely to borrow CDs which he uploaded to his iTunes library. These days he has a subscription to an audio streaming platform, so no longer visits the library. The other actually borrows books but, more usually, pays a small fee, fills in an online form and the library staff order a particular book for him, typically a biography of an obscure psychedelic band from the 1960s. He returns the book and, quite often, years later, his period of borrowing it is the only one logged.

Other friends mostly buy their books from Amazon, despite claiming to support local bookshops and shedding noisy tears in

* Department of Culture, Media and Sport.
† CIPFA, the Chartered Institute of Public Finance and Accounting.
‡ International Federation of Library Associations (IFLA)/United Nations Educational, Scientific and Cultural Organisation (UNESCO), Public Library Manifesto, 1994.
§ Statista, international data base company.

the name of libraries and the beleaguered book trade. Everyone but the very principled does this; it's almost impossible to resist, even though we know it earns Jeff Bezos, Amazon's founder, chief executive officer and president, $230,000 per minute.* The same as everyone else (I'm offering 'we all do it' mitigation already), I have bought books from Amazon for convenience and also because, while I enjoy bookshop banter, I sometimes have quiet, shy days better suited to clicking on a few links and my books arriving through the letterbox.

Our local library considers itself a 'community hub'. After the Hatchard Incident, we tried it out. As we entered, the boys fell anxious, taking hold of my trousers at the knees. There was a lot going on in the various sections: a re-enactment of a book called *Katie Goes to London*, with kids yelping and a mum dressed as Big Ben (painted cardboard box over her head with a hole cut out) repeatedly shouting 'Bong'; an underfed poet wiring up a PA – one *two*, one *two* – getting set to read from her new 'collection of proto-verse', *The Gutters of the Heavens Hang Over Me*; a dishevelled figure slumped over the *Daily Jang*, snoring loudly, and, over by the computers, a group of teenagers singing/talking along to a hip hop/grime track on YouTube. I doubted this tableau was on the mind of letter writers and campaigners when they went all sepia-swoony about libraries.

A few friends had also done as I had, making a return to libraries during their parenting years; it reminded them of their own childhood and they imagined it to be a nurturing, wholesome environment for their offspring. The return was usually short-lived. They could easily afford to buy their own books and, in truth, much as they espoused 'community' and 'inclusiveness' they didn't really want to spend downtime with noisy teenagers, the hung-

* Bloomberg Billionaire Index.

over homeless, shouty poets and a woman with a box over her head pretending to be Big Ben.

Bustle, the American online women's magazine (fifty million readers per month, each dipping in for news, politics and entertainment – 'How to Wear a Straw Hat Like Meghan Markle') conducted a survey of libraries.* It discovered that a primary draw was that 'they offered safe refuges for the homeless and underserved populations'. On a similar theme, a librarian writing anonymously in the *Guardian*† revealed: 'I've lost count of the number of customers who have told me, "You are the only person I have spoken to all day."' She then listed a wealth of services and functions provided by her library: help in writing CVs; access to PCs for the unemployed; computer classes; 'rhyme time' sessions for toddlers; a meeting place for teenagers; art classes; carpet bowls; tea dances; a café, and dementia support sessions. 'One day they might pick up a book, but it doesn't matter if they don't. We don't mind,' she wrote.

The government allocates £919 million‡ for library provision in the UK. Maybe this budget would be more effectively used if dispersed (and supplemented) to sectors that have fallen within the libraries' remit: social services, playgroups, day centres, youth clubs, Citizens Advice et al. Libraries were best when they were libraries, housed in austere buildings (echoey stone steps, polished brass, and plaques dedicated to long-dead aldermen). They formed an umbrella to the world, keeping out the noisy, the ill-mannered, the non-book people. The only sounds heard were whispers or, at worst, the clatter of coins fed into a photocopier. Libraries have tried to offer too much to too many. And surely

* October 2017.
† February 2016.
‡ CIPFA, 2017.

it matters very much that visitors pick up a book, otherwise what is a library?

Meanwhile, at Castleton Library, where I once called regularly on my Raleigh Chopper bike, the Friends of Carnegie (Castleton) have fastened a photograph of Andrew Carnegie to the wall, the man who, in 1905, donated £2,500 towards the cost of the building. He stares down – crab apple cheeks, soft blue eyes, snowy beard. He'd be pleased that, even if the books have now gone, at least there is a reading room and a local history and heritage centre on the ground floor. A reading room here and there, village to city, might at least give people a chance to commune with books and remind us of the lost splendour of quiet in a public place. Much better for the soul and spirit than a *community hub*.

Each week I'd give Grandad a shave. He'd sit on a chair by the sink in the bathroom. The skin on the underside of his chin was soft and loose and the hair grew randomly – long and wispy in places, absent altogether in others. He smelled of sweat and soap. His nose was still strong but tiny creases pinched at the mouth. I'd sometimes accidentally catch the skin on his cheek and drops of dark, syrupy blood trickled down. He didn't complain and continued looking straight ahead. He seldom spoke but now and again remarked indignantly, almost as if he had woken from sleep:

'Haven't you done yet?'

I acquired an agent; I was still passionate about becoming a novelist. He was well connected, enthusiastic and hopeful. He even *looked* like an agent in round-rimmed designer glasses and expensive jeans, with floppy hair. He smelled lovely, as if he'd been marinated in the finest aftershave; I imagined publishers would want to do a deal with him if only to bring this cloud of musky fragrance into their life on a regular basis. He took me to a restaurant in Covent Garden where everything possible had been done to make it feel as if you'd stepped into a yurt on the foothills of the Tarvagatai Mountains. We sat in a section towards the back, past the drapes and bamboo blinds. He was charming with the waiters, making a show of pronouncing the order correctly. He said how much he had enjoyed the manuscript of a novel I'd written. He was confident he could sell it.

He soon began to receive rejections. *Trainspotting* by Irvine Welsh was popular at the time and he referred to it often.

'There haven't been proper working-class novels like his for years,' he said.

'It's more about the underclass,' I said.

'Well, you know what I mean. It's gritty.'

He took my response to be pedantry or, worse, facetiousness, but I was being matter-of-fact.

'He's good at what he does, Welsh, but he's a different writer than me,' I said.

'He's doing very well for himself.'

He grinned and it prised from me an opinion I'd been determined to hold back.

'Do you know why I think he's so popular? His books are bought mainly by squalor tourists. They get a vicarious thrill from reading about losers and heroin addicts and people shitting the bed. They're reading about all that stuff in their drawing rooms and wine bars, from a comfortable and safe vantage point. There's something morally questionable about that and it makes me uneasy.'

I could see he was piqued by my using the word 'shitting' (the irony) and I sensed that I was chopping away merrily at the ties between us, though he would remain my agent for another year or so. During that time, he passed on comments from commissioning editors, suggesting I develop certain characters, maybe 'take a look at the ending' and so on. I did as I was asked, acceding to his, and their, greater knowledge of the market.

I spent many hours, weeks and months working away in my backstreet den. I finally resubmitted my novel to the agent and he decreed that it had 'lost some of the sparkle and pace of the original'. All that time, wasted. On the train home from our meeting in London, I made a pact with myself. If I'd have had a knife, I might have conducted the ceremony in blood, daubing my chest and forehead: I would never ever again, from here to eternity, write by committee or to order, amen. I would do what *I* wanted and leave all other views over there, out of harm's way.

As a columnist for *The Times* and published author, it was assumed I could help fellow writers. I began to receive emails from people wanting to know how to write a book, how to get a deal, could I read their manuscript, offer any advice. I was uncomfortable in this position. I didn't have a book deal myself and my own novel had been rejected by the industry – what did I know?

A friend sent me a manuscript by Boff Whalley, a founder member of the band Chumbawamba. Unlike everyone else who had sent their work so far, Boff *could* write and I enjoyed it as I would a bona fide published book. As I proofread it for him, I knew instinctively that it wouldn't find a publisher. Instead of it being viewed as an admirable piece of work in its own right, publishers would look at Chumbawamba's fading popularity and surmise that sales of a book largely about the band would be negligible.

I decided to set up an independent publishing company where I would bring together all I loved about books. It would, much the same as record labels I admired – Factory, Rough Trade, 4AD, Mute – have generic branding so the reader could tell immediately that they belonged to the same 'family', one which cared fervently about the aesthetic of books and the quality of writing, much in the mode of Penguin. I called the company Pomona, named after the Roman goddess of fruit. I liked the rhythm and sound of the word and how the letters blended together.

The deal I offered authors was that Pomona would cover all production costs and, on reaching break-even, we'd share any profits on a 50–50 basis. I found a company to rep the books into shops and another to store and distribute them. I was reintroduced to Christian Brett. He had run a guitar shop in Rochdale but was now working as a typesetter. He saw everything in and around books to which I was oblivious, the structure and mechanics, from the weight, texture and colour of certain papers to the density of ink.

I imagined that within a handful of books the established publishing industry would note the vision and energy of Pomona and adopt it as an imprint and, also, should I not secure a deal in the meantime for my work, I could publish it via my own company.*

The first two books, published simultaneously, were a state-ment of intent: *Footnote* by Boff Whalley and a reprint of *Rule of Night* by Trevor Hoyle, with a new cover and foreword. Both conveyed confidence and attitude, fitting together well but in a way which was hard to delineate; I liked this subtlety. I wanted to forge Pomona in my own image, to reflect my taste, believing such an idiosyncratic approach would make it more noteworthy. I was convinced there were others out there with a similar interest in literature, sport, music and politics.

Grandad checked through his pockets constantly. He'd put every-thing he'd found in a long line on the coffee table in front of him, as a child might with a row of toy cars: a metal glasses case covered in threadbare red cloth; an inch-long oblong sticker with his name on (pulled from inside the case); a pair of black-framed National

---

* No one from the formal publishing industry has ever made contact. All deal-ings with agents have been on a negative or hostile basis.

Health glasses; a pencil rubber; 14p in small coins; a heavily creased piece of paper containing his phone number and address; a sweet wrapper; a dry cleaning receipt and an appointment card for the eye hospital.

He repeatedly counted his money. He'd carefully empty coins from his wallet and make neat piles on the arm of the chair. Gran limited him to a small amount because she thought it would stop him travelling too far if he tripped out without her knowing and caught a bus.

The Glory Game by Hunter Davies had been one of the first outstanding books about sport (*A Fan's Notes* by Frederick Exley and *The Football Man* by Arthur Hopcraft are two other fine examples). Davies contributed a football column to the *New Statesman*. I asked if I could compile a selection as a book. *The Fan* was the first of three books by Hunter published by Pomona. The others were *The Second Half* (more columns from the magazine) and *Mean With Money*, a selection of pieces 'wilfully short on practical advice but offering instead good humour and much-needed empathy in the face of high-handed and indifferent financial institutions' – lifted from the blurb.

Hunter was great fun. When we met, either at his home in Highgate, London, or at his country house in Lakeland (as he insisted it was called, despite almost everyone else referring to it as the Lake District), he was always eager, keen, hurry, come on, get a move on. He'd flagellate me with questions that no one had ever asked before (or since); you could easily expect about twenty fired at you on the journey from porch to his bedroom-office.

He had planted an orchard at Loweswater, nailing together a lookout post from old telegraph poles. As we chomped on apples indigenous to the area – Greenup's pippin, probably – I half expected him to suggest a game of hide and seek or king of the castle. He was boyish, but also shrewd, and still a wink-wink, cheeky smile hustler. On a walk to a nearby pub I asked how he had come to write the first and only sanctioned biography of the Beatles. 'I asked them,' he said. It was such a simple but powerful answer; I decided to adopt this same approach. He offered another gilded piece of advice: get the maximum returns from your work. By this he meant shaping existing material to suit a different medium or book. A quick look at Hunter's bibliography shows how well he has self-harvested, repurposing similar work to fit different briefs, especially in his writing on football and working-class background.

My brief was extended at *The Times* and I was commissioned to review books and write interview pieces. I met Alan Sillitoe in 2008 on the fiftieth anniversary of *Saturday Night and Sunday Morning*. I arrived at his house early and circled the streets, remembering when I had first read the book while at college, sitting upright on the bed in that tiny room at John and Joan's. On the day of the interview, it was a beautiful autumn morning, the air warm and the sun lighting up numerous shades of brown and green on the trees and hedges and shrubs.

'Sillitoe – Fainlight':* I took a photograph of the card inserted below the intercom. Sillitoe had just turned eighty. He was wearing a leather waistcoat and polished worker's boots. His inky, rapt eyes flashed brightly. He dutifully promoted the reprint of his classic novel but it was clear that he cared little for its status, sales or legacy. He was happy to let others proselytise on 'the working-class novel'. His impetus had been merely to write and the book had fulfilled this desire; more than fifty titles bore his name in his study, along with more books-to-be, stabbed out on an electric typewriter and then covered in a rash of annotation.

---

* Ruth Fainlight, an American-born poet, was married to Sillitoe for fifty-one years.

'It's something that comes from within you, the need to write. You're born with it,' he said.

Grandad was adding up his money and grumbled:

'I've only got a few bob here. Do you think someone's been at my wallet?'

He often thought he was staying in a hotel and was suspicious of the other 'guests'.

'Do you think he's had it?'

'Who?'

'That bloke who was here talking to me. No wonder he was all sweetness and light.'

'There's been no one here except us two.'

On another occasion Gran was dusting the sideboard.

'When's the other girl coming, the one who'll take over from you?' asked Grandad.

'It's me, Eveline. Who do you think I am?'

'You work here, don't you?'

'I'm your wife.'

Sillitoe was congenial company. He asked if I wrote, and when I said I did he was very interested. Afterwards I sent him a letter explaining how I was finding it difficult to place a novel with a publisher. Within a few days, I received a postcard from him. It meant the world:

Dear Mark, thank you for your letter. Publishers know nothing about good writing. In fact they hate it, as a threat to the trash that makes them money. It's a bad situation, because it wasn't always like this. I'm about to hand a novel in but of course there's no guarantee it'll be taken. I'm not complaining, having had a good run, but for younger writers, I don't know what the

240

answer is. I can only say again: keep on keeping on. And good luck. Life is fickle, but often changes in your favour. Sincerely, Alan.

Alan Sillitoe died in April 2010, aged eighty-two.

I'd kept in touch with Barry Hines via letters and a few trips to Sheffield. He told me he'd been working on a story called *Springwood Stars*. He spoke about his fondness for Bernard Malamud, the American writer who often employed magic realism in his novels and short stories; I imagined he had incorporated this influence into his own new work. He sent me a copy of *Springwood Stars* and during the week it arrived I put off reading it, storing up the pleasure until I could bear it no longer. This was a privilege afforded a publisher: being among the first to read a writer's new work.

I read the manuscript at a time I knew I would be alone in the house; it felt like a tryst. Within an hour or so of starting, I was deflated. The story was about a village football team embarking on a cup run in the 1920s and Barry had used this to explore social inequalities, master and servant. The plot and writing style was similar to Catherine Cookson in, say, *The Cinder Path* or *The Glass Virgin*. Cookson (lifetime sales: 125 million) was a splendid writer of people and place but had none of the blood-bite of Barry Hines.

I think Barry had sent it with a view to Pomona publishing it. I developed a cold sweat. New work by Barry Hines, the author of *A Kestrel for a Knave*, a book *everyone* knew, would be a major coup for a tiny publisher. Try as I might, I could barely find Barry in *Springwood Stars*, beyond its Yorkshire setting and fuzzy class discord. How did I tell Barry this? I didn't want to break a friendship so quickly formed. And who did I think I was, turning down such an esteemed author? Although only a few titles in, I had stayed true to my original pledge that I would only publish books I loved avidly. Was I about to betray this? I need not have worried. I phoned Barry and explained that it didn't quite 'grab me' as his other books had done.

'You're reet,' he said. 'It's just a bit of writing, that's all, something I wanted to do. I might scrap it yet, I'm not sure. It's been kicking around for some time and I've come and gone from it. It's like that sometimes, you come and go and then you think at the end, "That's reet good, is that" or "That's a load of rubbish – what was I thinking abart?"'

We kept in touch and, without even a formal contract, Barry agreed that Pomona could republish two of his earlier novels – *The Price of Coal* and *Looks and Smiles*, a book that, more than any other, encapsulates the gloominess of Britain in the early 1980s. To reread it, as I did to prepare it for the printer, is to find a shoebox full of old black and white photographs, fan them across a table and see the enormous difference between what you *thought* it was like back then and what it really was, such is the authenticity.

I often recall the anticlimax of the night I spent with *Springwood Stars*. I returned the manuscript, so I am unable to double-check, but it felt uneven, with plot strands trailing and inconsistent characters. And the soft tone was alien to the Barry I knew as a person and through his writing. I had the impression that he was subconsciously nursing himself, retreating from the present and drifting to sepia. Perhaps the manuscript was early evidence of the Alzheimer's disease from which he would later die. I stayed in touch with Barry through his illness, visiting him and his wife, Eleanor, at Hoyland Common and, towards the end, at the care homes. Eleanor was a good and dutiful companion to 'Baz', as she often called him, on a long path to his death in March 2016.

In July 2019, three years after he had died, a plaque dedicated to Barry was fixed to the wall of 78 Hoyland Road, where he had lived soon after publication of *A Kestrel for a Knave*. His role as an emissary of his class was acknowledged: 'Barry Hines, 1939–2016, author of *A Kestrel for a Knave* and other novels which gave a voice to working-class people, lived here.' His brother Richard unveiled it on a sunlit morning with Ken Loach and Tony Garnett, the director and producer of *Kes* respectively, in attendance, along with the mayor of Barnsley. Barry would have enjoyed writing up this little scene.

Every few weeks we'd have a family meeting about Grandad, whether he should go to live in a home or not. His behaviour was becoming more extreme. Gran had lived on her nerves for years and the worry was making her ill. Mum and Dad sometimes become very clear minded.

'He doesn't know where he is or who he's with half the time, so what does it matter anyway?'

Sporadically, though, he revealed hints of his former self: a sudden flurry of energy, an incisive remark or a memory drawn in great detail. He also still laughed, chuckling at his own unfathomable jokes. You weren't quite sure what it was all about but joined in because laughing with him felt great.

Pomona allowed me to revisit my past. Christian, my typesetter pal, shared my admiration for Crass. We decided a book of their lyrics would form a perfect memento of the band and the times during which they were active (1977–1984). We stayed at their headquarters, a wonky house on the edge of Epping Forest, with co-founder Penny Rimbaud and Gee Vaucher, the designer of the distinctive sleeve artwork.

I had remained captivated by Bill Nelson, another artist whose music had featured in my youth. I was a fan of his groups, Be-Bop Deluxe and Red Noise, and regularly visited his website, where he meticulously detailed his life. Every day, he recorded music in a home studio while enduring perpetual colds, supermarket shopping trips and visits from various tradesmen fixing up his house on the open flatlands of the Vale of York. This online diary was neurotic, philosophical, absurd and addictive. We met and agreed it would transfer well to a book format under the name *Diary of a Hyperdreamer*, which ran to two volumes.

On the day his first book arrived from the printer, I looked long at the cover, as I had the Be-Bop Deluxe album, *Axe Victim*, many years earlier. I had found the record in a tiny shop in Devon while on holiday. I remember feeling that there was *my* world, Mum and Dad, semi-detached, plain and ordinary, and there was this other world where mystical, mythical, faraway people created kaleidoscopic artwork and music. I was proud enough that Bill Nelson took my phone calls and was polite and friendly. To allow me to be his publisher was an honour and a circle completed, then to now, boy to man.

CHAPTER TWELVE

I'm not a fan of poetry. This might be down to my old English teacher, Mr Selwood, who believed that only one poet of note had ever existed: Wilfred Owen. He was completely in thrall to Owen's work and life story. Actually, it was one of his poems in particular: 'Anthem for Doomed Youth'. He told us how Owen had joined the Manchester Regiment in the First World War but disliked the other soldiers and referred to them in a letter home as 'expressionless lumps'. Owen later showed great humility by re-evaluating his opinion and saluting the bravery of his fellow soldiers. After treatment for shellshock, he returned to the front line but was shot dead in November 1918 while crossing the Sambre–Oise canal, a week before the signing of the Armistice to end the war.

'Dead, just a few days before the end of the war. How unlucky was that?' asked Mr Selwood. 'And he was only twenty-five.'

He had said this in other lessons and his eyes had turned red and watery on each occasion.

'You all right, sir?'

'I'm fine.'

'You don't look it.'

He made us study 'Anthem for Doomed Youth' assiduously until we could memorise every line. No other poet was mentioned, so we passed through our education knowing nothing of Wordsworth, Keats, Blake, Byron, Yeats or even Pam Ayres and Cyril Fletcher.

I have a particular dislike of poetry when spoken aloud. As soon as I hear the first gathering breath of a poet I snap off the radio. If I'm caught by surprise at an event and a poet is summoned to the stage wafting pieces of paper, I feign illness to escape the room – get me out of here, a poet is on the loose. I am wary of anyone self-identifying as a 'poet'; it feels such an indulgence, a job or role made up on the spot, the same as claiming to be a talker or a watcher. Poetry is the easiest art form to undertake but the most difficult to master. Only poetry can be both conceited and corny at the same time.

There doesn't seem to be sufficient challenge in setting down a poem, as there is a novel or play. Aren't we all poets? Can't each of us bash out a few lines and claim it is a fragment of our suffered soul or a new wide eye on how the snaking flow of a river or the freefall of the hawk, is an exemplar of life itself, should we take the time to look. And if no one can make sense of it and chop through the thicket of allegory, tough – it's *their* problem. If affirmation was needed, I received an email recently from a poetry press which kindly outlined its preferred material: 'We are especially interested in poetry that is aware of the plasticity of language, and which places connotation and ambiguity over denotation and precision of meaning. This sort of poetry invites interpretation and, consequently, results in a plurality of meaning.'

246

Despite myself, I have, among so many titles, a few poetry anthologies – a seam on a shelf about as wide as a breeze block. There lie the anointed few but, even here, it tends to be because of a specific poem or a handful, at best, by Walt Whitman, Christina Rossetti, Rudyard Kipling, Robert Frost, John Keats, the Mersey poets, Tony Harrison, John Betjeman, Patrik Fitzgerald, Mikey Smith, Philip Larkin and Benjamin Zephaniah.

Pomona, then, was most definitely not a publisher of poetry. Until the day a future poet laureate came to town.

'He's a bit like you,' said the man at *The Times*.

'What's that?' I asked.

'Bangs on about being northern, likes bands, writes . . .'

'But he's a lot more successful.'

'That's your lookout!'

And so I was commissioned, in 2008, to interview Simon Armitage. He was promoting his book, *Gig: The Life and Times of a Rock-star Fantasist*. We had a little bit of history. Not me and Simon, but him and one or two members of a little gang of punk-for-life idealists with whom I sometimes shared pub space. To them he was an interloper as much as he was a poet. Years before, dressed as an escapee from the Housemartins, replete with a PSW* haircut, he had travelled over from Marsden to make off with one of our best grubby stories.

Grandad went missing. The estate where we lived was meant to be open plan but over the years people had installed small fences and rows of conifers or laurels to mark borders.

---

* Polish shipyard worker. Many Haçienda regulars adopted a more austere version of the traditional short back and sides. Some even wore *chorąży* caps, suggesting they had recently returned from a stint unloading containers in Gdańsk.

One Sunday in early summer, the estate was buzzing with the sound of lawnmowers. I had the bedroom window open and could hear kids shouting and a ball bouncing in the street. Dad was in the back garden sitting in a deck chair. Mum and Gran were planting flowers together. I presumed Grandad had fallen asleep and they'd left him dozing in the living room. I went downstairs to check. He wasn't there. I ran through to the back room and shouted to them in the garden.

'Where's Grandad?'

'He's watching telly.'

'He's not.'

'He might be in the bathroom.'

'I had a look when I came downstairs. He's not there either.'

They raced in and gathered in the living room, running on the spot and shouting orders to one another. I was told to double-check all the rooms. I popped my head into Mum and Dad's bedroom. The window was open. I scooped away the net curtain to look out over the estate. At the top of the street I saw a figure dressed in an overcoat and dark clothes; everyone else was in brightly coloured T-shirts and shorts. It was Grandad, marching onwards. He'd taken a linear route, walking across lawns, brushing away conifers, striding over knee-high fences and shrub borders. No one was trailing him, asking why he'd trespassed or shouting after him that he was on private land. They seemed to have waved him through, wishing him well on his plucky bid for freedom. I shouted downstairs that I could see him.

Simon Armitage had worked as a probation officer in Rochdale, specifically Ashfield Valley, before becoming a full-time poet. He had returned in 1992 with a camera crew as the last of the tenants were moved out and the bulldozers were revving up to smash it down – less than twenty-five years after being built. He was filming for a BBC2 arts programme called *Words on Film*. He narrated *Xanadu*, 'an epitaph to the crumbling Ashfield Valley estate', on a damp and bleak, bone-chilling day. He stepped over the bashed-down doors and broken glass, the abandoned mattresses, taking extra care on the snow-covered decks. He went into empty, echoey rooms and stared through holes where windows had been, the walls coated in black mould.

'What's he going on about fucking cabbage for?' asked Gerald, one of the punk-for-life idealists

Gerald's hair was thinning but he still dyed it that bleachy mess of yellow, white and black. He was three or four stones heavier than his best pogoing weight of 1978. Button badges were pinned to the lapel of his purple jacket; it was tempting to press one and see if it was possible to time-travel back to one of the gigs he talked about so much, at the Electric Circus or Mayflower.

'Sixteen times he mentioned cabbage. I counted them. *Sixteen fucking times*. What's that all about? And what's he doing over here anyway? When did you last see him having a ride on an Alsatian dog with Mike Harding?'*

We were each hoping he'd close the rant with his usual sigh: 'It's like punk never happened.' We'd heard it so many times that we often joined in, shouting the line as if it were the chorus of a song. He didn't. Instead he shook his head and announced that any day soon, this week possibly, *he* was going to start writing poetry.

'It'll be proper stuff. I won't be rhyming cabbages with criminal damages, that's for definite.'

Gerald had referred to the section at the beginning of *Xanadu* where Armitage had used a technique called anaphora,

---

* The folk singer and comedian Mike Harding had a hit in 1975 with a song called 'Rochdale Cowboy', which included the line, 'Cos people laugh when I ride past on our Alsatian dog'.

a succession of lines beginning with the same words to build a rhythm. The repetition of 'the smell of the cabbage' was *knowingly* absurd, to draw in the viewer (or reader) and create intrigue: what's this all about? I didn't announce this to Gerald, of course; his half-cocked monologues could light up a dull night in the scruffiest pub like an electronic fruit machine gone haywire.

Interloper or not, Simon had caught the valley immaculately — the heartbreaking bloody mess and waste of it all. *Xanadu* was a tremendous piece of work.

We met in a café. He didn't order cabbage. Simon was good company. We shared a love of many of the same bands: The Chameleons, the Comsat Angels, Echo & the Bunnymen. He thought before he spoke. He was cool. I told him about Pomona.

'I've got something you might want to publish,' he said.

A year earlier he had made a documentary for Channel 4 called *The Not Dead*, a short collection of poems based on the testimonies of ex-soldiers. I recognised immediately that the profile and prestige of Pomona would rise considerably with Simon Armitage on its roster — don't knock the poetry. Afterwards, we walked to his car. I was feeling a bit cocky, pleased that the interview had gone well and with the unexpected offer of a book. I have little knowledge of cars but as he opened the boot to put in his bag I could see that his was of reasonable quality.

'Nice car,' I said. 'Do you make a few bob out of poetry, then?'

It was a daft, intrusive question.

'What the fuck has it got to do with you?' he laughed.

The Not Dead was well reviewed and sold well. Four years later we published another book by Simon, *Black Roses*, a 'poetic sequence' written in the voice of Sophie Lancaster, the twenty-

250

year-old murdered by a gang of youths in a park in Bacup, Lancashire, in August 2007. I was familiar with the story. I had made several visits to Bacup working on an article for the *Observer* magazine which ran on the first anniversary of the murder.*

When a book is in production (proofing, choosing a cover, liaising with the printer and the reps, for example), it is formless and intangible. Later, it is authentically 'born' and has all that is life – colour, mood, warmth, attitude, personality. I did not properly notice this with *Black Roses* because I was so painfully close to the story; the barbarism of the killing was too much to permit even a glint of art-light. Several years later, a repeat of the adaptation of the book was broadcast on BBC Radio 4. Within a few lines, I had to pull over and park the car. The story of Sophie was distressing (all over again) but I was also overwhelmed by Simon's dignified craftsmanship, how he had got the tone, the cadence, the truth, everything, *just right*.

'You're the fastest. Go and catch him up before he reaches the main road,' said Mum.

I bounded along the pavement and drew alongside him as he cleared the final fence.

'Grandad, Grandad,' I panted.

'What's up?' he asked.

'Gran wants you to come back to our house.'

'But I'm just nipping out.'

'She's worried about you.'

'Tell her I'm all right.'

He eventually agreed to return. As we passed, people smiled.

---

* Pomona also published *Weirdo. Mosher. Freak: (If Only They'd Stopped at Name Calling)* by Catherine Smyth. The author was a local reporter working in Bacup and the first to learn of the attack on Sophie Lancaster.

When Simon was made poet laureate in May 2019 I was asked by pals and journalists seeking an insight: what's he like? He is conscientious, I told them. He honours agreements, whether to sign a hundred books in an empty, chilly office on a Sunday afternoon or to approve cover artwork on a weekday evening in the Nook in Holmfirth. He'll be there. He is at ease in front of a camera or microphone, a skill probably learned from his father and grandparents who projected strongly and earnestly from the stage for the Marsden Parish Church Amateur Operatic and Dramatic Society.

The same as many successful people, he can sometimes appear to have adopted a persona two or three steps back from who he is with family or close friends. If he was too much of himself to too many, he would never get home from the reading or he'd find himself spending hours, precious hours, responding to emails sent by tender sorts beseeching him to critique their bloody awful poetry. Similarly, he is mindful of how he is perceived, what he agrees to and turns down. I asked him once to contribute a quote for the jacket of the Barry Hines books we published. He said he'd rather not. I expected that he'd give a reason (not that he was obliged to) but he didn't: no more was said. He has poise, self-assurance, built tall from a lifetime of approbation and high-level patronage and his talent goes before him, fills the room, so he sits within himself with no need to hustle or gossip or seek out new friends or consider what might make him popular or well liked. He is what he is.

I attended his fiftieth birthday party at the Picturedrome in Holmfirth. He danced most of the night until he ran out of people willing to shuffle around in close proximity. When he was made poet laureate he and his wife had celebrated by doing star jumps on their daughter's trampoline. All those years ago, the film of the poem, *Xanadu*, closed with Simon visiting the Hungarian Club in Rochdale. The place was Saturday-night busy and he was filmed dancing with happy Hungarians, forming circles of people, locked arm in arm. He has the same open and happy smile he will have nearly twenty-five years later at his fiftieth birthday party, one that reveals bafflement with the world but a love of it, too.

A friend recommended that Pomona reissue a book by Ray Gosling called *Sum Total*. Faber had published it originally in 1963 when Gosling was just twenty-three. The book was an audacious 'sort-of' autobiography, a very English take on the Beat writing of the United States, with long tracts of wondering and wandering while going nowhere in particular:

> I bought a ticket for London, but I don't know. I fancy going home for a start. Whisky – feel it burn all the way down. Cigarette – feel the nicotine cling. That woman in green, she needs some lessons in how to pour beer. The bloody trains they're late again. Not surprising, everywhere there's fog. I love You. I love You. Write it with the wet beer on the marble. I love You. That's why it's taken so long for me to get out of this place.

Gosling was better known for his television and radio documentaries, some on major themes such as divorce, illness and unemployment, but also reporting back from forgotten towns, collectors of garden gnomes, seaside resorts, caravanners and cafés. We met a few times. He'd turn up, hair messy, plastic carrier bag in hand, always acting as if newborn to the world: What's that for? Who's that? When was this built? Where does that bridge lead to? We'd walk to the nearest pub and he'd order red wine. He'd start a conversation at the bar with the person next to him or a member of staff.

'It's all right round here, in't it?' 'What's it like at night?' 'What do *you* do?'

We'd find a table, put down our glasses, but Ray was often

elsewhere, marvelling at a poster he'd found or a leaflet he'd taken from the rack at the door or pointing to someone he'd met on the way back from the toilets:

'He's from Immingham, that fella there. Worked on the docks for years. It's got the deepest waters of anywhere in the UK, has Immingham.'

He didn't have a mobile phone but instead left about four phone numbers where he could be contacted; at least two of them were pubs. I wasn't sure whether Ray's book would sell but meeting him and similar mavericks was one of the unexpected delights of publishing.

Gran couldn't face the trauma of dropping off Grandad at the home, so Mum and Dad did it. When she got back, Mum held a tissue to her face and sobbed noisy tears all evening, firing off volleys of frustration:

'He didn't know where he was. Why are we doing this to him? All the family should take turns at looking after him. It shouldn't have come to this. He's not done anyone any harm.'

At times, life can set an ambush. I'd recently read *By Grand Central Station I Sat Down and Wept* by Elizabeth Smart, an acutely autobiographical book that chronicles her pursuit of the hard-living, heavy-drinking poet George Barker. At her whim, words dance wildly as she tries repeatedly to grasp this lizard's tail of a man. A few days after I'd read it, *Granta*, the literary magazine, carried a cover piece about his bohemian family, written by Christopher Barker, one of four children born from the union of Elizabeth and George (Barker had fifteen children by several women).

I contacted Barker and expected I'd be one of several publishers to do so; it seemed obvious to extend the lengthy, expressive piece into a book. No one else had been in touch. I met him in a Soho pub, the kind his father had frequented forty years earlier. He told me he was primarily a photographer. His portraits of poets including Philip Larkin, Seamus Heaney, Lawrence Durrell and Norman MacCaig were held at the National Portrait Gallery.

Unlike his parents, he was not a gifted writer. Still, I had faith in the story of his life and the insight it provided into two totemic literary figures. I spent months shaping the work. In the edit, I was keen to maintain his integrity as both an author and person; there were one or two phrases and episodes that jarred in a modern context. The book, *The Arms of the Infinite*, was published but did not sell well despite strong coverage, including a four-page extract in the *Observer* magazine.

When I first set up Pomona I had been oblivious to a valuable source of income – the sale of foreign rights. I was contacted by a Munich-based agent called Klaus Gröner who quickly became a trusted and capable associate. He had a network of contacts at publishers across the world and, for a cut, sold rights on Pomona's behalf. We had an offer from the Wilfrid Laurier University Press in Ontario (Elizabeth Smart was born in Ottawa) for the rights to *The Arms of the Infinite* in Canada. The advance was small but would slightly offset some of the losses incurred. I was delighted to inform Barker that we'd had this interest. He seemed pleased.

While the deal was being negotiated I received a letter from a literary agent acting on Barker's behalf. It was similar to one or two others I would receive over the years, claiming that I had not honoured a particular aspect of the contract and should therefore surrender my association with a book so they could place it elsewhere. I had purposely made the contracts as simple and author-friendly as possible – just a few pages long – to reflect the genial ethos of the company. Unfortunately this meant they were much easier to pick apart and dismiss by agents more used to dealing on a very formal basis. I wrote back and explained that I had no knowledge of any issues with Barker and had done all I could for the book, losing £2,000 and scores of hours along the way. She responded:

Dear Mark

Please don't talk about what you have given up in this martyr-ish way. This is your business and you have to take risks. Christopher has given you every opportunity to publish his book successfully and has earned not one penny. He is mourning what he has given up and what you have sold from under him. This is his life story, his parents' story. You didn't ask for his approval or even inform Christopher of the deal and he isn't going along with it; he has contacted me and asked me to help him out of this very disadvantageous situation he finds himself in. I think I have proposed something which will give everyone what they want including you and I hope you reconsider my generous suggestion. When WLP realise that you did not have the rights you have licenced [sic] to them in the eyes of the law, I doubt they will want to go ahead anyway as doing so is a very risky choice on their part.

I relinquished the rights. Had I continued the fight, I would have become increasingly frustrated; my emotional investment was far too high. Besides, this was a squall compared to what was to come.

Two days later, Grandad went missing. He'd been left on his own in the home's garden; they'd been told repeatedly to watch him closely because of his tendency to wander. I was away at college in Sheffield and unable to join the search party. I wish that I'd left straight away and been with them. I'd have given anything to be the sharp-

eyed hero once more, the first to see him shuffling out of an alleyway between garages or sitting down, having a rest on a grass verge by the road.

My fixation with J.D. Salinger meant I often cascaded through websites seeking new insights into his work. A regular stop-off and by far the best was Dead Caulfields, where there was considerable depth of information and it was updated regularly. I contacted Kenneth Slawenski, the site owner, and asked if he would consider writing a biography of Salinger. We were both aware of Salinger's fiercely private nature and tendency to litigate but thus far no one had contacted Slawenski to object to his website; I took the silence as tacit permission for the material being made available, in whatever format. Even if the book merely reproduced the text from the site, which Slawenski had done a fine job collating, it would make an interesting compendium.

Slawenski set to work diligently on the manuscript and sent me regular updates. Scores of emails passed between us. I enjoyed the exchanges. He was thankful for my interest and support, always polite. Again, he wasn't a natural writer but he was a grafter, applying himself conscientiously and whittling away at the story. He had a tendency to overwrite and repeat himself but this was easily excised; at least the detail was there, if not the colour. Importantly, he did not try to replicate Salinger's style, as many had done before, to disastrous ends. Slawenski was his own man: industrious to laborious, safe hands at the lathe. He continually asked for more time as he gathered new information – a month here, six months there. Finally, after six years of toing and froing across hundreds of emails, he delivered approximately 180,000 words of text. This was far too much; I wasn't sure whether it was even possible to bind a book of such size. I shortened it to approximately 150,000 words without reducing its quality or integrity.

257

The final revised manuscript was presented to Christian Brett at Christmas 2009, ready to be typeset. I had done most of the PR on the other books with help from friends but I realised this was by far Pomona's most high-profile title. I wanted to give it every chance to succeed and took on an established publicist, Nicky Stonehill. She had organised the press campaign for my biography of Marianne Faithfull nearly twenty years earlier. On Tuesday, 26 January 2010 – the date is important here – I was briefing Nicky. At the end of our conversation she asked Salinger's age. I told her he had turned ninety-one a few weeks earlier.

'You know what I'm thinking, don't you?'

I said I did.

J.D. Salinger died the next day of natural causes at his home in Cornish, New Hampshire. My emotions were conflicted. Although Salinger had not published new material since June 1965 (a story called 'Hapworth 16, 1924' in the *New Yorker*), the world, my world, immediately felt diminished. His death, however, had left me with one of the hottest books in publishing. I rang Alan Jessop, the head of Compass, the repping firm which sold Pomona titles into shops. We hadn't yet decided how many copies of the biography, now called *Salinger: A Life Raised High*, to have printed. Alan was ebullient; he grasped the significance of the situation immediately. He advised that the *initial* run should be 5,000 in hardback. I asked him if he was sure. He said he was sure he was sure. I fed off his confidence; he knew the market. He was a good sort, too, and had been a loyal supporter of Pomona. I used up my savings to have the book printed: more than £10,000.

Despite extensive press coverage with mostly good reviews, the biography sold few copies. Klaus, as usual, performed admirably, selling the rights across the world, from Brazil to Taiwan and many stops in between. These deals brought in small advances, from £400 to £1,500, and chipped away at the deficit.

An email came through from Random House in New York, 'the largest general-interest paperback publisher in the world'. It was keen to acquire the rights to the book for the United States. I looked at the email again. And again. I informed Slawenski; I was so happy for us both after all our hard work, the commitment and belief we'd shown. He, too, was distraught about Salinger's death but the book, and particularly this forthcoming deal, was a fitting tribute to our idol, and to us. I did the deal by email, fully aware that I had an excellent book at the optimum time and was negotiating with a company based in the country where it was set and about a subject stitched into its very fabric. The sales in the UK remained a trickle; it appeared that while people wanted to read books *by* J.D. Salinger, they were not interesting in *him* per se. I found this unfathomable.

On the second night Grandad was missing, I had a dream. Snapshots of images tumbled like photographs falling from the sky. Grandad was walking, stumbling. Two hands were pressed together at the sides with the palms open. They contained a cluster of speckled birds' eggs. Next, he was lying down, his face resting in an expanse of shallow water. This water was inside him too, filling him up, stopping him breathing. Darkness fell in the dream. It wasn't night-time darkness where there is a thread of light at the bottom of the door or a stop-start flickering of light on a distant hillside. This blackness was total. I had a sensation of rising; a gentle, effortless levitation: peace and release. I woke and looked at the clock by my bedside. It was 3.30 a.m. I fell back to sleep.

I received an email from an agent who said she represented Slawenski. Within seconds, via the internet, I learned that she was extremely high-ranking. The company for whom she worked was based on Broadway, a few blocks from Central Park – where a crucial scene is played out in *The Catcher in the Rye*. The tactic was the same as that applied by the other agent: discredit the existing contract so as to disqualify it, and, on this occasion, claim back *all* the monies accrued in advances and sales. This time, I could not walk away; there was far too much at stake.

Over the course of a summer, I was bombarded by emails and told to tip up all manner of paperwork across the various foreign deals that had been done. I was even made to send copies of my bank account to show that the 'in' payments matched those I had declared in Slawenski's royalty statement. I could have refused all this, stood my ground, but because I had nothing to hide and it had the cumulative effect of revealing my candour and honesty, I went along with it. I was rattled, though, and it ruined the summer. Occasionally, as I bolted the lock-up door behind me at the end of the day, I pondered on the absurdity of my having these high-level negotiations from dog shit alley in Rochdale all the way to Broadway, New York. At one point, exasperated, I rang Slawenski in New Jersey and asked why he had done this; it was the first time we had spoken.

'You know what these agents are like,' he said.

I said that she could only act on his instructions and that he bore responsibility. He continued to issue platitudes.

The story of the book took another turn, for the better. And then, the worse. The contract – which did, in fact, hold up – saw Pomona retain film and television rights on the same terms: 50–50. Danny Strong, an American media mogul (actor, writer, director, producer), expressed interest in the film rights. He had played a major acting part in the television series *Buffy the Vampire Slayer*. The procedure with film rights is that a relatively small advance is paid initially, with the balance – often sizeable – to follow when the film is made or goes on general release.

The film, titled *Rebel in the Rye*, went into production and had several leading actors in place, including Nicholas Hoult to play Salinger, and Zoey Deutch as Oona O'Neill, with whom

Salinger had a short relationship when he was twenty-two and she sixteen. The film was premiered in January 2017 and went on release in the United States in September of that year. A month later, allegations of sexual harassment and assault were made against Kevin Spacey, who had played Whit Burnett – the lecturer and magazine editor who had fostered Salinger's talent. Netflix cut all ties with Spacey. Any work with which he was associated was tainted, including *Rebel in the Rye*. The film had only a limited release and its subsequent poor box office performance meant no payments were triggered to Pomona.

The fallouts with authors were draining but rare, thankfully. More onerous was the sheer volume of work: the contracts, the AIs (advance information sheets), the ISBNs (international standard book numbers), the metadata required for Nielsen and Amazon and others, the hi-res and lo-res PDFs of the covers, the barcodes, the blurbs, fulfilling orders from the website, logging into PayPal, liaising with the typesetter and printer, maintaining a decent stock of padded envelopes, working out royalties and securing publicity for the books – phew. And, after all that, the financial rewards were minimal, if any at all. Only madmen and dreamers venture forth.

The cost of producing books is not prohibitively expensive. A paperback novel of typical size and pagination will cost about £800 to typeset and £2,500 to have 2,000 printed. If a book sells at £10, the retailer may ask for 50 per cent discount (Amazon more). The repping and distribution charges are approximately 25 per cent. This leaves £2.50 to be shared by publisher and author, once the printing and typesetting costs have been covered.* Plainly, the margins are tight. One temptation to help move

* Costs are correct at the time of printing.

towards profit is to have extra copies printed on the first run — the cost of the second 1,000 may be just 30 per cent of the first 1,000. This is a great boon if the extra 1,000 sell, but usually they don't and, a year or so later, they will incur storage or pulping charges and become a liability. As I discovered.*

I heard of Grandad's death on a humid afternoon in June. I'd arrived back from journalism college to spend the weekend at home. It was a sunny day, the sky empty and blue. I levered my bag from my shoulder, put it down. I waited for a phone box to come free at the train station. Dust was scattered across the pavement and discarded tickets had turned yellow and brittle in the sunlight. The phone became free. Dad answered.

'I've got some bad news, son,' he said. 'They've found your grandad. He's dead. They think he fell and banged his head.'

Silence. I couldn't understand.

'Are you still there? Dad?'

'I can't talk, I'm upset.'

He'd put the phone down. The hum of the dialling tone sounded exasperatingly neutral. Dad and Grandad had never seemed especially close but his voice breaking down and those shuddering sobs taught me so much about him in just a few seconds; how much he kept hidden.

A major, established publisher has many departments and a great deal of expertise to call upon. An independent has to carry out these functions themselves. I quickly discovered that this arrangement meant that almost everything that went wrong was ultimately my fault. If the barcode was left off or positioned incorrectly or they used one belonging to a different book and we

---

* See later.

needed to put a sticker over the existing one: my fault. If the precise protocol on delivery of information to the reps was too late or too early, thereby affecting orders: my fault. If there was no text on the rear of the dust jacket for the J.D. Salinger biography: my fault. If the kindly English teacher I'd asked to proofread a book was irritating the author because of her pernickety nature: my fault. If the artist commissioned to work on a cover became stroppy about a fluctuating brief: my fault. If an author was accidentally sent double his due royalties: my fault (and my loss: this happened). If the website chap was unable to update the site: my fault. If someone had ordered a book and, six weeks later, had still not received it: my fault. If a book received barely any media coverage: my fault. (I tried to address this last issue by taking on a publicist for one particular book. His normal rate was £7,000 per book. I told him all I required was his contacts and goodwill among journalists – I would write the press release, send out the books and so on. As a special, one-off deal, he offered to do it for £3,500. He didn't secure a single item of national press.) When a PR charges £3,500 to publicise a book and delivers nothing: my fault.

The success or otherwise of each title seemed arbitrary. One or two had extensive press or accidentally caught the news agenda but still sold a few hundred. Hunter Davies's first football book (*The Fan*) sold out the 3,000 print-run, but his next (*The Second Half*) sold about one-tenth as many. Everyone I met expressed a fondness for Barry Hines but few bought his books; perhaps they were fans solely of *A Kestrel for a Knave* rather than his wider work. There are other books of his – *Unfinished Business, First Signs, Elvis Over England* – that barely anyone knows about. The music books (Crass, Bill Nelson, Stuart Murdoch, David Gedge, Mark Lanegan, Bob Stanley, Joe Thompson) sold largely to a pre-existing audience and, while this helped the profile of Pomona, it sometimes felt as if we were supplying merchandise as much as books.

I didn't put authors under pressure to promote their books. I remain smitten with the idea of a writer being a pathologically shy, monosyllabic genius, living on biscuits and bacon rind, afraid of their own shadow but still able to script reams of gorgeous, rich, sparkly prose. I'm actually put off by authors who are overly comfortable with addressing an audience; I want writing to be their *only* means of communication. I must concede, though, that when a writer helped with promotion, it increased sales.

Maybe there isn't a correlation between publicity for a book and sales, or even a reason why one book sells well and another doesn't. The vagaries of the trade may be the bigger factors: an enthusiastic rep who secures a major order; a retail buyer who disproportionally supports a certain publisher, or a book that, by chance, falls within an existing discount offer (say, three sports books for the price of two). These will all skew sales figures. No book we published sold more than 3,000 copies and this seemed to be our ceiling, suggesting we didn't have the machinery (whether marketing or sheer profile) to push on beyond this figure. I soon accepted that the near-invisible, sleight-of-hand magic between major publishers and retail was out of our reach, another world.

Grandad's body had been found at the bottom of a ravine. The police said he'd probably died the first day he went missing. He'd banged his head when he lost his footing at the top of the slope and the momentum had carried him down. Gran was reassured that he'd died quickly; it was all over in seconds.

Mum and Gran went to the inquest. Gran was worried that the young care assistant who had been on duty when Grandad went missing might lose his job. She said she'd be careful what she said in case it got him into trouble. Afterwards, they saw him sniggering with his mate outside the court room and it angered Mum.

'He didn't give a monkey's,' she kept saying.

The saddest hour running Pomona came on the day a truck arrived carrying about 3,000 unsold books, most of them the Salinger biography. At the time I was recovering from a slipped disc in my back and had arranged for a few pals to join me at the lock-up. The truck was due at about 1 p.m. and I'd asked them to send a reasonably small one to fit down the alley and pull up outside the door. The driver got caught in heavy traffic and was two hours late, by which time I was on my own. The truck was massive. The nearest he could park was about 200 metres away. My back was aching. The pile of books was huge. The driver was unaccompanied. He said he was under 'no obligation whatsoever' to help unload the books. I said my helpers had left because he had arrived so late. Amid grunts and grumbles he untied the fastening around the pallet of books. We carried packs from the truck to the lock-up in near silence. He lugged two or three at a time; I could only manage one.

'What's up with you?' he asked.

'I've done a disc in my back.'

'You'll do another in a minute with this lot.'

We finished after about an hour. I was exhausted; my back had gone into spasm. I looked at all these unsold bloody books and felt sorry for myself. What the hell was I doing? It felt as if it was punishment for a crime I had no memory of committing. And all this hadn't finished yet. How was I going to get rid of 3,000 books?

I'm still shedding them, slowly. They would sell if given a chance but the system is such that retail space is taken up almost wholly by major publishers. I have sold some to remainder companies but they pay pennies for each title and the cost of carriage uses up most of the margin. I have put them on the Pomona website for 'free' but have to charge postage and packing, which means they are often more expensive than books bought in charity shops or remainder stores. I even tried giving them away at a train station

265

but was moved on by a man with a walkie-talkie and told I needed a licence. I said I wasn't doing any harm or breaking the law but he said he could report me for 'being a nuisance in a public place'.

Currently, I have a two-pronged approach to reducing the pile, which has grown by a further 2,000 after another overstock delivery. Firstly, and with great reluctance and distress, I am systematically throwing away scores of books (how it pains to write that sentence). I do this by either filling the recycling bin at home or driving to the local refuse centre. I am wary of doing the latter because I was 'caught' about a year ago. I had secreted copies of Hunter Davies's *Mean With Money* inside cardboard boxes. I tried to place them as gently as possible into a skip but a sharp-eyed operative saw the books spill out.

'What are they?' asked the man in a yellow jacket.

'Some books I'm getting rid of.'

'They're all the same.'

I nodded.

'How come?' he asked.

I was silent for about three seconds of deep thought, during which time I realised there was no plausible reason for having multiple copies of a single book unless you were a daft, inept publisher who had massively overreached by printing far too many copies of a certain book. I started out on this explanation but hadn't got far when he interrupted:

'So you're a trader, then?'

How did you convey that you *were* a trader but not in the conventional sense (i.e. you didn't make a profit) so shouldn't really have to pay traders' rates to have your goods recycled, especially for an item that had already caused you to lose an awful lot of money. The man in yellow towered over me (it might have just felt that way). My mind was in a whir, my tongue still.

*

Several witnesses at the inquest said they had seen Grandad shortly before he died. He was easy to spot in his suit on a scorching day, walking through a wooded area close to a cemetery. A council gardener saw him emerging from bushes and shouted for him to move on. He thought he'd been stealing birds' eggs. The pathologist's report said it was unlikely that the blow to his head had caused death; it might have left him dazed but was fairly inconsequential. Grandad had drowned. The most likely time of death was during the middle of the night on the second day he was missing, the time I had woken from the dream.

I sensed a strange elation as Mum told me what the inquest had revealed. I was a little spooked, too. It felt as if I'd been chosen as a messenger, since I'd dreamed everything in explicit detail. I felt I'd been entrusted to pass on something specific and vital: at the point of death, he'd found peace at last.

As I started to explain that I was a *kind of* publisher, the operative's attention was snagged by an old chap carrying vintage toy cars in his arms, about to deposit them in the 'metals' skip; they clearly had a sell-on value.

'Pal, pal,' he shouted, before making his way across to him.

I quickly got into the car and drove off with a strange mixed-up feeling of relief, happiness and then a curious sadness. I kept thinking of the journey those books had gone through to end up in a skip in Rochdale, all the work and money, love and hope, and here I was, dancing away in near joy at having successfully dumped them without incurring a fine. They hadn't been read. Or even opened. This was madness.

The other way I am relieving myself of hundreds of books is to pack various titles into carrier bags and drop them at charity shops. Here again, there is a frisson of jittery wrongdoing. I often have to park on yellow lines or constantly tour the same town-centre streets while my nephew races to shops he has located on his phone. I have had to speed off a few times as traffic wardens (or whatever they're called these days) encroach the car. At least these books stand a chance of being read and making a little money for the PDSA, the Springhill Hospice and the Bacup Fellowship of Churches, even if it adds to my financial (petrol costs, tipping my nephew) and time deficit; fifty-two bags in a day is our current record.

Down at the Red Lion I have the occasional moan about it all. By the second pint, when I've done with my (publishing) tales of treachery, impecuniousness, bureaucracy and disappointment, I cheer up. I buy another round. If anyone asks, and they occasionally do, I tell them why I do it. It's like this: there is a moment when the books first arrive from the printer, usually best enjoyed in a quiet room and alone. If all has gone well with the production, it can be transcendental. A notion – nothing more than that, intangible, hopeful – has led to this wonderful item that you now hold in your hands, which wouldn't exist if you hadn't done all the acts of midwifery between idea and artefact. This is further enhanced if the book is your own.

I published my novel, *The Last Mad Surge of Youth*, in May 2009. Several major publishers had come close to taking it on during the previous two years, including one that suggested a change of ending might seal the deal. But I wanted it to end as it did. Besides, experience had shown that compromise got me nowhere or set me further back from where I had started. This book was all me. I could hold it aloft as a shining light to everything I'd wanted to achieve down to the last detail, from the size of text, the type of paper, the cover shot, the blurb, every single word, sentence and paragraph. The reviews were unanimously good. *Q* magazine chose it as its novel of the year. *The Times* and the *Guardian* enthused.

I thought back to what the agent had told me years earlier, when he'd not been able to sell my first novel. He said that no one had a *divine right* to have a book published. I said nothing at the time because I was afraid to appear conceited, which I'm not any more. I wanted to say that, actually, a passionate love of books, a commitment to them allied to a natural and cultivated talent qualified, as near as damn it, to a divine right. Who else was in the queue? No one begrudges a genius, of course, but there are lots of mediocrities out there and plenty of well-connected opportunists.

As I offload Pomona overstock I am, as ever, simultaneously adding to my personal book collection. Friends who visit often remark that the house is becoming 'like a library'. And it is. In the hallway there is politics. Front room, back wall: rock and pop and show business. Front room, nearest wall: local history and biography. Front room, other wall: novels overspill. Living room, corner next to gas fire: hardback novels. Living room, other corner (kept in a cupboard that doubles as a bookcase): recent additions. Kitchen: cookery books. Top of stairs: Penguins, fiction. Landing: books I have authored or with which I have a link, and copies of *Granta*. First bedroom: sport (in a huge bookcase). Second bedroom, wall on left of door: more hardback fiction, more politics and economics. Second bedroom, other wall: humour and outsize hardback novels – the depth of shelf space is greater here than anywhere else in the house. Office/ spare bedroom: fiction, paperback, non-Penguin. Loft: various in sealed plastic boxes. Garage: more of everything, again in sealed plastic boxes. Also dotted around the house, are various To Be Read piles.

A week after the inquest, the news report of Grandad's death appeared in the Middleton, Moston and Blackley Guardian, *the paper where I would start as a trainee journalist a year or so later. In the short piece he was named as* Joe *Duffy and his address given as the home where he'd barely spent a night. This was technically correct but must have hurt Gran after the thousands of nights looking after and looking out for him in their own home.*

Over the next week or so, the West Indian ladies from two doors down called on Gran to say they had prayed for Grandad at church; the young woman living across the street who was beaten by her boyfriend most weekends ('I've told her lots of times to leave him, that he's a bad 'un' – Gran) pushed a note of condolence through the door and old Harry, from round the corner, said he'd do any jobs for her that needed doing or get one of his lads to, if he wasn't well enough.

'Aren't people kind?' said Gran.

John W. Duffy was sixty-eight when he died.

I have arrived here – 3,500 books – by stealth. It's easily done if you acquire books on a regular basis, seldom discard any and are lucky enough to live into your mid-fifties. I also have a couple of specific interests, sport and music, about which I have hundreds of books. I could happily read biographies of ex-footballers, ex-cricketers, ex-boxers and ex-rock stars for the rest of my life, though I would consider it the same as gorging on sweets rather than 'proper' nourishing meals (i.e. novels).

If, for the sake of simple maths, it is assumed I began amassing books at the age of thirteen, it means that in the intervening 2,236 weeks I have added, on average, just over 1.5 books to my collection per week; it suddenly doesn't seem such a remarkable tally. In fact, I am mystified how anyone can go through life and manage *not* to bring home 1.5 books per week.

I have bought mainly from second-hand bookshops and charity stores. Over the past decade or so, books have become a cheap currency. They are everywhere. Book crossing is the act of releasing books 'into the wild' for a stranger to find. A local church, for example, has cardboard boxes full of hundreds of books left on pews, with an honesty box on the windowsill. A free-standing cabinet full of books has been installed in a herb garden next to a park in Todmorden, a town close to where I live. While folk rest on the benches enjoying the aroma of lavender or rosemary, they can borrow a book to read or take it home and bring another as a swap next time they are passing. On the town's main Facebook page, more than 600 posters have 'liked' the idea and nearly a hundred have passed positive comments, though one, 'Anna' fires a bullet of wary realism: 'There are some real magical people in todmorden shame they have to live among some total arse wipes though xxx' [*sic*].

On a recent drive out, in the leafy village of Colton (population: 212), North Yorkshire, I passed a phone box which had been converted into a book exchange. I had no knowledge of this trend even though BT has been operating an 'adopt a kiosk' scheme since 2009, which has seen more than a hundred lined with shelves and filled with books. They are in villages with splendid names that sound made up by J.K. Rowling while giddy on Earl Grey – Feock (Cornwall), Westbury-sub-Mendip (Somerset), Sheepwash (Devon), Dinder (Somerset), Little Rissington (Gloucester), Hemmingford Abbots (Cambridgeshire).

Back in Colton, I had to go in and out of the box at least five times and take about twenty photographs, such was my incredulity. Books in a phone box? And free of charge? I wanted to sit on the grass verge nearby and take stock, think about where I was and where I'd come from, young to middle-aged. The last time I had used a public phone was when I called Dad and he told me Grandad had died. Before that, I was about fifteen and in Rochdale town centre, probably cadging a lift back from the college disco. I remember the sturdy door, heaving it open and trying not to gip when snared by the overwhelming stench of urine; it was always a pleasant surprise if the phone was intact and working, and not vandalised. 'Mum can you pick me up?'

*

Poor Rochdale. After the shutdown of the 1970s and 1980s, the wrecking ball was let loose all over town. In some places, mill walls were left standing without a roof. As kids, we walked through, pretending to be a liberating army, the first in after the bombs had dropped. We shouted so our voices echoed. We'd find cotton spindles and pretend they were mortar bombs, throwing them at pigeons roosting in gaps where windows had once stood.

Despite poor conditions and low pay, the mills had provided social and structural identity and regular income. Rochdale is now post-recession, Anytown UK, devastated by the impact of the coronavirus pandemic, much the same as many of the UK's poorest regions. It is spotted with litter-strewn retail parks and circled by mad-busy dual carriageways. The people are defeated. It's in their faces. They are tired, worried. Every other passer-by seems to be coughing or limping. On weekdays, shopping arcades used to be free of men of working age but they are everywhere now, buying two-for-a-fiver microwave lasagnes and bumper packs of crisps. Kids yell to one another or into mobile phones. Tracksuit terrors strut past, wrangling panting pit bulls.

At least the hills and the moors remain, ever so. The landscape up there is hewn from millstone grit and soft peat. Curlews make insistent calls. Sheep scurry by. A walk through the microclimate of rain, sunshine and perpetual wind leaves you changed, slapped into an altered state of mind. Afterwards, cheeks glowing, legs tingling, it's a joy to sit down in the coarse grass and suck on a spitty self-rolled cigarette or snack on a biscuit dipped in flask tea. In summer, on those rare days when the wind relents, there is no greater pleasure than finding a spot, perhaps among the ferns, and making camp with a book (Thomas Hardy, Laurie Lee, perhaps, or H.E. Bates). No one will pass, no one will see you, and it allows a temporary but exquisite escape.

Up there, as the sun fades and day is done, the streetlights of Rochdale flicker in the nightfall sky like a gas ring on a huge cooker. Among close friends I have heard several monologues delivered at this point. Originally, years ago, it was how they were going to leave this runty little town behind and all it stood for. London or Manchester or Anywhere Else was their destination and a life bigger, better. Then, the tone changed, became bitter. They called it Shitdale or Rochdull. 'I should have left this place years ago,' they'd say. I never had this urge. I had my own head to wander around and more than enough books, teeming with characters to meet, places to visit. And Rochdale wasn't so bad. When darkness falls fully, the best vantage point is from the car park of the White House pub on the A58, the top road to Halifax. The streetlights merge below and it appears as if this golden spread has been specially ladled from the Pennines. When you're so far away, you don't see the litter, the graffiti, the mess and the mucked-up-ness. All you see is light.

PART TWO

Where Am I Going?

CHAPTER THIRTEEN

Google, the world's proxy, pulsating brain, estimates that 132 million books have been published in 'modern history' (presumably the last 250 years or so). The quantity is ever growing, with 2.2 million* new titles added each year across the world.

Such colossal numbers mean that even the most avid and dedicated reader is only ever going to catch a droplet of this waterfall of books. All the same, and in defiance of statistics, many people label themselves 'well read' or let others paint the compliment upon them. This concept of being well read is a cultural stance, a judgement from on high. Up there, looking down, is a cabal of the advantaged and highly educated and, because they speak with most authority and articulacy, their taste becomes the defining taste and, should you share it, you are deemed to also be *well read*.

* UNESCO.

Robert McCrum is archetypal. He was an editorial director at Faber & Faber from 1979 to 1989 and editor-in-chief from 1990 to 1995. He was literary editor of the *Observer* from 1996 to 2010. His father, Michael William McCrum CBE, was vice-chancellor of the University of Cambridge and headmaster at Eton College. There's more. Robert McCrum's mother, Christine fforde, was the daughter of Sir Arthur Frederic Brownlow fforde GBE, headmaster at Rugby School and chairman of the BBC for seven years. When the *Guardian* resolved to define the term 'well read',* Robert McCrum was summoned from his study. He kindly outlined that 'three kinds of reading define the well-read mind'. These were 'the classics of Greece and Rome' (his words); the 'Anglo-American literary tradition' and a classification he referred to as 'great writing in translation'. Of the forty-five writers he cited in total, I have read fifteen; I hadn't heard of six of them. I am, therefore, by his definition, one-third of the way to being well read.

McCrum's list, his largesse, is informed by the experiences of his own life. He was a boarder at Sherborne School in Dorset (founded AD 705, motto: *Dieu et Mon Droit*, God and My Right). On home visits between terms he might have found his father thumbing through a book he had authored with a chum from Cambridge University, possibly *Select Documents of the Principates of the Flavian Emperors: Including the Year of Revolution, A.D. 68–96*. Another evocative essence of the McCrum homestead is conjured by the recollection of his 'strongest childhood memory': 'The sound of rooks in the beech trees overlooking our garden in Cambridge.'† McCrum's eminence is such that he was also asked by the *Guardian* to nominate the '100 greatest novels of all time'

---

* 'The 100 best novels: from Bunyan's pilgrim to Carey's Ned Kelly', *Guardian*, August 2015.

† Interview, Pan Macmillan website, September 2017.

(October 2003); the '100 best novels written in English' (August 2015) and, altering the theme slightly, the '100 best nonfiction books of all time' (December 2017).

This is the way of the publishing world. It draws predominantly from the highest echelons, from proprietors to editors, agents to interns and then across to reviewers and broadcasters who filter ('gate-keep') and publicise books, or not. The industry is principally based in London, so staff members live in the capital or Home Counties. They are university educated, often from the Russell Group, and have names seldom heard at my old school: Allegra, Antoinette, Aurelia and Arabella – and that's just the As. They will each profess a love of books and affirm their open-mindedness, but instinct will draw them to literary themes and settings and characters recognisable from their own backgrounds; it happens across all creative media.

At least several leading figures have acknowledged what they classify as an 'inclusivity issue'. Penguin Random House UK (PRH) introduced an 'inclusion tracker' in 2017 with an aim to 'reflect UK society by 2025'.

'We are determined to publish a wider range of voices and books to more fully reflect the diverse society we live in,' said its CEO, Tom Weldon, a graduate in history from Oxford University. 'I feel sick in my stomach when I realise books and publishing don't reflect the world we live in. I fundamentally believe in books and in the power of books to shape culture and it is depressing and wrong that culture is driven by a narrow sector of society.'* Weldon has implemented two critical policies at PRH to stymie elitism and cronyism: he has removed the prerequisite of a university degree for recruitment and banned personal referrals for work experience.

* *Bookseller*, June and November, 2017.

Unlike ethnicity or gender, which is easy to discern – a person's name is usually enough – class is difficult to distinguish. An easy categorisation might be based on ancestry or education: what are your parents' occupations? What kind of school did you attend? Or on social etiquette: what do you call the evening meal: dinner, tea or supper? Or perhaps, diction: how do you pronounce the word 'class'? Weldon, as an insider, is an apposite force for change. If grievances are raised from elsewhere, the lower orders perchance, they are accused of cooking up a right old broth of jealousy, self-pity and victimhood – sour grapes, chips on the shoulder – and this has been, until recent years, a reflexive rebuttal; it indemnifies the industry from criticism so that self-serving cliques remain and no one stops to think who is running this precious business, how they are running it and who it is for.

Robert McCrum, bibliophile and accomplished writer notwithstanding,* typifies the select few granted hugely disproportionate influence. He is one of many, born to privilege and designated a 'taste-maker'. Will Self is another – pupil at University College School (one of twelve independent schools affiliated to Eton College); son of Peter John Otter Self, professor of public administration at the London School of Economics, and grandson of Sir Albert Henry Self KCB KBE, deputy chairman of the Ministry of Aviation and chairman of the Electricity Council.

When asked to tender book recommendations, these writers are fulfilling an enticing commission and doing so playfully and provocatively, with a genuine desire to share the delight of reading. Unfortunately, these endorsements can have the opposite effect and narrow the culture, forming a consensus that is the antithesis

---

* His book, *Every Third Thought: On Life, Death and the Endgame* (2017), a treatise on death, includes excellent reflections.

of the role books should play. Much worse, such lists and assumptions of 'well-readness' foster elitism. Haruki Murakami, author of *Norwegian Wood*, agrees: 'If you only read the books that everyone else is reading, you can only think what everyone else is thinking.' The philosopher Arthur Schopenhauer mocked the notion of a literary canon: 'Oh, how alike one commonplace mind is to another! How they are all fashioned in one form! How they all think alike under similar circumstances, and never differ! This is why their views are so personal and petty.'

McCrum's background and life experience is exceptionally rarefied. Most people do not have the desire, patience or even the capacity to read, say, *The Birds* by Aristophanes (one of his recommendations), first performed in 414 BC. For the benefit of the uninitiated (most of us), it opens with a conversation between two middle-aged Athenians, Peisetaerus and Euelpides, as they meet on a hillside. Peisetaerus begins:

> He told us that these two birds would show us the way to Tereus, the hoopoe who once was human and turned into a bird; and he sold us that Son of Tharreleides there, the jackdaw, for an obol, and this crow for three obols. But they turn out to know nothing but nipping.

The argument runs, and it may have validity, that within these 'classics of Greece and Rome' lie the seed of every story and every character written thereafter, but too often it feels a currency that jangles only in the pockets of the extremely well educated. Most of the rest of us are at the window, locked out, wondering what an obol is, who Tereus is, and how exactly a hoopoe turns into a human.

At times, becoming well read can feel a duty or obligation; this should be resisted at all costs. If someone sets about the chore, from A to Z – Adams (Douglas) to Záborský (Jonáš) – it is a measure of fastidiousness rather than intelligence. Also, who can recall the characters, plots and scenes even from a book read as recently as just a few years ago? One or two episodes may jab themselves into the memory bank but mostly the recollection will be elemental, the *feeling* you had while reading a book or were left with, having read it. To continue wearing the well-read badge will mean rereading all those same books, and more, on a loop, constantly refreshing the memory.

There is another arrow often fired at the conscience and credibility of the supposed well read: your reading is not of suffi-cient breadth in terms of ethnicity and gender. In my collection the ratio of female to male writers reflects the general trends in publishing. In broad terms, 5 per cent of authors, fiction and non-fiction, were women in the twentieth century and before; 25 per cent in the 1950s; 40 per cent by the 1970s and today there is parity. Shirley Jackson, the American novelist, subject of a biopic in 2020, provided a snapshot of society's view of female authors in her memoir of 1953, *Life Among the Savages*. She recalled a conver-sation with a receptionist as she attempted to book into hospital to deliver her third child:

'Occupation?'
'Writer,' I said.
'Housewife,' she said.
'Writer,' I said.
'I'll just put down housewife,' she said.

I have never thought to positively discriminate by an author's race or skin colour but my collection again probably mirrors the wider general trend. More than 87 per cent of authors are white, with 4.2 per cent identifying themselves as black and 1 per cent 'Asian' (of the Indian subcontinent). These figures are from the United

States* — none are available for the UK, although it is assumed approximately 10 per cent of authors are non-white in proportion to the total population; this is likely to increase under the influence of the Black Lives Matter movement.

I'm happy to be considered one-third of well read; it feels about right. I have never set myself up as anything more but people presume if you own a lot of books or review books for newspapers and magazines (as I have done) that, at the very least, you have heard of, if not read, every writer with whom they are familiar.

'You've never heard of . . . I *am* surprised.'

This chastisement is effective and I often investigate said author. For example, the Red Lion caucus was joined one evening by a friend of a friend. He made musical instruments from 'found' pieces of wood; he showed us pictures of them on his phone, and they were very impressive. There was an enforced break in the conversation as Elephant Bob (one of the locals, a big bloke) interrupted to talk about crisps; it's by far his favourite subject. The landlord had sourced some crisps from Belgium, the last box apparently, flavoured with a cheese called Postel.

'You've got to try them,' he said. 'This particular cheese was invented by monks at an abbey. They age it for nearly two years and, mixed with the potato, it has a lovely hint of nutmeg and cloves.'

We all nodded, exaggerating our interest. As he moved on, bumping into one or two tables (Elephant Bob!), there was a few seconds of silence before the instrument maker summoned a standard, filling-the-time, fallback question.

'What books are you reading at the moment?'

* Data USA, a platform with access to shared US government data.

This was the joint-first worst question I could be asked, along with what was I listening to *at the moment*. I dreaded it. I'd invariably discovered seven new bands *that week* on top of the five the week before and, all in, I could only remember the names of two of them, I think, probably. And books? Were we talking about the five in the boot of my car that I'd already dipped into or the three on the front seat, before we even get to the various piles growing higher than termite mounds all over the bloody house? Thankfully, before any of us could answer, he volunteered his own list, though he'd altered the criteria to his three best writers *of all time*.

'Forced to choose,' he said (odd, when he'd done the forcing), 'I'd go for Les Murray, Charles Willeford and Marguerite Duras.'*

I sensed that none of us had heard of these authors. Now, what to do? We could say nothing, to hopefully convey that we knew their work but preferred to talk of other subjects; we could go all-out duplicity and feign to know of them and were happy to discuss their work ('I much preferred Murray's early output, his naïve period'), though this risked inadvertently revealing our fraudulence, or should we be honest and say it: never heard of 'em. My policy, though rather wily, has always been the latter because it makes the person supplying the information feel good about themselves, and their response, whether helpful or patronising, provides a gauge to their personality. As I expected, being a writer and owning so many books, I was volunteered as the most suitable first-responder. I swerved the question with aplomb.

'Nutmeg and cloves? Who wants that when you can have prawn cocktail or Thai sweet chilli?'

*

* Les Murray is an Australian poet, Charles Willeford an American crime writer and Marguerite Duras a French novelist.

I have had similar experiences to the one outlined by Shirley Jackson; it is not exclusive to women. Whenever you tell anyone that you're a writer, the reaction is invariably the same. They stare. This saucer-eyed scrutiny says: 'You? A writer?' Sometimes I wish they'd just say it:

'Well, you don't look like one!'

Obviously writers don't walk the streets declaring their profession to passers-by. They keep it to themselves, coaxed into admission only on certain occasions, such as when away on a writing retreat. Denial is futile. Who else but a writer is holed up alone in a remote cottage out of season, stabbing away at a computer keyboard for four or five days? After staring you up and down, they – the cottage owner or cleaner or local shopkeeper – will ask:

'What's your book about, then?'

This is easy enough to answer if the work in progress is non-fiction, but a novel is another matter. My first thought is: I don't know what it's about. That's what I'm trying to find out by writing it.

'This and that,' I reply.

People can't bear vagueness.

'This and that, what?'

I make something up. They nod, unconvinced. They gawp some more and return to their original theme:

'A writer, hey?'

When they've gone, I ponder: how do they expect a writer to look? What's the mental image? In films, male writers tend to be lighthouse tall, middle-aged, scruffy, bearded and wearing either a corduroy or leather jacket, whatever the weather. They play jazz records and drink gin or whisky. They grumble and mumble and rub their foreheads while trying to remember where they've left their keys or cardigan, as if, outside of their work, they make no sense of themselves, or life. There is no similar stereotype for

285

female writers in films, which says much to the issue raised by Shirley Jackson back in the 1950s.

Being away on a retreat, cut off from all responsibility, warm and well fed and able to indulge in writing, borders on the sensual. When the writing goes well, treats are in order. This can be a flick through a magazine (as a reward, maybe, for 300 words completed) or tea and a chocolate biscuit (500 words). Switching on the television is risky. A sneaky ten-minute viewing can often stretch to an hour or more. Another bad idea is a trip to the local pub. The alcohol might help, you tell yourself – loosen up the writing. When you get there, you usually find yourself in the vicinity of a handful of stocky blokes in wellies and wax jackets. They speak in a local dialect and have clearly known one another since being knee high to a piglet. You find an uncosy corner and nurse a pint. After a few minutes you start to wonder if the barflies are talking about you, mocking you even. They keep looking over. *Don't they?* On your return to the cottage (bolting the door), the impact of all this self-reflection bleeds into the writing. What started out as a light-hearted novel goes night-dark, P.G. Wodehouse to Franz Kafka, and all because of the gassy, grassy pint and those *Straw Dog* extras down at the St Buryan Inn. It gets cold and you start to regret being so stingy. If a place is offered for rent appreciably lower than the others, it will be run-down, under-heated, dusty and spooky. Alone-happy can soon swap places with alone-neurotic.

Eventually a rhythm sets in. You eat when you're hungry, sleep when you're tired. It's best to cook simply. A week of microwave meals does no harm, probably. Plates and cups should be washed immediately after eating. It's therapeutic, especially if the water is warm and soapy. The days are slow yet somehow pass quickly. The exact minute when night drifts in, trading places with the afternoon, becomes noticeable outside the window; this oneness with nature is uplifting. It's best not to take books with you, for fear of adopting another author's voice and losing your own, which will add a schizophrenic element to your work; this might not be so bad for thriller writers.

My main period of intensive reading, when I seemed to glide from one novel to another without a break, was up until my late twenties. A book was always to hand wherever I went, in my coat pocket or in the side pocket of my holdall, on the arm of the chair, by my bed at night; always there. Much the same as a mobile phone in modern times, it was an object of distraction, something to place in my hands, set my eyes upon and use to drift away from the world around me. A book became a shadow self, so I seldom felt alone. The train might have been running late by two hours. It didn't matter. Nothing mattered. I could make camp on a bench on the platform or in the neon-lit café next to the taxi rank a few hundred yards from the station. I had a book and, if I had a book, I had me, wrapped up tight, safe from boredom, contented. No one, aside from the madman, picks on someone with a book in their hands. It is a statement: here is someone living a life parallel, happily withdrawn, no harm to anyone, not worth the agitation of a disagreement and then a fight. Move on, nothing to see here.

Afterwards, I still read but life became busier, fuller, especially when we had children. After a couple of hours of Biff, Chip, Kipper and Floppy the dog* and *We're Going on a Bear Hunt*†, with the boys squeezed into a chair next to me, the inclination to return to a novel was appreciably reduced. A glass of wine or can of beer and an hour or so of soporific television formed a much easier slip

---

* Characters from books written by Roderick Hunt and illustrated by Alex Brychta.

† A children's picture book written by Michael Rosen and illustrated by Helen Oxenbury, 1989.

road into sleep. The next morning, the day stretching long and wide, the same vow as the day before was made again (along with the routine self-rebuke for being so weak yesterday): tonight I will read a book.

Around that time, my thirties, was probably when I began to accumulate books at a rate considerably greater than my capacity to read them. Life, much as we try to keep it at arm's length or delude ourselves that it falls under our dominion, often 'blindsides you at 4 p.m. on some idle Tuesday'.* The *big stuff* — bereavement, divorce, illness, heartbreak, a global pandemic — crashes randomly before us, splat, and reading becomes impossible with a head and heart weighed with pain and worry and regret. And the *good stuff* can impact on our reading, too: a new relationship, an urge to travel, an exciting project or an irresistible call for a reinvention of self.

Books don't mind. They are patient. They await your return.

* From an essay in the *Chicago Tribune* of June 1997, written by columnist Mary Theresa Schmich and later featured on the hit single 'Everybody's Free (To Wear Sunscreen)', by Baz Luhrmann.

CHAPTER FOURTEEN

Here, in this house, my house, books are for ever. They're everywhere. It is difficult to find a place where a book or several books don't fall within the eyeline. There will be a trail of set-down books leading the way to wherever I am in the house and by the sixth or seventh title a visitor will have a good idea of my personality. If it sounds like a mansion, it's not – you can fit a lot of books in a house of normal size.

Outside, away from here, books are not so omnipresent. The consensus is that the book is fighting for its life. Over the past decade sales of new books (print and e-books combined) have fallen by more than a third in the UK. Admittedly, these figures are skewed somewhat by the phenomenon of the Harry Potter series, which sold more than 500 million worldwide in the previous decade. All hail Lord Voldemort and Professor Albus Dumbledore.

Set against books, demanding attention and consuming days,

is a marching army of louder, brighter, faster, more easily accessed forms of amusement. Where, forty years ago, 'home entertainment' consisted only of a television, radio and record player, there is now enough cultural sustenance to last multiple lifetimes. The PC, laptop, mobile phone and iPad alone are, or can be, a portal for (as good as) the *everything* of modern living, namely shopping, banking, reading, writing, corresponding, photography, designing, recording, matchmaking, studying and sex. Spotify (and other streaming services) allows instant access to most of the world's recorded library of music. On our 55-inch widescreen full HD, smart LED televisions with infrared extenders and five years' warranty we can watch hundreds of channels. We can also, via Netflix, YouTube, Amazon Prime Video and Apple TV, view almost every film, pop video, concert or television programme ever made. These same devices are also utilised for video games, an industry which, since 2018, has matched the music and film business in revenue terms – it generates approximately $43 billion per year in the US and $140 billion worldwide.* What chance the book, so one-dimensional and frail?

Such is the ocean of choice on offer, people feel anxious, overawed, unable to alight on a single entertainment and so 'surf' from a film to a television programme to a podcast to a song, a magazine to a book, and then back again. They make high demands, fast-forwarding to the chorus, skim-reading to the 'interesting' sections, undertaking internet searches if the pace drops in a film, perhaps researching that very film. Warnings about the 'grasshopper mind' were first issued more than a century ago. Press adverts told us this person 'nibbled at EVERYTHING and mastered NOTHING'. Russell Brand, the 'award-winning comedian, actor, author and public thought

---

* Bloomberg.

leader' (from his website), outlined a similar malaise: 'There are things that I'm not doing that I should be doing or that I *am* doing that I shouldn't be doing and some deeper aspect of me is aware of this and trying to correct it.'

Previously we had a subconscious belief that *we could get round to everything* whether it be a film, music or reading material. The pathways through to us were few (letters, conversations, the radio) and this led to the illusion that we knew about all that existed. Now, on an average day, via Twitter, email, Facebook and scores of other sources, we are sent recommendations about, or links to, songs, films, newspaper articles and much more. We are left wired and tired because by instinct we want to experience all these but can't, and so we are perpetually frustrated and disappointed, as if we have let ourselves down. This feeling is exacerbated because we know time is finite; all will end. Under this kind of pressure, a tension is created where nothing seems good enough, grand enough, for the moment we are in.

Scientists have discovered that when we switch from one device to another it causes an increase in cortisol, a stress hormone that works with certain parts of the brain to control mood, motivation and fear. Adrenaline is also released, leading to mental confusion or scrambled thinking. A random, ever-changing focus causes the body to also create dopamine, a neurotransmitter, and this quickly becomes a loop where the brain is rewarded for losing focus and constantly searching for external stimulation. Even worse, the prefrontal cortex has a *novelty bias*, meaning its attention is easily snagged by the new and colourful and shiny. If, while watching television or working at a PC, we check the internet, click on our email account or send a text, each of these activities tweaks the novelty and reward-seeking areas of the brain, causing a burst of endogenous opioids (effectively a close relative of methadone), to the detriment of our staying *on task*. Instead of reaping the substantial rewards that come from sustained, focused effort, such as reading a book, we instead receive empty prizes for completing a thousand small, sugar-coated tasks.*

The printed book has already had a head-to-head skirmish with technology. At the time, it was forecast to send books the way of the fax machine, VHS player and fold-away maps. I resisted buying an e-reader – 'a device that you can carry with you and use to download and read texts and books in electronic form'.†
They were introduced in 1998 and hundreds of reports and think pieces ran across the media, most claiming an 'X' had been marked on the jacket of the printed book: doomed.

Typically, J.D. Salinger was an early objector, insisting that his work should be available only in print. After he died, his son, Matthew, relented, claiming he had received a letter from a woman with a hand disability who could not manipulate physical books; his father would not have been so easily swayed. Maurice Sendak, the author and illustrator of children's books including *Where the Wild Things Are* and *Little Bear*, was unequivocal: 'Fuck them, is what I say. I hate those e-books. They cannot be the future. I will be dead, I won't give a shit.'‡ Ray Bradbury, author of *Fahrenheit 451*, felt the same. He told the *New York Times*: 'They wanted to put a book of mine on Yahoo! You know what I told them? "To hell with you. To hell with you and to hell with the internet."'

The new, in whatever guise, has a particular appeal, especially if it is considered hi-tech and is sparkly and sleek and can be held in the hands, tumbled from one palm to the other, slipped into

---

* Information drawn largely from *The Organised Mind: Thinking Straight in the Age of Information Overload* by Daniel J. Levitin, 2014.
† *Collins Dictionary*.
‡ *The Colbert Report*, US late-night news and satire programme, 2012.

the back pocket – they are purposely designed to embrace this fetishistic element. When first introduced, e-books sold almost as many as printed books. Sales peaked in 2012 and have waned since, currently making up 16 per cent* of book sales despite being heavily pushed by Amazon, which accounts for 95 per cent† of the market. The data suggests that many were intrigued by the e-book, bought one, but have now reverted back to print books, or combine both.

I couldn't see a single feature of an e-reader that was an enhancement of a printed book, apart, at first, from when on a foreign holiday. If we were off to Branscombe or Filey by car I could jam thirty books into plastic bags, and often did, but this wasn't possible on a plane with increasing pressure to take hand luggage only, which meant a case about the size (but not the weight) of three house bricks. What use were two or three books on holiday? They were quickly read and nowhere near enough sustenance to service the many moods of a week laid low, given to reflection. The answer, I was told (by several people – it *was* 2011, when these devices were supposed to be chasing printed books into the sea, never to be seen again), was a Kindle. An obliging friend uploaded onto his device a few of my favourite books and others I'd not yet read. I remained open-minded and disallowed myself any scepticism over this piece of borrowed kit. Whatever the means of delivery, this was still literature, words gathered together and lined up to tell a story or create a mood, or inform.

During the outward flight I switched it on and was impressed that the format emulated the printed page so faithfully; it would be the only time I looked on a Kindle with fondness. Words on a

* Nielsen.
† Amazon.

screen reminded me of work and I was looking for a non-existent keyboard, ready to start proofing, snipping a word or sentence here and there, cut and pasting whole paragraphs. On a practical level, despite negating the need for lots of books, it was a disaster. The glare from the sun made the screen almost invisible. I put on my sunglasses but could barely see the text. I fiddled with the brightness but at every increase in light words left the screen and faded to white. On the beach I was worried sand might get into it or I'd drop it into a rock pool. More than anything else, it became *something else to fret about*, much the same as a mobile phone, debit cards or passports. Holidays were about shedding worries and responsibilities, letting go. I gave back the Kindle. Not for me, thanks.

Whatever the pressures and competing distractions, the book trade is still with us, still functioning – 191 million new books were sold in the UK in 2018,* creating revenue of nearly £8 billion† and employing nearly 200,000 people.‡ Books survive because their perceived weakness is an absolute strength. They are a quiet, meditative pleasure, a necessary antidote to the clang and clamour of everything else happening within the average household. A book left in a room, ready to be picked up or among others in a bookcase, is a symbol of downtime to come, a respite. Much the same as a walk in the countryside, it is a pure delight that doesn't alter – it was there before, last week, last year, even when you were a child. And it awaits your return, loyal to the memory.

* Statistica.
† Creative Industries Council, a joint forum between the creative industries and UK government.
‡ Creative Industries Council.

A book is genuinely organic – it was made from trees! The sensory greeting will always be the same and with that comes familiarity, reassurance. Run your fingers along the cover and feel its texture, whether it is matt or laminate and the title or author's name is embossed. If it is hardback, put it on its side so it can stand tall and strong. Cradle the paperback in your hands, careful not to damage the spine. Hold the book to your face. The inky cover will smell different from the pages inside. The sounds – opening the covers, rustling the paper – will enchant. After an hour of reading, a fair number of pages will stack up next to your thumb and, although you know it doesn't really matter, this will feel a wholesome achievement, the same as having a jog or eating a healthy meal.

As you read, reconnecting with yourself and the author and the wider world of books, you are assured that what you see, hear and feel is everything; nothing else is going on. A book is honest. Unlike a digital screen and its associated paraphernalia, it does not have an unseen eye and a spider's web network busy sharing and scheming your profile to sell you more, always more. And neither does it have a multitude of distractions, fired at the synapses of your brain, imploring you to send an email, check your Facebook page, update your anti-virus software or look, once more, through the folder of your holiday snaps from 1998. A book pulls none of these tricks, pecuniary or emotional, and is what it is, stays what it is: words on a page.

After the busyness of a working day and a home filled with activity, the act of reading can become a near preternatural experience. But, gentle warning – if it is a designated 'holiday' from self, a sequestrated joy, there is a great danger that reading will become a corridor to the next stage in relaxation: sleep. The conditions favourable to sleeping also apply to reading: quiet, warmth, solitude, a comfy chair, not being hungry or thirsty and, most of all, having peace of mind. I first started drifting off while reading in my mid-forties; it was another stage in life, much the same as needing glasses to see small print or rising carefully from chairs to avoid a back spasm.

Many people read as an intended prelude to sleep and take a book to bed to help them wind down; some believe that the left–right (and back again) movement of the eyes across a page can work as self-hypnotism. A pattern can set in where a book is so associated with sleep that it is a job to stay awake and read at any time of day. The answer is to break the connection or at least disturb the pattern. At the first sign of sleepiness, an elongated wink or the head dropping, it helps to stand and stretch or at least change position in the chair. If this doesn't work, walk around the room or take a drink, open a window or jog on the spot to get blood moving more quickly around the body. A healthy, normal heart rate when sleeping is between sixty and eighty beats per minute for an adult, so a higher rate will fend off sleep. If all this fails and there is no limit on time, snooze and read and take equal pleasure in both.

The converse problem is a wide-awake and alert mind communing with a book that is undeserving of such attention. How long do you give a book? This is presuming it is sharing house space with you, so the title, cover, blurb, author's photo and perhaps the first page (read in the shop) have already passed muster. Whether recommended by a friend, well reviewed in a newspaper or bought on impulse, it's personal now: you and the book. Subscribers to Goodreads (ninety million members, Amazon-owned) said they completed 38 per cent of all books they started. This is an extraordinary commitment but they will be a benevolent lot by virtue of the fact they have joined what is virtually a global book club. They probably eat all their greens and exercise even when they have colds.

Among friends, I was surprised at how much of a bad book

they were willing to stand. The recurring number of pages they cited before passing judgement was a minimum of fifty, but sometimes a hundred. Hari Kunzru, author of *The Impressionist* and *Gods Without Men* said:

> I used to force myself to finish everything I started, which I think is quite a good discipline when you're young, but once you've established your taste, and the penny drops that there are only a certain number of books you'll get to read before you die, reading bad ones becomes almost nauseating.*

Arthur Schopenhauer had many peculiar views (women were, he claimed, 'childish, frivolous and short-sighted') and was brilliantly partisan about books. 'Life is too short for bad books,' he wrote. 'A few pages should be quite enough for a provisional estimate of an author's productions. Bad books are intellectual poison; they destroy the mind.'

I'm with Hari and Arthur. I *always* judge a book by the first page. If the writing is awkward, forced, unfathomable or pretentious, I move on. Otherwise I know that trying to make sense of it, let alone enjoy it, will be like viewing the world through someone else's glasses. If I get past the first page, I give most books a further fifteen to twenty, regardless of whether I bought it at full price or found it discarded on a train. I don't owe the author anything but he or she owes me a fair exchange for that most valuable commodity: time. Besides, when I was more generous and benevolent, not once did a book improve substantially to contradict or invalidate my original thoughts. Sometimes, I remain unsure after the twenty pages but I make a decision by

* *New York Times*, March 2017.

deferring a decision. I'll put it down with every intention of returning to it, giving it another chance, but I won't remember the route back. By then, more recently purchased books will stand in the queue before it or I'll be pulling out books from my collection, flipping them from spine-out to front, and back into my world.

I am a bibliophile and not a bibliomaniac. There is a world of difference. Bibliomania is a mental illness with an inventory of established symptoms: an overwhelming desire to collect books irrespective of genre, subject or author; amassing multiple copies of the same book; and hoarding them randomly so that living areas often become hazardous and unhygienic. Untreated, social alienation develops and, perhaps most disturbing, a lack of interest in reading.

The condition was first cited by the Anglican clergyman Reverend Thomas Frognall Dibdin in his satirical book published in 1809, *Bibliomania; or Book Madness*. Dr Max Sander, of the Northwestern University Pritzker School of Law in Chicago, outlined the curse:*

> Some people think that collecting old books is a kind of mild insanity. The collector, on his side, smiles upon the ignorant who cannot understand the enjoyment of collecting. The philosopher says: 'Ne quid nimis', go not too far. But of all adages this one is the most difficult to follow. The bibliophile is the master of his books, the bibliomaniac their slave. With the development of bibliomania, the friendly, warming flame of a hobby becomes a devastating, ravaging wildfire, a tempest of loosened

---

* *Journal of Criminal Law and Criminology*, 1943.

and vehement passions. We are then in the presence of a pathological, irresistible mental compulsion.

The modern diagnosis of bibliomania is that it is a type of OCD and has two forms of treatment: cognitive behavioural therapy and medication. It is not intrinsically life-threatening, although a house crammed with books can be a harbinger of insects, mice and rats, and a fire hazard. The Collyer brothers (Homer and Langley) were two eccentrics who packed 25,000 books and tons of newspapers into their home in Harlem, New York, in the 1930s and 1940s. They had to slide on their bellies through tunnels to navigate the building; it did not end well.*

Psychiatrists believe books function as a carapace, putting a barrier between the collector and any trauma or unhappiness they may have sustained. Hoarding books can be viewed as a self-made source of anxiety, much the same as self-harming, to skirt the real source of distress. In effect, hoarders are choosing a pseudo-concern rather than confronting real issues often dating back to childhood – sexual abuse, hostility or having possessions taken by force; studies show that hoarders report a greater incidence of such violation. My version of this would have been someone hurling my PG Tips card collection to the wind. Or telling me that books would leave me myopic and friendless and I'd suffer chronic bouts of impetigo and scabies. They meant well.

The bibliomaniac largely views books as he might bricks, albeit with slightly different shapes, colours and textures. He (they are almost always men) builds walls and barriers from them

---

* Langley died when a 'tunnel' collapsed on top of him. His corpse was found near an early X-ray machine and the jawbone of a horse. Homer, who was blind, subsequently starved to death, unable to raise the alarm and trapped within 120 tons of junk.

in his home. Hoarders of a more general nature do this with discarded items or even refuse, but by using books the bibliomaniac believes it is much less of a transgression from 'normal' behaviour. The difference is that while most houses contain a limited number of books that have been read, or soon will be, usually neatly organised, his collection fills every room randomly and eventually *becomes* the house.

Meanwhile, a bibliokleptomaniac or bibliomane is someone with a compulsion to steal books. The most famous is Stephen Blumberg, aka 'the book bandit'. He embarked on lengthy road trips by Cadillac during which he stole 23,600 books worth $5.3 million from 327 libraries and museums across the United States and Canada. He said he was on a mission to 'liberate' rare books and materials kept hidden from the public as part of a government plot. His modus operandi was to pretend to be a visiting member of a university faculty (using the name Matthew McGue) and ask whether he could see certain antique books and papers, which he referred to specifically by name to verify his credentials. In a tweed jacket and with dishevelled hair, he looked the part, though staff later recalled that he was 'slightly smelly'. He was rumbled many times but made numerous escapes, often via ventilation ducts in ceilings and elevator shafts. He was finally caught in March 1990, aged forty-one. The 'Blumberg Collection', kept at his home in Ottumwa, Iowa, weighed 19 tons. W. Dennis Aiken, an FBI special agent, said a '50-ft hole in the ground encased in concrete' would be needed to stop Blumberg stealing books. He was jailed for seven years and fined $200,000. On his release, he began to steal again.

The world's largest personal collection of books is held by 'John Q. Benham'.* He lives in a detached two-storey property in

---

* *Guinness Book of World Records*. He is also known as John Lawrence Benham, Yochanan John Lawrence Benham and Messianic Rabbi Benham, Ph.D., Th.D.

Avoca, Lawrence County, Indiana, and is said to own more than 1.5 million books. They are piled, floor to ceiling, throughout the house and take up most of his garage space (which previously held six cars). Mounds of books covered in tarpaulin are also deposited on his land. Benham lives a quiet, insular life among woods and fields and is barely known, even by locals. He collects his mail from the local post office, often at night.

'I met Mr Benham once or twice more than twenty years ago, when I was helping price collectible books for a local charity book sale,' said an Avoca resident. 'At that time, he had an arrangement with the organisers of the sale to pick up all unsold books afterwards, in order to preserve them. He also mentioned that he was a Messianic Rabbi, but I'm afraid that I don't know any more about him than that. I haven't seen or heard from him for some time.'

Benham has not done any media interviews or, so it appears, even spoken to friends and neighbours; it remains a mystery why he has accumulated so many books.

Umberto Eco, the author and philosopher, had a personal library of more than 30,000 titles. He said that he, and other bibliomaniacs, encased themselves in books as a signifier of unrealised knowledge. His intellectual hunger, curiosity and humility was burnished, he claimed, by the constant reminder of all that he did not know, held in those books.

CHAPTER FIFTEEN

I booked in to get myself checked out, just to be sure. I visited, separately, a psychologist and a life counsellor. I'd had similar consultations before, for fear of flying, so my unease about possibly having too many books seemed, by comparison, a relatively minor issue. The psychologist was Jennifer and the life counsellor, Lisa.

They both lived in substantial detached houses on private estates. Jennifer asked me to take off my shoes at the door; she was ready with the slippers. She had big fuzzy hair trained into a top knot. I passed a shiny Buddha figure on the way to the 'consulting room' (her spare bedroom). She was smiley and nodded almost every time she blinked. She asked whether I 'treasured' books. I answered that I cherished the *concept* of books and reading but not individual books – I could always buy another copy if one got damaged (I've accidently dropped books down the toilet and in the bath before, for example).

She blinked some more. After six seconds (I counted them) she said she was surprised by my answer. She asked me to continue.

'I don't see them like that,' I said. 'They're not artefacts, they're books. It's great if they've got lovely laminated covers and the rest of it but it's what's inside that matters. I'm not interested in first editions or rarities. I don't buy them as investments. I'm not sure I like people who do that actually; they seem completely different from me.'

She asked how I felt when I saw and then entered a bookshop. I smiled. I was thinking of a quote by Alfred Edward Newton, the American book collector who turned most of his manor house in Pennsylvania into a library:

> Even when reading is impossible, the presence of books acquired produces such an ecstasy that the buying of more books than one can read is nothing less than the soul reaching towards infinity. We cherish books even if unread. Their mere presence exudes comfort, their ready access reassurance.

I considered saying this aloud or at least paraphrasing it but thought it could be viewed as showing off, which might swerve us into a whole new area of counselling, or, worse, that I had learned it by rote as a self-protective mechanism, gathering evidence for the defendant. In this case, me.

'I get a thrill,' I said. 'Well, it's like two, possibly three, thrills. First off, I get the thrill of seeing the shop, anticipating what is inside, and this reminds me of other thrills I had, possibly as a child — that same feeling of seeing a bookshop or even books for sale somewhere: garden centres, jumble sales, places like that. And so it's kind of a nostalgic thrill, a memory of a thrill, sort of. And the third thrill is the one of being excited about the actual books I'm going to find in there. It's a definite chemical tingle going around my body.'

'Does it matter what book or books you find in there?'

'Definitely. I feel I'm actually quite choosy about what I buy, which might sound odd considering I've got so many. I always believe I'm going to read every book or at least try it out.'

'These books you already own,' she started. 'If I were to take a quick look at them, what would I learn about you?'

'There's a fair bit of variety.'

'Really?'

Actually, was this true?

'I don't own many of what you might call contemporary novels,' I said.

'Who or what kind of writers are we talking about?'

I began listing them.

'Donna Tartt, Ian McEwan, Kazuo Ishiguro, Hanif Kureishi, I suppose. I like most of their stuff but, actually, now I think about it, they've been around for years. I bought Sally Rooney's book, *Conversations with Friends*, and that one with the brilliant cover – *The Girls* by Emma Cline. I wanted to like them and really tried but I couldn't. If I'm honest, they annoyed me. In fact, a lot of modern books annoy me.'

I wondered whether she'd heard of these books and writers, if it made any sense to her. Most people didn't keep up to date with literature.

'Do you think there is an element of you venerating the past, holding on to it, and your collection represents this?'

'Not really. I'd love to find new writers I like. There's nothing more inspiring than finding something new and brilliant.'

'Does it bother you, from where you source your books?'

'I'm happy enough to get them from anywhere . . .' I stopped for a second. 'Come to think about it, I'm not any more. I didn't used to mind spending hours in damp basements under shops where books were scattered across tables or piled into towers from the floor. They would always be dimly lit with a single bulb hanging by a frayed cord, casting shadows across peeling-off posters from 1968. These days, if it smells musty or I see mould on the walls or little trays of poison put out for mice, I leave it. I'm also fussier about the books I buy. If they're not in reasonable condition, I won't pick them up. I can't stand it if they're foxed or creased or the pages have gone yellow and dry in the sun.'

She asked what 'foxed' meant.

'It's those spots that you get on old paper. It probably got its name because it's that reddish-brown colour, the same as a fox's fur.'

'I see,' she said. 'Now, what do you think books have given you that maybe other things haven't?'

I'd already thought about this many times and had an answer – a rather grand one.

'This might sound a bit pretentious but bear with me,' I said. 'Over the years I've sat down with many people who exceed my intelligence and speed of thought. They can better tell jokes and remember stories. They are more popular. Among these and everyone else, I have always felt, whatever the force around me, positive or negative, a sort of stillness which I believe comes from books.'

'How would you describe this stillness?'

I was at my magniloquent best; it might have been that Buddha statue or the soft, dainty slip-on slippers:

'The tranquillity is the husk and to break it open is to find patience and self-confidence and, I suppose, happiness within myself. If it were a picture, at my best, especially if I've been reading a lot, we're talking daisies dappled in sunlight, clouds in a clear blue sky or sparkly, flowing rivers – you know, that stuff you get on the cover of self-help books. Another thing is that when it comes to my turn to speak, the words usually come to mind ordered and incisive and fall that way from the lips: this is down to books. I had no schooling to speak of, so a few hundred novels read over significant years of my life, aged fifteen to twenty-two, and many more afterwards, were my educators.'

I was hoping she would pick up on this last bit so I could waterfall my life story, how I felt I was a weird cuckoo kid placed with the wrong parents and had been failed by the education system and how I'd missed out. Basically, all my self-pitying stuff, laid on good and thick. I caught her glancing at her watch and realised there was only a few minutes left. Time for her summary. According to Jennifer, I *collected* books rather than hoarded them, so this meant I 'swerved any serious mental health issues'. That said, 3,500 was rather a lot and she counselled, in typical psych-speak, that I should monitor my behaviour to ensure it didn't become *uncontainable* or *impact negatively on other aspects of my life*. At the door, I handed back her slippers.

Lisa's consulting room was a summer house at the bottom of her garden. There was a pleasing smell of creosote and wood heated by the sun. She was younger than Jennifer, in her thirties. She had very long hair, so straight that it looked as if it had been ironed. As she spoke, introducing herself, she crossed her legs and I noticed she was wearing black plimsolls, the type I'd not seen since school. She clearly had me down, straight off, as a hoarder. She handed me four laminated cards containing quotes vouching for the majesty of decluttering.

'It's all on these,' she said, as if any agenda of life, crackpot or effectual, was unimpeachable so long as it was printed in a font of suitable gravitas, laid on pristine white paper and sealed in thin plastic. The quotes, obviously lifted from the internet, read:

'The benefits of decluttering go beyond just the tangible benefits of a clutter-free, tidy home. Decluttering can become an important way to practice self-care because it helps you take control of your home, your life and your "stuff" to improve your overall well-being.' *Melissa, Simple Lionheart Life, a tea-drinking, yoga-loving mama whose favourite place to be is at home.*

'Clutter stops that energy flow and creates stagnation, exhaustion, and exasperation. Having stagnant energy in your home is like rolling a boulder up a hill and having it roll back on you each time you stop to rest: everything requires lots of force, and nothing is fun. When you dig through mess, you're likely to excavate a lot of deep emotional residue that's buried in your clutter. Everything from bad memories to broken dreams can get uncovered in a deep clean, and each one you confront creates more room for the truly new.' *Dana Claudat, designer and Feng Shui Master.*

'Clutter can even become a psychological crutch. You may start worrying that you need an item "just in case", and you may become paralysed at the idea of not having it. In this way your clutter will be feeding into your anxiety, and you will become anxious as you contemplate removing it. At this point you'll have invited a trigger for anxiety into your own home!' *Kylie Browne, organising advocate. '80s music fan. Busy Mom. Amateur over-thinker. Thrives on coffee and chocolate.*

'Clutter leads to anxiety, embarrassment, family stresses. When you relieve the problem and learn to throw things away, you feel better.' *Dr Robert London, a New York City-based mental health professional.*

'Is it proved, all this?' I asked.

'Decluttering is widely held to be beneficial to the state of mind and general health.'

'*Widely held?*'

'Well, I suppose it would be very difficult to present absolute empirical evidence,' she said.

I'd seen pictures of these declutter zealots on the internet. They were trying hard to exude happiness and healthiness, in their white T-shirts, tight jeans and stuck-on smiles, but they actually looked poorly. Or possessed, at least. And most of them were promoting their books: clutter sold to you by a declutterer.

'I think these people are weird,' I said. 'They don't look like me or anyone I know.'

'Don't you think so?'

Hadn't she noticed? Maybe all her friends smiled like that and wore white T-shirts and tight jeans.

'I think there's something wrong with them,' I said.

This was the good thing about therapy. The financial transaction meant they were duty bound to listen carefully and kindly, so you could let loose much more than with friends; not that this would help alleviate my 'condition', from which, I knew, I wasn't really afflicted. The downside was that you always resented them a little because the sessions cost about £1 a minute, at least, so you had to constantly weigh up whether it was worth being a bit rude or antagonistic to someone when it was starting to add up.

'They're like a cult,' I said. 'They've thought something up, agreed to it and now they're all devout about it. I bet if you did a survey you'd find that they had, even after all their decluttering, more mental health issues than your average person. If you take away a person's belongings or make them feel it's not normal to have many, it rubs out their history, reduces them. It makes us all the same. I love going into people's houses that are full of mementoes [I was thinking of my aunty Lizzy and her dolls and some of the wonderful nutcases I'd interviewed when working for local papers – the man with a model zoo installed in his bath, for example], where you can't move for bumping into Portmeirion pottery or photo albums or the entire back catalogue of *Mad* magazine. It shows that a person has got personality, that they've been to places and collected stuff. And it also speaks of their ties to family and community and what they've achieved in life. I'm not talking Mr Trebus, that's different altogether.'

'Who's Mr Trebus?' she asked.

'He was this bloke on a telly programme, *Life of Grime*, from years ago. He filled his house with newspapers, boxes and bags. Almost up to the ceiling in every room.'

She made notes and then asked:

'Do you think your attitude is a tad defensive?'

I hated the word 'tad'.

'I agree it could be construed as being defensive but I don't honestly believe I've anything to defend. I'm not a hoarder, I know that, and I'm not in denial that I'm a hoarder.'

'What would you say is the single most important issue that is causing you concern about owning 3,500 books?'

'I suppose I'm trying to make sense of why I've got them and keep adding more and yet I know I haven't got the time left to read them.'

'Do you sometimes get a sense of anxiety or panic when you think about this?'

I said I did.

'Have you ever considered meditation?'

'Not really, but a few years ago I had some EM-something done to me.'

'EMDR – eye movement desensitisation and reprocessing?'

'That's it. I had to keep following the end of this woman's finger while she did all these squiggles.'

'Did it make you feel better afterwards?'

'No, I felt sick.'

I thought she was going to laugh but she held it in.

'If you don't mind my asking, why were you having this treatment?'

'I didn't know I was until she whipped out her finger and started drawing these figure eights in front of me. I'd gone to see her because I was feeling stressed, overawed.'

'Do you have a partner at the moment?'

I said that I did.

'Do you live together?'

'Yes.'

'In your previous relationships, were you left?'

This seemed intrusive, but I didn't mind.

'As in, dumped?'

She nodded.

'Twice,' I answered.

'How did you respond?'

'I was quite a wreck.'

'People often use the term "heartbroken". Would you go that far?'

I was at a loss to know what this had to do with books.

'Yeah, I was devastated. It took me by surprise on both occasions.'

'Sometimes people say they feel a kind of heightened state of awareness at such times. Would you say that stood for you?'

I remembered that I'd been hugely affected by song lyrics at the time. I'd parked the car once or twice to shed a tear. Well, several tears. I told her this.

'Did you find the same held for reading, that you saw things more clearly or felt it had more resonance to your life than before?'

'Not really. I was hardly sleeping or eating and this made me too restless and fidgety to read. I couldn't concentrate on anything. My reading, or not doing, is a good barometer to my state of health and happiness.'

'Do you worry that you might be left again and you are storing up all these books because they can provide succour in a time of extreme grief?'

This was an interesting theory.

'Possibly. I do believe books offer that, as much as anything else.'

'Offer what?'

'A sharing of emotions, someone else going through the same thing. When that happens in a book, a description of a certain feeling that you thought only you had, it's incredible.'

'How incredible?'

'Like when you see a beautiful sunset over the sea, something that only comes along now and again in your life.'

'How were you throughout the lockdown during the coronavirus pandemic?' she asked.

I imagined this had become a standard question in mental health circles.

'Not good.'

'Why was that?'

'I felt lonely. I know everyone did but I was particularly bad.'

'Why do you think that was the case?'

'Is it okay if I swear?'

'Go ahead.'

311

'I felt the government fucked it up. In fact, I felt the whole world did. I couldn't believe or accept what was going on, the hysteria, the mass compliance.'

'Did you ever feel this was to do with you rather than anyone else?'

'All the time. I always question myself, too much probably. It makes life complicated. Like I said, I felt lonely, as if everyone else was going mad and I was the only one sane, but everyone else thought it was me that was mad. I think a few friends were a bit worried about me actually.'

'Do you think this was ultimately about control and you were at your most reduced at that time, completely powerless?'

I could see where we were going. I hated the term but knew she was about to use it.

'Is there a little bit of the control freak about you?'

'I would have hated that thought until a few years ago but I don't care any more,' I said. 'I'm quite proud of it, in fact. I'm happy to be considered a control freak in a world where everything is always getting fucked up by people who don't know what they're doing.'

'Don't you feel you could change things if you really wanted to, even on a small level?'

'Probably.'

'What's stopping you?'

'Two things. It's all too far gone and I'm sort of shy. I've not been trained to speak in public. I'm not confident enough. You've got to be born to that kind of thing.'

I was hoping, again, to start letting it all out, summoning the cuckoo kid who'd gone to the worst school in the world and was told he was the size of an ant, day after day (weekends included). She cut across me as if cauterising a wound.

'We shouldn't really linger on the pandemic or force parallels. It let loose a global paranoia.'

She'd brought it up!

'Fine,' I said.

I'd had only limited experience of therapy and considered most of it similar to a one-on-one conversation in the Red Lion with a good, long-standing pal. Occasionally, though, a nugget of gold would tumble, so true and powerful and helpful that it didn't matter whether it was gleaned from a New Age manual or if a Hopi Native American had said it to a Cherokee on a rickety bridge over Alamuchee Creek in Alabama. Lisa was about to more than justify her fee. Here comes the gold.

'On one hand, by having such a collection and planning to read all these books, you are making a fantastic statement of hope and revealing an investment in future self,' she said. 'Even if you recognise you probably won't have time to read them all, you are already forming a relationship with mortality which we all must do at some point in our lives. The snag is the frustration you say you feel that comes with this realisation. This is something you need to deal with and accept. I sense that some of this dissatisfaction is because, for whatever reason, you have not read as many of these books as you'd have liked and you spend a lot of time projecting yourself into the future: a time and place where and when you will finally do all the reading that you've always wanted to do. I also think you see books subconsciously as a safety net. Everyone has a primal fear of abandonment and you have suffered this twice in your life. Most people experience this or similar and the pain is such that, in many different ways, they make preparations so that it either doesn't happen again, and that can go as far as avoiding future relationships altogether, or setting down to themselves a clearly defined coping mechanism. I think, to you, books are metaphorical friends and part of the reason you have so many is that, ever so slightly and in a perfectly normal way, you have lost a little bit of trust in the world. I think you believe that if you are ever left again or suffer from circumstances outside your control, these books will help assuage the pain and get you through.'

She pulled out a thin drawer in the desk positioned directly beneath her computer keyboard. Not more cards, I thought. Please don't dilute the magnitude of what you've just delivered. Let it be.

'Have a read of these,' she said, and handed over two more cards.

'The true definition of mental illness is when the majority of your time is spent in the past or future, but rarely living in the realism of NOW.' *Shannon L. Alder.*

'If we as a community believe in anything, we believe in feeling good in the moment. The felt presence of immediate experience. This is what has been stolen from you. By capitalism, by religion, by linear thinking, by strategising. We're always about to be happy. Or we're always about to be free. And while we're about to be free and about to be happy, life passes us by. This is because western ideologies are always ideologies of delayed gratification. It comes after death, after retirement, after coitus. It's always after something that it comes. Well, I've got news for you, this kind of thing is chasing your own tail. The felt presence of immediate experience is the only world you will ever know. Everything beyond that is conjecture and supposition.' *Terence McKenna, ethnobotanist, mystic, psychonaut, lecturer, author, bibliophile and butterfly collector.*

'Can I keep this one?' I asked.
   'Which one?'
   'The quote by Terence McKenna – I've never heard of him before.'

'He was a bit of a guru figure.'

'*Was?*'

She must have detected the disappointment in my voice.

'He died a few years ago.'

A silence passed between us which wasn't at all uncomfortable. She finally spoke:

'What are you going to do with the card?'

'I think I'll put it on the wall somewhere at home.'

'Do you often do that?'

'I've only really done it once before.'

I was thinking of the passage by Sylvia Plath I had framed all those years earlier.

'Does it speak to you particularly, then?'

'Yes.'

'What is it about the quote?' she asked.

'What it sums up, I suppose.'

She nodded.

'What are you thinking right now?'

(I don't know what happened next but everything felt changed. I had a feeling I'd only experienced twice before – the night I dreamed Grandad's death and a time when I had visited the Cuevas del Drach in Majorca. I was thinking back to then: walking the pathway through the winding caves and arriving at a huge underground cavern containing a clear, still lake. We sat on wooden benches in what was effectively a natural auditorium. The lights were turned off. It was complete darkness. Suddenly, music started, Albinoni's *Adagio*. A handful of small boats came into view with shadowy people inside carrying candlelit lanterns. It was so peaceful you sensed your heartbeat slowing down, almost to a stop. There was no panic accompanying this; it felt the perfect way to go, to lose who you were and submit to the dark and quiet.)

Lisa moved slightly in her chair as if to nudge the bewitchment.

'I asked what you were thinking?' she said softly.

'That the best thing you can do in life is to leave behind something like that statement so it can help others. And when you read it, you should try and act on it because it's so urgent and heartfelt.'

AFTERWORD

My dad had a friend who could sup pint after pint and tell tale after tale. He was a lorry driver by trade but really should have been a comedian. Or a philosopher. He'd have everyone laughing but then stop abruptly to issue a truth that would fall like a hot cinder. One night in the Royal Oak he raised his hand to call for quiet around the table. He looked straight at me.

'How old are you now?' he asked.

'Twenty-two.'

'Make sure you enjoy your life, kiddo, because it goes like that . . .'

As he said 'that' he clicked together his thumb and middle finger. I nodded but thought it was a pretty dim remark. Everyone knew a life lasted days and weeks and months and years, as good as for ever. Ever since, as time has passed – a great deal of it and quickly, very quickly – that click has got louder.

By writing about my life through books I've seen clearly that the dust of time has coated many of my stories and much of the scenery. Comprehensive schools? CSEs? Typewriters? Mills? Public telephones? Latch-key kids? Angry young men? Libraries? Video recorders? Pot shire horses? Skinheads? Cassettes? Local newspapers? All gone or going. In this rush to tomorrow it is surprising that books have survived, and look and feel as they always did. I dare say it (for I love them so much) but they may even be immortal.

When people see or hear of my collection, a handful of which bear my name as author, they often ask whether a working-class kid of today would still seek to find and define him or herself through books and writing. The very term 'working-class' has been largely excised from our vocabulary and is redolent of foggy and rusted times past. As much as Margaret Thatcher and her government were despised by many in the north, you knew where you stood. She branded a fierce boundary between workers and bosses, blue collar and white, haves and have-nots, us and them. When you walked around a town such as Rochdale, where huge factories blotted out the sun, the terraced houses all crammed together, you knew your place, knew your class. Men in boiler suits queued for dinner-time butties at the corner shop. Guard dogs barked on the other side of wire fences in mechanics' yards. The air was often scented with the sweet-sharp tang of heated metal from one of the foundries. A gigantic gasometer was jammed tight to the streets near the town centre, much like an abandoned UFO. Everywhere, all of us: working class.

A culture existed to bolster this shared sense of class. *Coronation Street* was on the telly. Films were being made about it by, among others, John Schlesinger, Tony Garnett, Ken Loach and Mike Leigh. Plays were written by Shelagh Delaney, Arnold Wesker, Jack Rosenthal, Willy Russell and Jim Allen. During my growing-up years, Barry Hines, Alan Sillitoe, Stan Barstow et al.

had already published their most street-smart work but were still reporting back from working-class life with regular novels. John Lennon had even donated a theme tune, 'Working Class Hero', which told us it was 'something to be'.

So, there was a place I belonged, both literally and culturally. I was validated and inspired. And then everything changed. While no one was looking, the working class became smudged, disavowed and discarded; it was no longer something to be. We were sold aspiration, moving on and up, lured perhaps by the legend of classlessness advanced by the United States, which has always held disproportionate sway over little Britain.

If 'working class' is no longer a status recognised by the wider public, the publishing industry, with only 10 per cent of its personnel drawn from the NRS (National Reading Survey) grades D and E – 'non working' and 'working class' – might be forgiven for ignoring its existence. 'Publishing is an upper-middle class industry whose output caters to upper-middle class tastes,' affirms Chris McCrudden of the PR and marketing giant Edelman. This is why so few novels are by authors from a background of manual labour, writing about their lives. There are exceptions. Authors are granted specific shelf space if they fall within the subgenres of: female, 'misery lit', black, ethnic, gay, Welsh, Scottish or Irish. Such writers routinely frame the working-class experience along the way.

When I asked friends to nominate contemporary writers from, let's call it SCFKAWC – the Social Classification Formerly Known As Working Class – that fell outside these subgenres, the list was paltry. In fact, it barely qualified as a list. Publishers have at least acknowledged the need to avert their gaze from London-centric 'middle-class' novels. The hope is that novels from SCFKAWC become *normalised* so that authors naturally place their stories and characters in a traditionally proletarian (I've been avoiding that word; it wears a scruffy overcoat) setting without it seeming a mission statement or call to arms.

319

Maybe none of this really matters. When I began reading and then writing, I had no awareness of class. As a child, you think everyone's family and environment and way of living is the same as yours. Reading is a beautifully natural experience, much the same as walking or talking: you just do it and, if you enjoy it, you do it some more.

My generation, the same as those before it, had an intimate relationship with boredom. I can still recall whole days of having nothing to do, watching the rain from the window, the streetlights flickering on, and day turning to night. My parents were usually elsewhere – another room in the house, at work, out. I had the television, of course, but there were only three channels and, aside from a few hours in the late afternoon, there was little of interest to kids. This meant I stared into space a lot, thought a lot, and all this staring and thinking led to reading and then writing.

These days our children are bombarded. They receive much more attention from adults than ever before and are gifted an array of fast, flashy, flashing gadgets. Their route to books is difficult to navigate amid the glare and noise. Although my sons grew up in the book cave I built, they were typical. Until their mid-teens they surrounded themselves with all manner of electronic devices. Slowly they inched towards the books, almost as if seeking respite from the onslaught of stimulation, their brains spying the flatlands and gentle contours of an hour or so spent reading.

The creative urge remains, ever will. A novel is a bold and unique statement to the world, but now there are many ways to chronicle, interpret or pursue a creative life, and all within easy reach. Computers and phones are mediums of expression for illustrators, designers, photographers, musicians and film-makers, for example. When he was ten years old, my nephew devised an animated version of a day in his life and uploaded it to YouTube. This was done in a couple of days – a novel can take years. Who has the time?

Mine was probably the last generation of collectors. We spent vast amounts of money and used up thousands of hours assembling our cultural insignia – vinyl, cassettes, video tapes, CDs, DVDs, books – only to find it superseded by invisible, intangible digital versions. My kids have none of this paraphernalia and ephemera and view my holding on to it as quaint, an indicator of the schism between generations.

That night in the Royal Oak, my dad's drinking pal was astute in relating the swiftness of the passing of time but made no claim to know what would happen between then and now. No one does. Much of it is maybe, probably, perhaps. A few years ago, a record dealer said he would kindly 'relieve me' (i.e. without payment) of a few hundred vinyl albums; I declined. Soon afterwards, he offered a sum for them in excess of what most had cost originally. There had been an about-turn, he said. The kids were buying vinyl again.

In the UK, a new or revised book is published every three minutes over an average day; more than enough to line the walls of thousands of houses. No one can say for sure who, in the future, may install their own personal libraries, their age, gender or class. And who knows the authors of these books. Tomorrow's readers may not genuflect, as I did, to Barry Hines, Elizabeth Smart, Alberto Moravia and J.D. Salinger. Different literary heroes, friends within pages, will pass this way soon, kiddo.

APPENDICES

Between the covers
(Items found or notes written in books in my collection.)

A pencil drawing of a fireplace, in *Felicia's Journey* by
William Trevor

In a neat hand, a fireplace has been drawn with measurements
included. The cream woven paper is folded precisely and carries
a watermark of an acorn and oak leaf. The sketch has been done
by someone who cares about their work. I've known tradesmen
scribble plans on an Indian restaurant menu or outline the costing
of a fitted kitchen by overwriting on newsprint. When my sons
were young they had a name for these workmen or similar among
my friends: greasy burger blokes. One day, I ran through a list,
asking whether they were greasy burger blokes or not. They were
too young to be condescending or snobby and I realised that it

was an accolade to be judged one – it meant you had qualities considered 'blokey'. I had to ask: 'Am *I* a greasy burger bloke?' They burst out laughing.

A bookplate bearing the name Edna Scholefield, in *Bernice Bobs Her Hair and Other Stories* by F. Scott Fitzgerald

A bookplate is a printed label stuck into a book, usually on the reverse of the front cover. They are also known as 'ex libris', meaning 'from the library of'. They are a branding for the book's owner. Book collectors generally disapprove of them. The designs are often viewed as tacky and incongruous to the book's content (fairies and unicorns are popular) and the adhesives used to affix them are acidic and damage the pages.

Others, the Bookplate Society especially, celebrate them as works of art. William Hogarth adorned his with cherubs and garlands of flowers. The peculiar drawings of Aubrey Beardsley ('I have one aim, the grotesque. If I am not grotesque I am nothing') were often adapted and used as bookplates – cats sitting atop heads, enormous genitalia and levitating nymphs.

Bookplates denoting a title that belonged to an acclaimed writer are extremely collectable. Rudyard Kipling's featured a dignitary reading a book while in a carriage on the back of an Indian elephant. It had been drawn by his father, John Lockwood Kipling, a fine artist who contributed illustrations to *The Jungle Book*. Other writers with their own bookplates included Lord Byron (disappointingly, considering a life so well lived, a coat of arms); Charles Dickens (a lion); H.G. Wells (a balloon in the night sky); Ernest Hemingway (a hut in the woods and a matador jousting with a bull, all angles covered); Samuel Pepys (rope and anchors) and Jack London (a wolf, of course).

In her book (now mine) Edna Scholefield has gone for a

charming pen and ink drawing of flowers, trees and, in the distance over the meadow, a farm building. I ponder on Edna – was there ever a name more synonymous with ladies of a certain age? I do an internet search, optimistic because of her relatively unusual surname. I find a death notice from the *Bradford Telegraph and Argus*: 'SCHOLEFIELD Edna (nee Buck), on November 24, 2015, died peacefully at Herncliffe Care Home, Keighley.'

I live about twenty miles from Keighley. I have visited every book and charity shop between there and home, many times. We might believe the covers of a book can turn into wings to fly high and far, but I imagine most, the same as most people, make short journeys during their lifespan. I think there is a very good chance that it is the same Edna Scholefield.

Four words and their meanings written on the end page, in *Brighton Rock* by Graham Greene

The previous owner had clearly been on a mission of self-help. He (or she) has written: *calcined* – burn to ashes; *ewer* – water jug with wide mouth; *ordure* – excrement, obscenity, foul language; and *plantain* – herb with broad flat leaves.

Jotting down words in the back of a book is a terrific way to increase your vocabulary. Incidentally, of the four words, I knew the meaning of two (plantains and ordure), could have guessed at another (calcined) but had no idea as to 'ewer'.

A library sheet showing various date stamps, in *A Clergyman's Daughter* by George Orwell

The book was issued by Richmond College Library under the auspices of, deep breath, the City of Sheffield Metropolitan District Education Department. I have no memory of a library at the college but this is indisputable evidence of its existence. I must have taken out the book soon after arriving at journalism college because the return date is 22 Jan. 1982 and I started there three weeks earlier.

I'm pleased with my younger self for being so keen: seventeen years old, away from home, lost in all this newness (residence, people, places, study) and I'm clearly determined to keep on reading. I'm not a habitual stealer from libraries (and get shirty when people talk about this as if it were a badge of honour) but I'm glad this didn't go back on the shelves. What else do I still have from 1982 that I can date categorically? To think, when I hopped off the bus and walk-jogged over the college field, singing songs by the Jam ('Strange Town', in keeping with my situation, but, because I was missing my girlfriend, more often 'Monday' – 'but a sunshine girl like you, it's worth going through'), fancying myself young and smart, that book, this book, was in my black Adidas bag slung over my shoulder. It's creased and the spine is lined but this is to be expected when something has journeyed from 1982 to now.

A note written to 'Daphne' on the first page of *The Wit and Wisdom of the Talmud* by Rabbi Dr Reuven Bulka

'Dear Daphne; May this booklet help you find many answers. Mardochai.' An intriguing dedication that poses several questions: who were Daphne and Mardochai? What was their relationship? What was Daphne seeking? Did she find it? The Talmud, according to Dr Bulka, 'expounds and elucidates' the Bible which, in turn, gives Judaism its 'form and character'. The homilies inside span the prosaic ('one should not remove stones from his domain by throwing them in the public thoroughfare') to the philosophical ('Man should always be flexible as the reed

326

and never stubborn as the cedar'), taking in the absurd ('Even if you hang the heart of a palm tree on a pig, it will still do its thing').

A bookmark for George's Booksellers of 89 Park Street, Bristol, in *England, My England* by D.H. Lawrence

A splendid ink drawing of George's is featured, with two cars parked outside, presumably early in the morning, because the streets are otherwise empty. The text says that the shop has been selling books since 1847 and has 350,000 volumes. It can also 'rebind or repair any book for you'.

George's once formed a hamlet of bookshops with six outlets along the same street, each dedicated to a different type of book: general retail (spread across four floors), academic, second-hand, two for art books and, later, another for computer books. Blackwell's had bought the store in 1929 but the branding and public support was so strong, it continued as George's.

In the mid-1990s it was finally rebranded to fall within the Blackwell chain but closed in 2010. A year later, the corner plot was taken over by celebrity chef Jamie Oliver and became one of his short-lived Jamie's Italian restaurants which went into receivership in the summer of 2019. Most of the building is now taken up by the Bristol and Bath Rum Distillery.

George's lives on, if in name only, in these bookmarks blown like seeds on the wind and caught within the pages of books – I've seen several over the years. Marvel at the drawing of its grand headquarters, check out the sincerity of the copy ('Orders and inquiries by post from any part of the world receive our careful and immediate attention') and imagine, just imagine, a building, a street, containing *six* bookshops, all called George.

A dedication, in *Malone Dies* by Samuel Beckett

'Happy Birthday Dad, Love from, Mark Nov 1975.' A book given as a gift is a long-standing tradition, of course. What was the nature of their relationship, I wonder, where this outlandish novel about illness and death, sex and violence, was considered a suitable present? Maybe son and dad needed a pretext to enjoy badinage ignited by a fireside reflection on existentialism, allegory, tangential plotting and the psychology of ennui.

A large newspaper photograph of Edith Sitwell glued to the first page. Another, the size of a postage stamp, loose inside, in *Taken Care Of* by Edith Sitwell

Dame Edith Sitwell, in her own words, was a 'throwback' descended from 'queer and remote sources'. She garlanded herself with bizarre headgear, huge gemstone rings, extravagant scarves and brooches as big as horse brasses, presumably to distract the eye from her unusual features. When Edith was young, her father, Sir George Sitwell, a former Conservative MP, persuaded her to wear a brace to reduce the size of her nose.

She would seem, then, an unusual quarry for a reader perusing newspapers, armed with a pair of scissors and tube of glue. But there she is and almost life-size: the knife-stab eyes, high forehead, painted-on eyebrows, thin and long nose (the brace didn't work, alas), each a supporting player to a perpetual glower. The smaller photo is more of the same but closely cropped so she appears to be tap-tapping at the camera lens.

The shock of the Dame is well worth bearing, for the prose beyond the photograph is wonderfully mischievous and as sparkly as her oversized gems. Although better known for her poetry, the autobiography – which she was unable to proof because she died in December 1964, a week before it went to the printer – is one

of the finest of her generation, shamelessly acerbic and enter-
taining. Of D.H. Lawrence, she writes, 'Mr L looked like a plaster
gnome on a stone toadstool', while the writer and artist Percy
Wyndham Lewis is so conflicted, 'He had to appear in different
roles in order to impress himself, and, if possible, others.'

A few handwritten lines on the first page, in *A Clockwork Orange*
by Anthony Burgess

I'm not sure why anyone would use a novel as a substitute notebook.
Perhaps the desire to get the words down immediately, there and
then, was too pressing to resist. It reads: 'The clothes I wear, the
hours I sleep, the friends I have, the work I do, the books I read,
the music I listen to, how to spend my leisure time.' Maybe it is a
section of free verse, a list, or a pastiche of a Talking Heads lyric.

Written on the first page: 'Neil Inglis 25/9/79. Read by
20/11/79', in *Daisy Miller* by Henry James

I shared 'digs' with Neil Inglis in Sheffield. He is the 'Neil' of the
Willie Donachie incident. He was from the north-east, proud of
it, and enjoyed a pint. The subject matter of the book doesn't fit
with Neil, although you shouldn't really prejudge the literary
taste of a man from the north-east who is proud of it and enjoys
a pint. The novel is a period piece where a coquettish, wayward
young woman (Daisy Miller) is pursued by an educated but lonely
socialite (Frederick Winterbourne). Neil must have lent me the book
and I clearly failed to return it. His practice of dating the receipt
of a book and the date of reading is a commendable idea, much
the same as listing unfamiliar words. He managed to read *Daisy
Miller* in less than eight weeks although, at eighty-eight pages, it
is a dainty book.

An imprint from an ink stamp, on the title page of
Tibetan Secrets of Youth and Vitality by Peter Kelder

Most people, if it is their custom, write their names in their books in pen. Christopher Puddy has gone further and made a special stamp, similar to those once used in libraries to date loans of books. The text reads: 'This book belongs to CHRISTOPHER PUDDY. Please return it promptly So [*sic*] others may benefit from it.' Maybe Christopher runs an independent library of self-help books and the entreaty is heartfelt: its speedy return ensures others can be enlightened to the 2,500-year-old Tibetan rites − basically an exercise programme to delay ageing. If, however, it is a ruse to limit its loan period to friends or even put them off borrowing at all, surely this goes against the spirit of the book.

A bookmark/postcard for the CIS (Co-operative Insurance
Society), found in *The Wayward Wife* by Alberto Moravia

The design and typeface suggest it is from the late 1960s or early 1970s. Eight insurance plans are listed including 'Fire & household comprehensive', 'mortgage protection' and 'savings for young men'. Once filled in, the card was to be sent to the Co-op at Miller Street, Manchester 4.

A line drawing of the CIS Tower is featured on the card, a building which was visible from my grandparents' flat, about a mile away in Collyhurst. They were proud that Manchester had such a 'skyscraper' and Grandad often visited the site to see the different stages as it was built over a four-year period. A contractor told him it was a copy of an office block in the United States. He was correct. The Inland Steel Building in Chicago, built in 1958, was the blueprint. Grandad always claimed the CIS Tower to be, at 387 feet, the highest building in Europe. This wasn't the case but, for nearly a year after it was built in 1962, it was the tallest in the UK. Now there are seven taller buildings in Manchester alone and the country's highest, the Shard, is nearly three times its size.

Acquired but not read. Until now.

(On purchase, I had every intention of reading these books but they were each swallowed up in my collection, lost in the crowd, until my year of reading avidly.)

The Autobiography of Alice B. Toklas by Gertrude Stein

Friends recommending books or lending them unbidden is always fraught. I seldom do it because I don't want them to feel obligated although, in practice, I find they often remain unread anyway.

A friend of a friend enthused so much about this book that when I think of it, I think of him, even though his counsel dates back almost forty years. Books can often function as aides-memoire, helping recall a specific person, place or memory.

The photo of Gertrude on the back cover is a mile-high warning. She bears a quarrelsome expression which may relate to her fringe; it appears to have been cut by either a love rival or a friend wearing oven gloves. Ostensibly about salon life in Paris at the turn of the twentieth century and the arty types she meets, the book is actually all about Stein, channelled supposedly through the pen of her partner, the Alice B. (for Babette) Toklas of the title.

Stein makes reference to her 'grammatical solecisms' probably in a bid to honour or at least validate a text desperate for the breath of commas, quotation marks and capitalisation. Has there been a sloppier sentence in a book dubbed a 'modern classic' (by Penguin) as: 'There are a great many things to tell of what was

331

happening then and what had happened before, which led up to then, but now I must describe what I saw when I came.'

Where she forgets herself and dims the self-love, Stein is much better company, especially at the end when she writes vibrantly of Ernest Hemingway. Forty years is a long wait, much the same as 200 pages before Ernest shows up with an infusion of energy and engagement.

Zen and the Art of Motorcycle Maintenance by Robert M. Pirsig

Robert Pirsig, whose mother was of Swedish descent, led a one-man crusade to see the term *'kulturbärare'* adopted internationally. The Swedish word translates as 'culture carrier', meaning a concept or person who moves culture forward: this was how Pirsig viewed his bestselling book. He made no claims that it was a classic (though many scholars disagreed) but acknowledged that its timing (1974) was apt – the counterculture era had waned and the materialism personified later during Ronald Reagan's presidency (1981–1989) was taking hold. People, especially the young, were seeking a moral map.

Zen and the Art of Motorcycle Maintenance is ostensibly about a month-long trip by motorcycle from Minnesota to California, taken by Pirsig with his eleven-year-old son, Chris, and family friends, John and Sylvia Sutherland, who return home after just nine days. Pirsig received 122 rejections before the book was taken up by William Morrow & Co., though its senior editor, James Landis, fretted that neither William Morrow nor Pirsig would earn back the advance. Pirsig did little promotion, fearing it might trigger mental illness that had dogged his early adulthood. Despite this, the novel sold 50,000 copies in the first month and a million within a year.

Earlier, at the age of ten, Pirsig was discovered to have an IQ of 170, which placed him in the top 1 per cent of the population for his age. His writing is heavy with the cargo of this outsized IQ and the novel, whether dressed up as philosophical, spiritual or an odyssey, is a battleground between his linear, mechanical intelligence and low-lit emotional acumen. This war is the book and everything else ancillary. When his perfunctory side is triumphant, which is often, the descriptions of the workings of a motorcycle engine and the various routes taken are tedious. His emotional side takes hold occasionally and coats sunshine to the text, especially as he points his version of fatherhood at Chris. Even here, there is struggle. He knows what a father *should* be but spends too long analysing, scrutinising, until the moment is gone and the kid confused, let down.

Almost fifty years on from first publication, it is difficult to fathom the impact and popularity of *Zen and the Art of Motorcycle Maintenance*. Maybe the blend of Socrates, Plato, Homeric heroes, the Gordian knot, Hegel and *The Iliad* riveted onto a Jack Kerouac-style road trip was enough to consider it a path-for-life, the way to go.

The Satanic Verses by Salman Rushdie

Salman Rushdie is a prodigiously talented writer. Everyone agrees. Words dance at his behest; his imagination is as wide as the sky. But here, the book that caused all that fuss, he is a magician who dishonours the Magic Circle. He uses his gift to show off, confound – only those as smart as he can open the door to this dense, dizzying prose and make sense of it all, or profess to. That it was chosen, in 1988, as the Whitbread Novel of the Year and was a Booker Prize finalist is disheartening, a firm push against the literary Everyman in favour of the elite. Did anyone *really* know what it was all about?

Wolf Solent by John Cowper Powys

The cover features a luminescent garden, painted by Stanley Spencer. The marriage to the prose is supreme, for a reference to a flower, the smell of grass or a metaphor drawn from the natural world is rarely more than a paragraph or two away. Wolf Solent, the protagonist, is a thirty-four-year-old history teacher who leaves London to settle in Ramsgard, Dorset, a fictional town based on Sherborne where Powys was brought up in the 1880s. There follows a beautifully rich evocation of a long-lost rural England. The writing is ornate, occasionally too much so, but it is also brave and sensual, unafraid to stand shoulder to shoulder with D.H. Lawrence or Thomas Hardy. Powys is a man who knows of love: 'He [Solent] discovered that to talk to Christie was like talking to himself or thinking aloud. And he recalled how he had been struck, the very first time they met, by this ease and naturalness with which the lightest thought flowed back and forth between them.'

The book is long, at 614 pages, principally because Powys is determined to relate every feeling, and describe, in sumptuous detail, all that his characters stumble upon. There is also a great deal of dialogue, much of it delicious gossip and calumny. The cover painting, incidentally, *Bellrope Meadow, Cookham* (1936), is from the permanent collection at, of all places, Rochdale Art Gallery.

Half of a Yellow Sun by Chimamanda Ngozi Adichie

Only the bravest authors set their books against momentous events – war, famine, natural disasters. The challenge is to make, within the same story, both the small and the colossal equally believable and compelling. Adichie almost succeeds but is let down by ambition as she flits over different time periods and calls upon too many characters. The main focus is the Nigerian Civil War of 1967–1970 and its impact on a diverse group of people, from Richard Churchill, an English writer studying Igbo-Ukwu art, to Ugwu, a sweet village boy led inexorably towards atrocity during the conflict. The book won the Orange Prize for Fiction in 2007 and was deposited as a mainstream exemplar (despite the harrowing subject matter) of a book with literary aspirations that would also have popular appeal.

Farenheit 451 by Ray Bradbury

Few books carry a commendation from a former president of the United States. Barack Obama, no less, sings that *Fahrenheit 451* 'reshaped our culture and expanded our world'.

Bradbury wrote it in nine days on a rented typewriter and this probably accounts for both its strength – urgency, energy, flashes of remarkable insight – and its weaknesses: a hotchpotch of a story that never settles and, after one about-turn too many (about three-quarters in), the reader loses heart and trust.

The novel, published in 1953, is a device for Bradbury to explore themes of alienation and totalitarianism, stirred by McCarthyism. In a pallid future-world, firemen are authorised to seek out and burn books and properties where they are stored. The protagonist, Guy Montag, has an epiphany: 'And for the first time I realised that a man was behind each one of these books. A man had to think them up. A man had to take a long time to put them down on paper.' Montag meets former English professor Faber and the dialogue between them is the book's principal drive. This discourse is conducted mainly through a transmitter earpiece; Bradbury was similarly prescient, with his depiction of flat-screen televisions and ATMs.

Many of the issues Bradbury explores are still resonant

today, if not more so – a fractured society, the masses overloaded to indifference by the media, rampant narcissism and a disregard for the counsel of history. Within the chopped-up, haywire plot there are occasional gems: 'The good writers touch life often. The mediocre ones run a quick hand over her. The bad ones rape her and leave her for the flies.'

The Corrections by Jonathan Franzen

Most readers do it. They guess at a writer's personality: what's he (or she) like? Would I want him (or her) as a friend? Franzen, via several supercilious declarations (most contained in his '10 Rules for Novelists' – 'you have to love before you can be relentless'), is widely perceived as overly smitten with his own reflection.

The characters in *The Corrections* are afflicted with a world-weary smugness that falls across generations of the Lambert family. They are so well drawn in their egotistical grotesqueness that it is almost impossible to divorce them from Franzen and imagine him as anything but, as Americans have it, a blowhard ('a person who likes to talk about how important they are' – *Cambridge Dictionary*). This is unfair, of course, because he may well be writing these people *away* from him, in effect uncoupling flaws from his own personality. Or he may simply have the knack of relaying insipid people with precision; in conversation on radio or television, Franzen is affable enough.

The Corrections has won numerous awards and become a bestseller. Franzen is regularly cited as an author of the Great American Novel alongside titans such as Herman Melville, Mark Twain, William Faulkner, F. Scott Fitzgerald and Cormac McCarthy. He is a confident writer, which is not the same as being a great writer. There is a sense, even in the otherwise laboured opening chapters, that he is in cool control, the pen held in a safe hand. He tarries at will, confident the reader will stay with him as he tells us, for instance, what breakfast Caroline has made for her husband, Gary (the Lambert's alcoholic, depressive banker son) – 'cinnamon toast, sausage links, and a bowl of oatmeal topped with raisins to resemble a face with a comically downturned mouth'. This level of detail builds the story tall but is often indulgent and, elsewhere, chases it down rabbit holes, slowing the pace, which is otherwise sprightly, considering its length of more than 600 pages.

Pride and Prejudice by Jane Austen

I tried, I tried. I wanted to challenge the prevailing view of Austen appealing solely to a female readership. I was also eager to take myself to the ballrooms and drawing rooms of Regency England, places where my imagination has never hitherto wandered. Accordingly, forsooth, I compelled myself to go there.

Many novels can make the past feel as if it has pulled up a chair next to you and, within minutes, you are there, marvelling at all you share and sense, despite the years between. Peopled by snobs, gossips, opportunists and egotists, Austen's world (the early 1800s) should be deliciously enthralling but it feels mythical; all puffery and inconsequential chit-chat and speculation going nowhere, slowly. The measured courtship of Elizabeth Bennet and Mr Darcy clearly has a charm and there is a beguiling morality tale in here, but much else is wearisome.

TBR: To Be Read

(Whenever To Be Read became TBR, I was elsewhere, possibly buying books. I kept hearing TBR and pretended I knew what it meant until I had the courage to ask someone who would explain in the least condescending way.

The English language has approximately 200,000 words – more than most others – but the word most apposite for these TBR piles is Japanese: *tsundoku*. It combines '*tsunde-oku*' (letting items pile up) and '*dukosho*' (reading books) and was originally a slang word dating back to the nineteenth century.

I have several TBR piles of various heights around the house and at a given time I estimate that I'm making my way through about ten books among them. A writer's TBR pile differs from the general reader's because some of the titles may have been sent to review or bought for research. The content of each pile is listed exactly as it stands, or topples.)

TBR Pile #1 – coffee table, front room

Playing for Keeps by Alec Stewart. While drifting in and out of shops in the pleasant Lancashire town of Clitheroe, I encountered the wonderful sight of about twenty-five hardback sports books, mainly on cricket, each in pristine condition. This had clearly been someone's cherished sports library, featuring autobiographies of, among others, Marcus Trescothick, Kevin Pietersen, Shane Warne, Matt Prior, Ricky Ponting, Andrew Strauss and the former England captain and wicket keeper (hence the title) Alec Stewart. I was excited. I wanted them all.

Putting together a tower of books, I asked their price. 'Twenty-five,' said the lady at the cash desk. If bought new, they would have cost approximately £20 each and, as I had stacked up twenty, I had £400 of books before me: £25 for the lot was a reasonable deal. I'm not sure of the look on my face as I did this adding up, but it caused her to shout over: 'We can't go any lower than 25p per book, love.' They were 25p *each*. Madonna's 'Vogue' was playing on a golden oldies radio station and I was tempted to swank around the shop voguing, such was my glee. And then I felt sad, two times over. Sad that someone had been divested of such a collection (had he or she died?) and also on behalf of the charity (RSPCA) and all who worked there. Filling two plastic carrier bags to tearing point with twenty hardbacks and placing £5 on the counter felt an act of larceny or, at the very least, moral dereliction. I fished in my pocket for a £10 note with every inten-tion of paying double the asking price. I made two dips but could only find a £5 note. At my side the queue of customers waiting to pay was growing. Flustered, I handed over the fiver. The shame of it.

Landscapes of the Metropolis of Death by Otto Dov Kulka. I bought this solely because of the arresting cover, a monochrome pastiche of a classic 1970s image. The designer, Jim Stoddart, is mentioned in tiny print below the barcode. I found his website and emailed to offer my appreciation of such great work. I think it's important we do this; talent has to be encouraged.

How Does It Feel? – A Life of Musical Misadventures by Mark Kermode. I'm not sure how I ended up with this or even if it's my book. I have several friends who, when they visit, feel compelled to leave books for me to read. This is a lovely and kind gesture but when I've already got scores *to be read* it can steer me towards that tipping point or TBR, O (To Be Read, Overwhelmed). I share a passion with Mark Kermode for the icy, shimmering Sheffield new wavers the Comsat Angels, but I'm not sure I could last a whole book of his smarty-pants prose. Besides, I have an issue with the publishing industry offering patronage to those already established in other fields – comedians, television presenters, musicians, broadcasters, film reviewers et al. Let the writers write, I say.

All Dressed Up and Nowhere to Go by Malcolm Bradbury. A well-packaged (cool cover, strong and clear typeface) collection of essays first published in 1982. The lukewarm blurb ('He restores belief in the power of laughter') won't help it escape the lower reaches of the pile.

I'm Not with the Band by Sylvia Patterson. Memoirs by music journalists are a staple of my collection. I know from reading her regularly in the *NME* and elsewhere that Patterson's will be funny, truthful and visceral – a favourite word of music writers.

The Ethnic Cleansing of Palestine by Ilan Pappe. My youngest son recommended this while studying at university. Lit by his passion, I ordered it immediately. I *will* read it but the titles above and below in the pile are more frothy and attractive, and much less harrowing, of course. The small typeface doesn't help its cause – why do they do that? Surely more pages could be added to accommodate a larger typeface. An anglepoise lamp or sunny day is an essential accessory.

Into the Void, on Tour with The Coral, 2016–17 by Nick Power. A book I was sent to review by a music magazine. I have kept it at hand to revisit occasionally. Power writes in a loose-limbed, Beat-powered shambling mode and holds no excising knife to his tale; he tells it as it is, all of it. I used that sentence in the review.

TBR Pile #2 – corner table, front room

Bertrand Russell's Best by Bertrand Russell. Much the same as George Orwell, Russell writes in a brilliantly structured way where even lengthy and complex theories are unfurled straightforwardly. Russell has a vivacity and wit greater than Orwell, however, and this plays well in shorter work such as these pieces on six hefty life subjects: psychology, religion, sex (and marriage), education, politics and ethics.

Greatest Churches and Cathedrals of Great Britain by Sue Dobson. In another life, or possibly this one, I plan to visit every cathedral in England, to feel small and insignificant beneath roofs so high they seem halfway to heaven. When it's raining and dark, the world gone winter, I'll read this book and marvel at a vocabulary all its own – misericords, quires, lierne, transept, spandrels et al.

The Seasons, a Celebration of the English Year by Nick Groom. I'm drawn to books on a single narrow theme, intrigued to see how a writer can expand and indulge, tilling for enough material and creativity to sustain interest over several hundred pages (exactly 400 in this case). On one or two pecks, I was disappointed to find this is largely a compendium of poems and other writings which, while informative, skirt the greater challenge of either a personal account or an imagination set free to marvel, in this case, at the soil, fields, hedgerows and skies of England.

Beyond Words by John Humphrys. The tracks leading back to Humphrys's days on the *Penarth Times* and *Western Mail* are still evident. His titles are often available in remainder bookshops and, for the price of half a pint of beer, it feels similar to my calling on a journalism lecturer from forty years ago. I'm set for a few droll anecdotes, a bittersweet reflection on times gone and a reminder of how best to construct a sentence.

Images of Mullingar by Ruth Illingworth. A friend offered to plot my family history and, flattered, I gave him every encouragement. As I expected, on both sides, there were generations making do and getting by in urban settings, the women chambermaids or servants, the men bicycle repairers or labourers. The only real discovery of note was that my great-great-grandparents had left Mullingar in County Westmeath, Ireland, to relocate to Manchester in 1850; this accounted for my mother's maiden name of Duffy. In commemoration of my new-found Irishness, my girlfriend bought the book as a Christmas present. On the cover are the 'Presentation Sisters'— four bespectacled nuns with wimples as big as tablecloths, photographed in 1958.

Child of Satan, Child of God by Susan Atkins. Few could resist a book about 'a young and attractive woman desperate to find happiness. Alcohol, drugs and promiscuity didn't satisfy her . . . she was looking for more.' The *more* Susan Atkins found was the doomsday cult leader Charles Manson, later responsible for the murder of nine people. I routinely avoid sensationalist books but succumbed here, influenced by the television documentary *Inside the Manson Cult: The Lost Tapes.*

The Moor, a Journey into the English Wilderness by William Atkins. Moorland, squelchy and peaty in winter, dry and bracken-scratchy in summer, lies in three directions a mile or so from where I live. I spend a fair amount of time either on these moors or thinking about them. One of my favourite books is *Millstone Grit* by Glyn Hughes, who tramped the nearby Calderdale moors, stopping to jot down sweet thoughts and prose, leaning against his rucksack in the coarse grass. I met Glyn a few times. He was eager, keen, looking always to engage and listen or, better still, tell a tale of his own.

A few pages turned of Atkins's book reveals a journey over various English moors, recalling fables and folklore but with enough faithful description of paths and copses to save you getting out your walking boots and doing it yourself. Proxy adventuring is a thriving sector of the publishing world.

The Forgotten Dead by Ken Small. Unknown to many — everyone was sworn to secrecy at the time for fear of damaging morale — more than 750 American servicemen died a few miles out to sea off the Devon and Dorset coast in April 1944. They had taken part in Exercise Tiger, a rehearsal for the D-Day invasion of

Normandy. The assignment, starting at Slapton Sands, Devon, went calamitously wrong and they came under friendly fire before being shelled by German E-boats. I had heard of the disaster while researching a story and made a pilgrimage to see the Sherman tank which the book's author, Ken Small, had rescued from the sea.

Englischer Fussball by Raphael Honigstein. Sports books are my equivalent of throwing a packet of chewing gum into the trolley at the supermarket checkout or, at the petrol station, a car air-freshener shaped as a lemon or Christmas tree – easy, instinctive purchases. The blurb says it is 'a German's view of our beautiful game'.

TBR Pile #3 – toilet

The Winker by Andrew Martin. I was a fan of 'Northside', Martin's witty column which ran for several years in the *New Statesman*. His television programmes are charming too, usually about trains and travel. I have met him once or twice. He is, much the same as his writing, modest and wry and warm. I'm struggling with *The Winker*, though, as I did with another of his novels, *Bilton*. I'm not sure he knows what he's best at; the same as many of us. If I were his editor I'd commission him to wander around and, each night (in a cheap hotel room: keep him keen), ask that he write down as many thoughts as he can recall and everything he has come across – simple.

My Dear Mother . . . Love, Keith: The war letters of Keith Lysons 1940–1946. As a memento, a pal has published letters his father wrote during the Second World War while serving in India, Pakistan, Iraq and Egypt. It is surprisingly rich and I can recognise my friend in his father.

Hawkwind, Sonic Assassins by Ian Abrahams. I've long been

drawn to Hawkwind, for both their experimental music and radical outsider stance allied to an 'anyone-can-join-in' collectivism. Creative people working together outside of mainstream support is the purest embodiment of hope and commitment.

The Best American Short Stories 2019 edited by Anthony Doerr and Heidi Pitlor. My partner bought this for me while on a work trip to the United States. She left the receipt inserted in the pages. How delightful to know that at 9.37 a.m. on Saturday, 18 January 2020, someone called into the Harvard Book Store on 1256 Massachusetts Avenue, Cambridge, MA and thought to buy such an appropriate gift.

Iron Mask, the Story of Harry Bensley's 'Walking Round the World' Hoax by Steve Holland. Legend has it that in 1907 Bensley was offered £21,000 to push a baby's pram around the world while wearing an iron mask weighing four and a half pounds. Other conditions were that his baggage must be limited to a single change of underwear, the trip had to be financed through Bensley selling postcards of himself and, perhaps the biggest challenge of all, he had to return to England with a wife who had not seen him unmasked. Has there ever been a more bizarre story?

For Esmé – with Love and Squalor by J.D. Salinger. This has journeyed across several piles since I made a documentary for BBC Radio 4 about Salinger's time spent in England as a soldier during the Second World War. While making it, I revisited his haunts in Tiverton, Devon. The short story which lends its title to the book is an exemplary piece of writing. I have left it around for so long because I want to be reminded regularly of perfection. It has all of everything: narrative, characterisation, verve, intelligence, humour, emotional depth and honesty. If I could, I would read it every day and twice on a Sunday.

TBR Pile #4 – bedside table

Playing the Bass with Three Left Hands by William Carruthers. Spacemen 3, the band in which Carruthers played, went in for loud, one-chord, collegiate, droning rock of which I am fond.

I was drawn to the book because it was declared a 'Rough Trade Book of the Year' and published by Faber & Faber. Music released on the Rough Trade record label has formed a substantial part of the soundtrack of my life: The Smiths, the Go-Betweens, Jonathan Richman, AR Kane, Microdisney, Easterhouse, the Sundays, the Heart Throbs, Levitation, Zoundz and many more. (I once found myself sitting next to Geoff Travis, the label's founder, at an awards ceremony. I wanted to know so much. Was Jonathan Richman really so childlike or was it an affectation? How did AR Kane end up on David Byrne's record label, Luaka Bop? What was Terry Bickers, formerly of the House of Love, up to these days? He answered with a yes or no or nod of the head. I think I was getting on his nerves.)

Similarly, I have an allegiance to Faber & Faber. I see those sweetly beckoning lower case f's on the back of a book and I want to take it to a hushed place and read away the day. I fantasise about the ff gang, alive or dead – W.H. Auden, William Golding, Mario Vargas Llosa, Philip Larkin, Hanif Kureishi, Ezra Pound, Harold Pinter, Jean Cocteau, Sylvia Plath and Edna O'Brien – sipping sherry or slopping pint pots of beer, arguing and then making up, all loud laughs in a woody London pub on a winter's afternoon where it's not even 3 p.m. and everyone is sloshed happy.

Will Carruthers would seem an unlikely Faber & Faber author but he is part of a trend across many publishing houses. The demographic span means that those original fans of, for example, the Rough Trade-associated acts on my iPod, are now in their late forties and fifties and ensconced in senior editorial positions. Where, in 1988, on a trip to town between essays or the next lecture, they bought the limited edition 7-inch single and mused on the curious artwork and every line of the lyrics (predominantly mumbled or shouted), they can now commission the singer, drummer or roadie to tell the whole unexpurgated story of the band.

Along with Carruthers's book, Faber & Faber has published *Art Sex Music* by Cosey Fanni Tutti of Throbbing Gristle; *Clothes, Clothes, Clothes. Music, Music, Music. Boys, Boys, Boys* by Viv Albertine of the Slits; *Girl in a Band* by Kim Gordon of Sonic Youth and *2023* by the Justified Ancients of Mu Mu. The editor behind these, Lee Brackstone, left the company in 2019 after twenty-three years and was given his own imprint, White Rabbit, by Orion. He told the *Quietus*: 'I want to create an environment where music writing can experiment and take on literary value.' Brackstone had recognised that a potential readership known variously (though part of their shtick was a refusal to be classified, of course) as new wavers, post punks or indie kids, were literate and loyal to the ethos of forever youth espoused by bands and artists of that era. They'd been there, bought the T-shirt. And now they wanted the book.

Auschwitz, a History by Sybille Steinbacher. A glut of television documentaries and dramas had made me want to understand better, if possible, the rise of Nazism. I had avoided books on the subject for many years, afraid of becoming mired in the horror or somehow complicit by engaging with it. The effect of the numerous television programmes has been to defuse the ghastliness, almost as if by sharing it and belonging to a community of viewers, we had reduced its impact on the individual. I opened the pages of Steinbacher's book apprehensively, though there was little to fear. It is a concise, dispassionate read that does not gorge on the atrocities. I will finish it soon.

A Reading Diary – A Year of Favourite Books by Alberto Manguel. I was handed this by a friend in publishing. It is wistful and tangential and I dip into it often for writerly inspiration. He has a cool style, as if each word is splintered from ice. He's Argentinian and looks a bit like Bill Bryson. I'm not sure about his stripy tank tops.

A Cat, a Hat and a Piece of String by Joanne Harris. I bought this from 'the biggest bookshop in the North of England' – Waterstones in Deansgate, Manchester (three floors, 80,000 books, one restaurant). As I perused the store I realised that, for someone with so many books, I seldom visit shops selling new stock. Second-hand ones are so cheap. The charity shop nearest my home, for example, is currently selling *five* books for £1. And this sale is likely to continue because numbers appear to be plentiful – a notice on the wall asks customers to 'refrain from bringing in books, CDs and vinyls for the time being, thank you'. The Joanne Harris book cost me £8.99. I could have brought home forty-five books from the hospice shop for the same amount. I curse that I'm not a fan of Wilbur Smith, Lee Child or John Grisham.

Another reason I seldom frequent chain stores is because I know how it all works – that publishers often have to pay for a presence there on a sliding scale, from a full window display to a title being included on a table at the entrance within its 'three for two' offers. They sometimes ask publishers for 'marketing fees', which are effectively condition payments before a retailer will stock a particular book. I am amazed that most book lovers are unaware of these facts and believe the trade is homespun and wholesome.

Maybe these policies have to be set against the dragon of Amazon. Waterstones (which, laudably, doesn't charge for space or profile in its stores), has 283 outlets in the UK and Europe and employs more than 3,500 people, but in 2017 (the most recent available figures) returned a profit of £18 million – a relatively small recompense for investors, considering the admin and scale of the operation. In the same year, Amazon UK's profit was £72 million. This differential will be much greater, of course, after the coronavirus pandemic of 2020–21.

I have never bought up collections from a single source. The nearest I came was when a good friend died and his parents passed on his football books. The passage from his shelves to mine seemed to go against nature, however, and I find them difficult to open, let alone read; they still sing his name.

I had bought the Joanne Harris book because I was due to interview her for a radio programme. I skimmed it but, after meeting her, properly read the collection of short stories. Across each one, it was if Joanne was reading aloud to me; her rich, enquiring voice caught fast and firm in my head.

Walking the Americas by Levison Wood. If I'm asked what books I like, *really* like, I say I'm not overly concerned with story or narrative and much prefer books that ramble on, that are like someone talking to you or you're hearing their thoughts. Travel writing is the exception. The genre appeals precisely because I know there will be a good yarn. We'll meet people, visit places, get into scrapes and both of us will survive to tell (and read) the tale. Three travel adventures were among the first ten books I ever read as a young teenager: *The Long Walk* by Slavomir Rawicz and *Call of the Wild* and *White Fang*, both by Jack London.

Wood, a former major in the parachute regiment, undertakes epic journeys staring down bloodthirsty militia and bloodthirsty bugs with equal insouciance. He writes crisply and the journey is everything, which means you're resolutely *with him* rather than slowing up to wade through trench-foot prose. Other similarly gifted travel writers: Colin Thubron (especially *In Siberia*), P.J. O'Rourke, Jon Krakauer, Paul Theroux, Jan Morris, T.E. Lawrence, Dervla Murphy, J.B. Priestley and Bruce Chatwin.

The Long-Winded Lady by Maeve Brennan. The strapline at the bottom of the cover tempted me: 'Notes from the *New Yorker*'. The book is a collection of Brennan's columns, 'Talk of the Town', which ran in the magazine from 1954 to 1981. Almost everything connected with the *New Yorker*, across many decades, is worth reading. The association guarantees that it will be precise, sassy and a reflection of America at its most fascinating.

Pond by Claire-Louise Bennett. Once more, I have no idea how this arrived in the house and so close to hand, a few feet away from where I sit and write most days. Finding it now, as if for the first time, I can see why it magnetised its way into my hands and then a carrier bag. The cover carries limited text on a royal-blue background – merely the title, the author's and the publisher's name. Set upon matt rather than gloss, it brings to mind the austere record sleeves of New Order's single 'Ceremony' and album *Movement*, designed by Peter Saville.

Browsing a few pages, I know instinctively that I will enjoy the book because it is awkward and angular and hugely contemplative, if not outright indulgent: 'In many ways this aerated point of view appeared more troubling than the costive statement from which it had originated, and I was quite defeated in my efforts to distinguish anything amusing about it.' I have a predilection for writing that feels almost as if English is the author's second language.

This Is Memorial Device by David Keenan. I buy books like this mainly to test myself, my magnanimity and generosity of spirit. This is a novel about being in and out of bands in the late 1970s and early 1980s, very similar in theme to my novel, *The Last Mad Surge of Youth*. I'm madly jealous, of course, that it is published by Faber & Faber and I want to understand why I had to self-publish, while Keenan has had such tremendous support; it received widespread publicity. Ideally I will enjoy it immensely and it will lift itself imperially above petty rivalry. We'll see.

The Naked Civil Servant / How to Become a Virgin / Resident Alien by Quentin Crisp. Widely viewed as a *character* or *eccentric* above all, Crisp is overlooked as a supreme writer. Three titles bound as a single compendium will offer enough pathos and waspishness to fill several afternoons, complemented by tea and biscuits served on a fine china plate.

Rochdale, the Runaway College by David Sharpe. I found out about this other Rochdale a few years ago. The 'college' was opened in a high-rise block in Toronto, Canada, in 1968 and offered no structured courses, curriculum, exams or traditional teaching. It was an experiment in radical free living, taking its inspiration, bizarrely, from the Rochdale Pioneers, founders of the co-operative movement in 1844. Students could purchase BAs for $25 and MAs for $50. After seven years, it was abandoned. Crime was rife and, when police forcibly removed students, it was known as 'North America's largest drug distribution warehouse'. The book can't fail to entertain.

Eiger Dreams by Jon Krakauer. A collection of essays on mountaineering by one of the most respected writers in the field. Best read in a warm room, safe and sound.

The Moon is Down by John Steinbeck. A slim novel (112 pages) about the military occupation of a town in northern Europe. Steinbeck was the author of more than thirty books; this is among the last I have yet to read.

Infidelities by Kirsty Gunn. The blurb got me: 'These are tales of lust, deceit, resentment and regret.' The cover, however, is dreadful — an architect's floor plan of a house. The sticker on the back says it is from Oxfam and cost £1.99. Only a small gamble, then.

This Too Shall Pass by Milena Busquets. This too shall pass is one of my favourite phrases. Sometimes, when all the thinking and wishing and hoping is done and a situation has become out of control or hit home hard and painful, it is the only consolation; a sigh of acceptance set to words. According to legend, it was first uttered by Sufi poets in medieval Persia.

7 Miles Out by Carol Morley. She is the younger sister, by nine years, of the writer Paul Morley. I imagine it has been a challenge standing small next to someone able to talk so eloquently and confidently about Proust, Hegel and Nasher from Frankie Goes to Hollywood. Their father committed suicide when Carol was eleven and she turned to drink soon afterwards. She was promiscuous, traipsing through Manchester and London with her belongings in a duffel bag. Carol's work, her writing and film-making, is haphazard but presented with a great drowning heart.

Voices in the Evening by Natalia Ginzburg. I find it impossible to resist almost any novel by an Italian writer translated into English. I'm much the same with Italian films. I'm not sure how, but Italians do philosophical and ridiculous so well, often within a few pages or scenes in a film. They are always either thinking or talking or eating, sometimes all three at the same time. The precision of language embodied by Ginzburg et al. can make a novel shine, though I'm never quite sure if this is the author's talent or a gift from the translator. Either way, the book and the reader is the beneficiary.

On Writing: a Memoir of the Craft by Stephen King. I should read more Stephen King. Everyone says this but is deterred by either the sniffy reviews or a gnawing sense that the pleasure will be compromised through first encountering the film version; it is a trial to divorce a book from a film and not have two renderings running simultaneously in your head. This won't be an issue with a book about the craft of writing (note: he doesn't use the more commonplace description, 'art'). I imagine it will be a solid buddy book proffering good sense and well-told anecdotes.

ACKNOWLEDGEMENTS

I would like to thank, most of all, Kellie While, for her help and support in the writing of this book. Kevin Pocklington, my agent, expertly found it a happy home at Canongate, where Simon Thorogood, my editor, was brave enough to let it go its own way. Thanks to Leila Cruickshank, also at Canongate, for seeing it carefully home. Seán Costello did a fantastic job with the copy-editing. Jim Stringer and Richard Lysons gave valuable critiques to an early draft. Richard Whitehead, Austin Collings, Nige Tassell and Trevor Hoyle offered similar expert counsel. James Heward and James Wallace took care of other business on my behalf while I was absent. Dale Hibbert provided essential technical support. My two sons, George and Alec, gave constructive advice and support, as did friends John Abraham, Guy Patrick, Christian Brett, Gary Canning, Chris While, Terry Eves, Miles Moss, John Matthews, Julie Matthews and Bernie Wilcox. Lisa Edgar and Emily Wood generously provided a writing bolt-hole in a Cornish paradise. Bryan Ledgard kindly proffered alternative covers and help with various photographs. Thanks, too, Benjamin Myers, Ian McMillan, Mark Radcliffe and David Hepworth for the commendations.